The Network Design Process

Practical Computer Network
Analysis and Design

The Morgan Kaufmann Series in Networking
Series Editor, David Clark

Practical Computer Network Analysis and Design
James D. McCabe

Frame Relay Applications: Business and Technology Case Studies
James P. Cavanagh

High-Performance Communication Networks
Jean Walrand and Pravin Varaiya

Computer Networks: A Systems Approach
Larry L. Peterson and Bruce S. Davie

Forthcoming:

Optical Networks
Rajiv Ramaswami and Kumar Sivarajan

The Art and Science of Network Design
Robert Cahn

Switching in the Internet
Yakov Rekhter, Bruce S. Davie, and Paul Doolan

Gigabit Workstations
Jonathan M. Smith, Bruce S. Davie, and C. Brendan Traw

Internet Payment Systems
Mark H. Linehan and Dan Schutzer

Advanced Cable Television Technology
Walter S. Ciciora, James O. Farmer, and David J. Large

ATM Applications: Business and Technology Case Studies
James P. Cavanagh

Multicasting
Lixia Zhang

Practical Computer Network Analysis and Design

James D. McCabe
FSC End2End Incorporated

Morgan Kaufmann Publishers, Inc.
San Francisco, California

Production Manager Yonie Overton
Production Editor Cheri Palmer
Editorial Coordinator Jane Elliott
Cover Design Ross Carron Design
Cover Photograph © 1998 The Image Bank/Michel Tcherevkoff
Copyeditor Sharilyn Hovind
Proofreader Jennifer McClain
Printer Courier Corporation

This book has been author-typeset using FrameMaker.

Morgan Kaufmann Publishers, Inc.
Editorial and Sales Office
340 Pine Street, Sixth Floor
San Francisco, CA 94104-3205
USA
Telephone 415 / 392-2665
Facsimile 415 / 982-2665
Email mkp@mkp.com
WWW http://www.mkp.com
Order toll free 800 / 745-7323

Library of Congress Cataloging-in-Publication Data

McCabe, James D.
     Practical computer network analysis and design / James D. McCabe.
         p.   cm.
     Includes bibliographical references and index.
     ISBN 1-55860-498-7
     1. Computer networks--Design and construction.   I. Title.
TK5105.5.M398 1997
004.6´5--dc21   97-34934
                                                                         CIP

*To my Mom, for raising a pre-alpha dilbert
and still being able to smile about it*

Foreword

by David M. Piscitello
Core Competence

Networks are nearly as prolific today as PCs were 10 to 15 years ago. Businesses of every size, service, and marketplace have come to embrace networking as a means of sharing resources, disseminating information, advertising, conducting commerce, and extending their communities of interest through collaboration and joint venture. Elementary and secondary education systems are as "networked" today as many colleges and universities were as recently as five years ago.

Nearly every transaction engaged in over the course of one's daily routine involves networking—or can. You can bank, work, shop, gather news, invest, plan a vacation, and be entertained using networks. Networks, it seems, are everywhere.

Several factors contribute to the apparent ubiquity of networks. Personal computers are now business appliances and are fast becoming home appliances. The hardware costs of local area network interfaces and "hubbed" network connections is a small fraction of what it was only five years ago. And the skill and software required to install and operate a small to modest-size PC LAN is readily acquired. The design of such networks is, in most cases, straightforward.

Local area networks, it seems, are organic. As an organization grows, so does its network. Through processes that are characteristically similar to cell meiosis and mitosis, a network segments or combines with other networks, changing its shape, composition, and complexity. The process, however, is often more complex and seemingly chaotic than cell union or division. The resulting networks are not always exact regenerations of the original. For in addition to changes in physical characteristics (e.g., CPU and storage), network components frequently undergo changes in ways not as readily analogized to cell biology. The use, application, or "role" of a computer in a network can change: in many cases, computers become specialized and provide application as well as communications services. The relationship of the user of a computer to other users and server computers in a network can change. The geographical location of a computer in a network can change. The characteristics of the connections between computers may change. Depending on the number of hosts and LAN segments, considerable planning may be required so that multisegmented LANs deliver services to the users of the concatenated set of LANs.

LANs—or more precisely, the users of LAN computers—never seem quite happy existing in isolation from other LANs. For the users on any given LAN in an enterprise, there's always more and different and *indispensable* information on another LAN *somewhere*, whether that somewhere is down the hall, on the next floor, across campus, at a regional or main office, or at an international office, on a different continent. Users need to access this information—after all, the information is indispensable or *mission-critical*—and so wide-area connections must be established between LANs.

Accommodating growth and change in enterprise and multiorganizational networks adds a new dimension to what may already be a considerable technological challenge for an organization. Many organizations are not prepared to deal with change at all these levels. They often do not have and cannot produce clear definitions of user (application) requirements and information flows; without these, their ability to define appropriate service upon which to base physical and logical network design criteria is greatly limited. So standard operating procedure for network design is often more seat-of-the-pants than anything else.

Why? The answer is amazingly simple. Network design is a science with too few references and guidelines for practitioners. Chemists, biologists, nurses, and physicians have a wealth of references upon which they can rely for formulae, actions and reactions, prescriptive indications and contraindications. But there are few places to go where you will find a statement of the nature "if you observe symptom X and you apply this, then you should observe Y or Z" when you attempt to design or redesign a network. Network design is hardly as exact a science as medicine—and as my wife reminds me, medicine is not as exact as we would hope.

A common cocktail-party analogy I make regarding network design is that networking is a lot like plumbing. But there are guidelines and municipal codes that plumbers apply to size pipes for water mains, water supply distribution, and drainage. A plumber can better estimate the number of sinks, showers, washers, and tubs a main supply pipe of a given diameter can support at a given pressure than a network designer can estimate computers on a network, because the plumber has more exact information to work with.

A plumber needs to understand the number and diversity of water delivery systems (e.g., faucets and showerheads), where the delivery systems are located, and the amount of water pressure desired before determining the appropriate diameter of a main supply and internal delivery pipes. Similarly, network designers need to understand the number of users, the network resources consumed by the applications they use, and the individual and collective flows of information (which, unlike plumbing, is bidirectional!).

Just as municipal codes provide plumbers with guidelines for calculating pipe diameter to achieve a given rate of water flow, this book provides guidelines for calculating information flow. From them, the network designer and team will come to understand how to characterize service, identify service requirements, and develop an information-flow specification. Author Jim McCabe also explains how to develop criteria for evaluating network technology, and how to determine appropriate methods and strategies for physical and logical LAN interconnection.

Practical Computer Network Analysis and Design fills a much-needed gap in data-network reference literature. As a consulting editor for a professional series on computer networking, I have read dozens of books on network theory, and dozens more that describe protocol bits and their operation. The shelves of every bookstore I visit are bursting with how-to's for personal computer operating systems and software applications. These are important books for computer scientists, but to design a network that meets user expectations, one needs more.

This book is something special. Jim describes a systems approach to designing networks that is disciplined and exacting. I refused to relinquish my preliminary manuscript because it's quite frankly not merely the only practicum I've encountered for network design but it's also highly useful, and it has quickly become indispensable.

Contents

**CHAPTER 10   Logical Design: Network Management   255
and Security**

Preface

Computer networks have become a major influence in our lives in the last two decades. From using the Web to make travel plans to accessing remote databases for research to having a medical specialist in another state review your MRI images while you're still at the machine, networks have made many new types of communication possible. And we are becoming increasingly dependent on networks to accomplish our day-to-day tasks. Yet, as important as they are, network designs are often left to chance, with choices based on a popular vendor or a familiar technology. This was barely tolerable in the early days, when network designs were relatively simple, but today, with large, complex networks and savvy, demanding users, the network design must be well-thought-out, robust, and reproducible.

There are fundamental design concepts and guiding principles that are key to producing good, solid network designs. *Practical Computer Network Analysis and Design* brings these concepts and guiding principles to you. Presented in a logical, step-by-step fashion, they develop a foundation in network analysis and design. Whether you are starting to learn how to design networks or have been designing networks for years, this book should provide you with some new and interesting perspectives on the analysis and design processes.

As you may already know, many of the problems in network design appear to be straightforward on the surface, but when we dig deeper the problems become much more difficult, involving complex interactions between services, technologies, and protocols. Without understanding the design environment, relatively simple solutions, such as increasing bandwidth or buying higher-performance switches and routers, are likely to be ineffective or are too costly to be practical. And when we consider how the network should support the end users and their applications, coming to a solution can be painful for the designer.

Approach

This book will help you to define and understand your design environment. It examines the entire system, from end users and their applications to the computers and networks that support them, and takes the view of the network as a set of services in the design environment.

I provide you with a step-by-step procedure for doing network analysis and design. I have refined this procedure through years of designing large-scale networks for government, corporate, and academic environments, and have incorporated the ideas and experiences of expert designers throughout the process. I have also taught this procedure to a variety of network designers via corporate seminars, training courses, and conferences such as Networld+Interop. Many network designers have successfully used it and have helped to refine it with their experiences. Like an open standard for a technology or protocol, this procedure is the result of many contributions and offers you the cumulative experience of many designers.

In *Practical Computer Network Analysis and Design,* I tackle some of the hard problems in network analysis and design and have made an effort to address real design challenges, such as how to

- Evaluate and choose network technologies, such as ATM, Ethernet, FDDI, Frame Relay, SMDS, and xDSL

- Choose between ATM interconnection mechanisms, such as ATM LANE, MPOA, PNNI, and NHRP, or the variety of flow-based variants

- Determine when to route or switch in the network

- Determine when and where to apply routing protocols (RIP/RIPv2, OSPF, BGP-4), as well as classful and classless IP addressing mechanisms such as subnetting, variable-length subnetting, and classless inter-domain routing (CIDR)

- Start considering QOS in the network, and how to make QOS meaningful to the end users and their applications

In addressing challenges such as these, I provide guidelines, examples, and rules of thumb to help you in making the tough decisions. You may find some or all of them to be useful, and I encourage you to modify them to fit your design environment. As part of the examples, I present a case study that is developed throughout the book. As each chapter describes a part of the analysis or design process, you will see parts of it applied to the case study, reinforcing the concepts and guidelines. I also present a number of new ideas on how network analysis and design can be done. The early chapters discuss network services, requirements, and flow analysis, which I believe to be necessary in developing successful, forward-thinking designs.

I have written this book primarily for the folks in the trenches, to help you in making better design decisions. In several chapters you will find templates to use in listing requirements, mapping applications, and laying out the logical and physical designs for your network. These templates are available both in this book and via Morgan Kaufmann Publishers, at *www.mkp.com*.

How to Use This Book

This book may be applied at many different levels, from an undergraduate introduction to network analysis and design, to an in-depth step-by-step approach for graduate study, to application in customer and end user design environments. While all of the chapters are beneficial in the analysis and design processes, the practitioner may want to review the analysis concepts in Chapters 2 and 5 and focus on the guidelines and case studies presented in Chapters 3, 4, 6, and 7 through 12. Students who want an outline of the concepts will want to study Chapters 1, 2, 5, and 7 through 12, and those who want a practical perspective should review all of the chapters. The chapters are organized to allow readers to pick and choose topics to study, and to make it easy for readers to quickly locate guidelines, templates, examples, and case study.

Note that requirements analysis (Chapters 2, 3, and 4) and flow analysis (Chapters 5, 6, and 7) are structured differently than the other topics in the book. These topics introduce a substantial amount of new material to the reader. In order to make the material easy to digest and reference, I have segmented each topic into three chapters. The first chapter introduces the concepts, the second chapter discusses how the concepts are applied, and the third chapter provides any necessary templates, and present examples and the case study.

Support Materials

I have developed a number of support materials for you to use with this book. As mentioned earlier, these materials are available from Morgan Kaufmann Publishers, at *www.mkp.com*:

- A list of frequently asked questions (FAQ) and their answers
- A glossary of terms used in the book
- Pointers on current discussions on the analysis and design processes
- A pointer to where you can find the password-protected solutions guide
- Analysis and design templates

Acknowledgments

The material presented in this book is based on a compilation of practical experience from myself and other members of the networking community. This material has been accurately represented to me, and any errors within belong to me. The network analysis and design processes are constantly evolving, and feedback from you on how to improve these processes is most welcome. I may be reached at doowah@fsc.com. Useful feedback will be added to the FAQ available at *www.mkp.com*.

I owe a great deal of thanks to many folks that helped with the development of this book. First of all I would like to thank David Clark, the series editor. From being an inspiration to write the book, to providing helpful discussions, comments, and suggestions about the contents, David has been a great help.

Many thanks also to Dave Piscitello of Core Competence, for writing the foreword. Dave may not remember, but the first thoughts of doing this book were put into my head by him, who stated "Write the book!" at one of the Networld+Interop conferences.

The chapters on requirements and flow analysis are based on early work encouraged by Bruce Blaylock at the Numerical Aerodynamic Simulation (NAS) Supercomputing Facility at NASA Ames Research Center, and modified by the ongoing work of the Integrated Services Working Group (int-serv) of the IETF. Various portions of the book were written with input from Anthony Lisotta and Jude George of FSC End2End Inc.; ideas on network service metrics and how to measure performance in the network were developed with the help of Mark Turner of Sterling Software; and the comparisons and contrasts of the various ATM methods were developed with the help of Walter Gould of Cisco Systems. An early outline of the book was based on contributions from Anthony Lisotta and Jude George from FSC End2End Inc., as well as Alfred and Kelly Nothaft of Bay Networks.

Various versions of this book were reviewed in whole or in part by Eural Authement, Bay Networks; Pierre Catala, Texas A&M University; Mike Davis, University of Delaware; Jim Fossella and Mike Palmer, BT Office Products International; Walter Gould, Cisco Systems; Jude George, Arshad Khan, and Anthony Lisotta, FSC End2End Inc.; Mike Minnich, DuPont; Keith Nesson, FORE Systems; Dave Piscitello, Core Competence; Matthew Rice, First Boston; and Paul Williams, X-Stream. Many thanks to you for your generous help.

I owe a great deal to the professional staff at Morgan Kaufmann Publishers for bringing this book to completion. Jennifer Mann, senior editor, was a great source of help, patience, and understanding, while the team of Cheri Palmer, production editor, Yonie Overton, production manager, and Jane Elliott, editorial coordinator, made the process enjoyable. I cannot imagine what the process would have been like without their enthusiasm, patience, and hard work.

CHAPTER 1

A Systems Approach to Network Design

1.1 Introduction—Traditional Network Design

Network design is somewhat of an art, combining rules on evaluating and choosing network technologies, knowledge about how technologies, services, and protocols work, and experience in what works and what doesn't. However, as in other types of art, the success of a network design depends greatly on who is doing the design, and designs are rarely reproducible.

Traditionally, network design is based on developing a set of general rules (such as the 80/20 rule, the old adage "bridge when you can, route when you must"). These rules worked well when there weren't too many choices in technologies, interconnection strategies, routing protocols, and so on, and when the end users considered the networks to be more of a luxury than a necessity. But times have changed, and our notion of designing networks must adapt to the wide variety of options we now have for building networks and the many different types of services we can offer to our end users.

Traditional network design focused primarily on capacity planning. When end users experienced problems with the network, particularly congestion, a common solution was to "throw bandwidth at the problem." While capacity planning is still an important part of the design process, we now also need to consider how we can optimize delay in the network. And, in many cases, reliability means much more than redundant paths in the network or resilient routing protocols.

In this book we will explore how the design process has changed and continues to change. We will look at networks from a services perspective, discussing how we can design networks to provide many different types (and levels) of service to the end user. In taking this approach, we will place emphasis on the process of network analysis, which will help us to understand what will be required by the end users, their applications, and their computing resources. The processes of network analysis and design can be complex, but they are powerful tools that can help you to build better networks.

1.2 The Analysis and Design Processes

Network analysis and design is a combination of several factors: design goals, trade-offs, and the balance between architecture and function. First, these processes help us to set and achieve design goals, such as minimizing network costs or maximizing performance. In this book you will learn how to set design goals; how to map network performance and function to your design goals; and how to recognize when your design varies significantly from these design goals, by triggering "red flags" in your mind.

Network analysis and design is also about trade-offs. Trade-offs like cost versus performance or simplicity versus function occur everywhere in the analysis process, and most of network design concerns recognizing these trade-offs and optimizing the design between them. You will find that there are many ways to achieve design goals and that there is rarely a single "right" answer—although there are often many wrong ones!

These processes are also about hierarchies, which are the degrees of concentration of networks or traffic flows at interconnection points in the network. In general, as networks grow in size and numbers of users, applications, and hosts, hierarchies provide structure within the network. They occur in how the network technologies and services are sized and interconnected, as well as in network addressing and routing techniques. A key component of this book is understanding these hierarchies, learning how to know when and where they will occur, and finding out how to take advantage of them.

Along with hierarchy, there must be some consideration for the degree of redundancy (numbers and types of alternate paths) in the network design. As hierarchy provides structure in the network, redundancy balances this structure by interconnecting the network at different levels in the design, to provide greater availability and reliability in the network. This is perhaps one of the most fundamental trade-offs in network design, and it shows up many times in the analysis and design processes.

   This book begins by setting the foundation in services-based networking, which provides you with a number of useful definitions for network analysis and design. From there you will start the analysis process, consisting of *requirements analysis* and *flow analysis*. The analysis process prepares you for the design of the network, which in this book is separated into design of the logical network and design of the physical network. The last component of the design process is developing the addressing and routing for the design. The relationships of the components of network analysis and design are presented in Figure 1-1.

   The analysis and design processes will help you to identify the services and performance levels that your design must satisfy. Through these processes, you will design your network to provide the desired services and performance levels, and to choose the best network technologies and services to meet your design goals.

FIGURE 1-1. Components of the Analysis and Design Processes

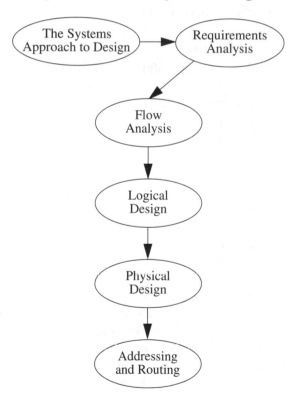

1.3 Network Services and Services-Based Networking

We begin the network analysis process with a discussion about network services and services-based networking. This is a relatively new approach to looking at networking (at least in the Internet protocol [IP] world), which reveals some interesting concepts that will be used throughout this book. As you shall see in this chapter, network services and service qualities are levels of performance (e.g., round-trip delay, available bandwidth, or reliability) and function (e.g., security levels, user groups for virtual networks) that are offered by the network to the rest of the system: the users, applications, hosts, and networks.

Services-based networking is the concept of developing network designs that take into account network services and service support. We are currently at the stage in network evolution where services are becoming important to the success of users and their applications. This is the generation of network services, which can be considered the third generation of networking.

Generation	Time Frame	Capability
First	1960s to mid-1980s	Basic connectivity/ interoperability
Second	mid-1980s to early/ mid-1990s	Performance (IP forwarding rates)
Third (current)	mid- to late 1990s	Network services (levels of network performance and function)
Fourth	2000 to 2010	Self-configuration/ administration

The evolutionary path of networking is leading to the introduction of rudimentary decision making by the network. It may be expected that, as early as the end of the decade, components of the network will have some capability to self-configure, operate, monitor, and manage, especially for those networks that must be configured or administered by end users (e.g., telecommuters or roaming users). Indeed, this will become necessary as the complexity and performance of networks increase, and as services offered by the networks become more sophisticated.

In this section we will examine systems and services, service levels and types, along with their characteristics and requirements. We will also discuss how services are provisioned and used in the network, and their roles in network design.

1.4 Systems and Network Services

One of our first challenges in the design process is to describe the system and network services that the network will support. Just what are systems and network services, anyway?

1.4.1 Systems

A *system* is the set of components that work together to support or provide connectivity, communications, and network services to users of the system. Generic components of the system include users, applications, hosts, and networks. Figure 1-2 shows how these components are connected in the system.

These components can be subdivided, if necessary, to focus on a particular part of the system. For example, users in a corporate network could be described as the network and computer support personnel, as well as developers and customers of the corporation's product. In a similar sense, applications may be specific to a particular user or customer, generic to a customer base, or generic to the entire network. Hosts may be subdivided to show the operating system, device drivers, or application programming interface (API). All of these components are combined to provide connectivity and communications between users and their applications, data stores, and computing devices. They also provide network services to the end users, such as real-time delivery of video and voice, best-effort delivery of data, or reliable delivery of mission-critical data.

The degree of granularity in describing system components is a trade-off between how detailed (and possibly accurate) you want the description to be versus how much time and effort you are willing to put into it. While the network is considered part of the system, for the purposes of designing the network, it will often be shown interfacing with it (since we don't know what the network will be at this time). When the design includes existing networks, they will also be considered part of the system.

FIGURE 1-2. Generic Components of a System

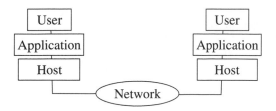

FIGURE 1-3. Traditional View of a System

Network designs have traditionally focused on providing connectivity between hosts. As such, the systems were described as the set (host, network) and typically did not consider the users or applications. Figure 1-3 shows (generically) what this set looks like.

This traditional view of a system is not complete enough for today's networks. In particular, we need to include users and their applications in the design. Experience shows that the degree of descriptiveness in the set (user, application, host, network) is usually sufficient to do a complete and accurate description for most end user or customer environments, yet not so large as to be overwhelming. In this set, users represent the end users, or customers, of the system. The end users are the recipients of the network services described in this chapter.

One reason for identifying components of the system is to understand how they interface with each other across component boundaries. By defining what the components of the system are, we are setting the boundary conditions between them, and what is to be expected across the system's interfaces. Using the set (user, application, host, network), Figure 1-4 shows some potential interfaces and boundary conditions.

While this description of the system is usually satisfactory for the start of most network designs, there will be times when you will want to describe more components or more defined interfaces in the design. As an example, consider the difference between a network using an asynchronous transfer mode (ATM) backbone with what is often referred to as a *native ATM network*.

FIGURE 1-4. Interfaces and Boundary Conditions

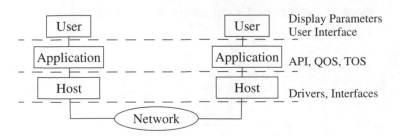

FIGURE 1-5. **Example of System with ATM in Network Backbone**

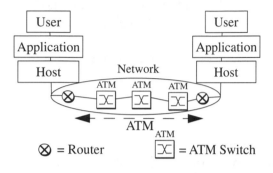

Figure 1-5 shows a design environment where ATM is used as a backbone technology. Here ATM does not directly interface with the hosts, applications, or users, but is usually isolated from them by routers. This is one of the scenarios described in the classical model of IP over ATM, discussed in detail in the design of the logical network. Within this system description, the ATM backbone is imbedded only in the network component of the set (user, application, host, network).

Figure 1-6, on the other hand, shows a native ATM network in which ATM is integrated into the host part of the set and will interface directly with the applications. In this case, the system may be better described as the set (user, application, ATM-specific API, ATM device driver, and network).

FIGURE 1-6. **Example of System with "Native ATM"**

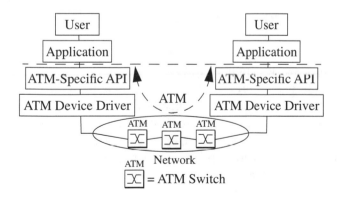

You should consider more detailed system descriptions when there is a need to identify system components that are likely to impact the delivery of services to the user. In Figure 1-6, the ATM-specific API translates application requirements to the ATM network. As part of the system description, the ATM-specific API is clearly recognized as being important. System descriptions can also be useful in showing where network addressing, routing, naming, accounting, management, or security may be applied.

1.4.2 Network Services

The concept of network services in this book builds upon the services work from two major networking organizations: the Internet Engineering Task Force (IETF) and the ATM Forum. These organizations are developing service descriptions for IP and ATM networks. They see network services as sets of network capabilities that can be configured and managed within the network. We apply this concept to network design, integrating services into the entire system. This will help you to take advantage of the services concept, by analyzing and designing based on services, and will also prepare you for the near future, when services will be configurable and manageable within the network.

Network services are defined as levels of performance and function that are offered by the network, host, and/or application, to the rest of the system, or as sets of requirements that are expected from the network by the end user, application, or host. Levels of performance will be described by performance characteristics such as capacity, delay, and reliability, while functions include security, accounting, billing, scheduling, and management.

It is important to note that the concept of services in this book is based on what the network can deliver to the system. Thus, it is not to be confused with services that applications may provide to the user (e.g., graphics rendering services). When the term "service" is used in this book, it is in reference to network service.

Network services in most of today's networks are based on best-effort delivery. In addition to best-effort delivery, we will examine some new types of services, including high-performance and specified (deterministic or guaranteed) services. These new services will require some different ways of looking at network design, and you will see how to incorporate these services into your design environment.

Network services are applied by grouping network performance and functional characteristics together, and using these characteristics to configure, monitor, and verify the service in the network, as shown in Figure 1-7.

FIGURE 1-7. Network Services as Groups of Characteristics and Levels

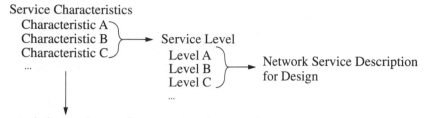

Characteristics used to configure services in network,
and as service metrics to measure and verify services

Service Characteristics

Service characteristics (individual network performance and functional parameters) are used to describe services that are offered by the network to the system (the *service offering*) or that are requested from the network by users, applications, or hosts (the *service request*). Service requirements are characteristics that are used to gauge the need of the system for services. Service characteristics and requirements are useful in the network analysis and design processes from two perspectives: in configuring services in network elements (e.g., routers, switches, host operating systems [OSs]) and in providing input into the network design.

Service discussions in this book focus on developing service requirements for the network and using service characteristics to configure, monitor, and verify services in the network.

In order for specified services to be useful and effective, they need to be described and provisioned end-to-end, at all components between end users, applications, or hosts. If services are not provisioned end-to-end, then some components will not be capable of supporting them, and the services will fail.

Services also need to be configurable, measurable, and verifiable within the system. This is necessary to insure that the end users are getting the services they are requesting (and probably paying for), and leads to accounting and billing for system, including network, resources. You will see how service metrics can be used to measure and verify services and their characteristics.

Services also are likely to be hierarchical within the system, with different service types, mechanisms, and levels applied at each layer in the hierarchy. By making them hierarchical, you can have general or nonspecific services in the network backbone, while placing more specific services close to the end users.

Service Levels

Service requirements or characteristics are grouped together to describe service levels for the network. This is done to make the service provisioning process easier, so that you can configure, measure, and verify a service level instead of a number of individual service characteristics. Service levels are also helpful in service accounting and billing. There are many ways to describe service levels, including *committed information rates* (CIRs), *classes of service* (COSs), *types of service* (TOSs), *qualities of service* (QOSs), and custom service levels based on groups of individual service characteristics depending on which network technology, protocol, or combination of these is providing the service.

Figure 1-8 indicates where service offerings, service requests, and service metrics are applied in the system. In this figure, the demarcation of services is shown between the host and network components. Depending on the service requirement or characteristic, however, the demarcation may also be between the host and application components.

Services and service levels can be distinguished by their degrees of predictability or determinism. In the next section we will discuss best-effort delivery services, which are nondeterministic, as well as specified (deterministic and guaranteed) services.

Services and service levels are also distinguished by their degrees of performance. You will see that service performance characteristics—in terms of reliability (i.e., availability), capacity (i.e., bandwidth), and delay (i.e., latency)—are used to describe services and service levels.

FIGURE 1-8. Service Level Demarcation

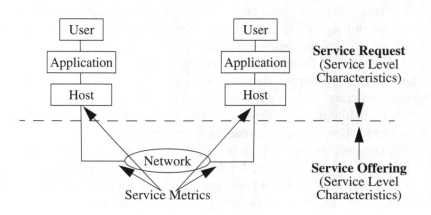

Determinism is sometimes equated to performance, but determinism is the ability to predict or guarantee a service, which implies knowledge about the state of the network, while performance is the relative levels of reliability, capacity, and delay in the network. Best-effort delivery services can be grouped into low- and high-performance, primarily for the purposes of capacity planning, and deterministic services can be grouped by various degrees of performance. The degrees of performance for best-effort delivery, deterministic, and guaranteed services will be coupled with the service metrics that can be used to configure, measure, and verify services in the network.

System Components and Network Services

Network services are derived from requirements at each of the components in the system. They are end-to-end within the system, describing what is expected at each component. Network service requirements are defined for each component: user requirements, application requirements, host requirements, and network requirements. Figure 1-9 shows each of these component services. Since the network component is what we are analyzing and designing, the network requirements are for existing networks that the design will incorporate or connect to.

These requirements add to each other, so that application requirements add to user requirements, host requirements add to application requirements, and all add to network requirements. Thus, requirements filter down from user to application to host, resulting in a service request that is a set of service requirements, or service levels, to the network. This results in a service offering that is end-to-end, consisting of service characteristics that are configured in each network element (e.g., router, bridge, circuit, etc.). In addition to providing performance and function to end users, network services also support the design and operation of the network. These are services such as network routing and addressing (described in detail in Chapter 12).

FIGURE 1-9. **System Components and Requirements**

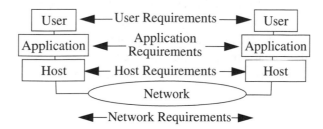

FIGURE 1-10. **Mismatch in Performance Between Network and Firewall Creates Performance Bottleneck**

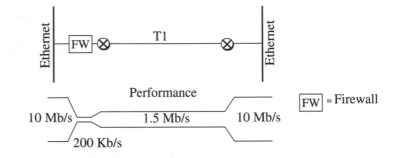

Network services are also necessary to keep the system functioning or to provide extra value or convenience to a system component (such as to the users). Some network services may focus on a particular function of one of the components, such as a client-server application or distributed-computing service. Examples of such services include network monitoring and management, security, and accounting. Services such as these are important in that they need to be considered an integral part of the network design. This may seem obvious, but traditionally services such as security and network management have been afterthoughts in network design, and their support from the network not considered until problems arise. Figure 1-10 shows the performance bottleneck created when a firewall that performs at 200 Kb/s is added to a network built with T1s (1.5 Mb/s) and Ethernets (10 Mb/s).

One of our design goals is to identify performance bottlenecks such as this before the network is implemented. By considering them early in the design process, we are more likely to understand their behavior and impact on the network and to design the network to accommodate their service requirements.

Element services describe low-level services that are configured within network elements or at interfaces between network elements. Element services are the most focused of the service descriptions, and also have the smallest scope.

Figure 1-11 shows the scope of end-to-end services and service characteristics at network elements in the system. When service characteristics apply to individual network elements, such as routers, switches, bridges, data service units (DSUs), and so on, their characteristics are often vendor-specific. In this book, we only discuss those characteristics that are part of public standards and that are not vendor-specific.

FIGURE 1-11. **End-to-End Services and Service Characteristics**

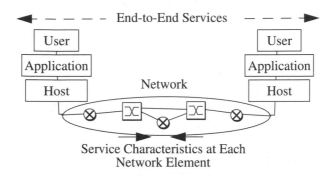

It is important to note that while standards-based characteristics are "standardized" on the basis of having their descriptions either publicly available (i.e., an IETF RFC), sanctioned by an organization recognized by the networking community, or generally accepted and used by the networking community (a de facto standard), the implementation of characteristics is open to interpretation and is often different across vendors and vendor platforms.

1.5 Characterizing Services

One of the goals of network analysis is to be able to characterize services so that they can be designed into the network, and requested from vendors and service providers. In addition to today's best-effort delivery services, we will also examine new types of services, specified (deterministic and guaranteed) services, as well as high- and low-performance services.

1.5.1 Service Requests

Service requests are distinguished by the degree of predictability needed in the service. Based on predictability, service requests are placed into best-effort (best-effort delivery) and specified (deterministic and guaranteed) groups.

Best-effort service means that there is no control over how the network will satisfy the service request, that no guarantees are presented, nor is the network obligated to do more than try. Such requests indicate that the rest of the system (user, application, host) will need to adapt to the state of the network at any given time. Thus, the expected service for such requests will be unpredictable and variable across the range of performance values. Such service requests either have no performance requirements for the network, or the requirements are nonspecific. Since these requests are nonspecific, they are not tuned to any specific user or application service requirements.

Specified service requests are based on some knowledge of or control over the state of the system. A specified service request may require that the service operates either predictably or within some specified bounds. These services have more stringent service requirements than best-effort services. In order for the network to provision resources to support a deterministic service request, the service requirements of the request must be measurable and verifiable. This is where service metrics are applied.

For example, if a specified service request is made for capacity to be between 4 and 10 Mb/s, then there needs to be a way to translate these service requirements into a service offering from the network, a way to measure and/or derive these capacity characteristics from the network, as well as a statistical method to control the information flow and the network to keep this service between 4 and 10 Mb/s.

Specified service requests can also be based on the ability to actually guarantee the service through the network. This type of service has the most stringent service requirements, and requires a mechanism (such as a service contract and policing) to guarantee service end-to-end within the system, even to the exclusion of other users, applications, or hosts (as in bounded access described earlier).

By the nature of specified service requests, each request will identify specific requirements for service. These service requirements are based on performance and function. Service performance requirements are described in terms of the service characteristics we discussed earlier (reliability, delay, and capacity), while service functional requirements are in terms of specific functions such as the need for multicast, security, or accounting. Service requests for performance will result in describing low- and high-performance services, and how to use these performance levels in the network design.

Service performance requirements are usually grouped into service levels. Service levels can be the same as specified service requests, but can also be closely related to well-known service offerings from the network, such as ATM QOS or switched multimegabit data service (SMDS) classes of service. Thus, service levels are a way to group service performance requirements into a specified service request that can be mapped onto a well-known or standard network service offering. As in Figure 1-12, a properly specified service will provide insight into which performance requirements should be measured in the system, as well as how to measure and verify service levels within the network.

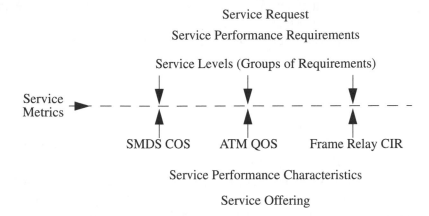

FIGURE 1-12. **Mapping Service Levels to Service Offerings**

1.5.2 Service Offerings

From the network perspective, services from the network are offered to users, applications, and hosts. These service offerings (as in SMDS, ATM, and Frame Relay in Figure 1-12) are the network counterparts to the service requests from the users, applications, and hosts.

Like service requests, service offerings are also separated into two groups: best-effort and specified. Best-effort service offerings are not predictable—they are based on the state of the network at any given time. There is little or no prior knowledge about the network, and there is no control over the network at any time. Most networks today operate in a best-effort mode. A good example of a network offering best-effort service is the current Internet.

The best-effort service offering is compatible with the best-effort service request. Neither the service request nor the service offering assume any knowledge of the state of or control over the network, therefore the network offers whatever service is available at that time, and the rest of the system adapts the flow of information to the available service. An example of a best-effort service request and offering is when a file transfer (via FTP) occurs over a best-effort network such as the Internet. FTP uses the transmission control protocol (TCP) as its transport method, which, via a sliding-window flow-control mechanism, adapts to the current state of the network it is operating over. Thus, the service requirement from FTP over TCP is best-effort, and the corresponding service offering from the Internet is best-effort. The result is that, while the FTP session is active, the performance characteristics of the network (Internet) and transport method (TCP) are constantly interacting and adapting, as well as contending with other application sessions for network resources. As part of its best-effort service, TCP provides error-free, reliable transmission to the application.

On the other hand, specified (deterministic and guaranteed) service offerings are predictable, bounded, or guaranteed. There is some knowledge of the network and possibly control over the network, in order to meet performance bounds or guarantees. Thus, *specified* refers to the ability of the network to offer a measurable and verifiable service, and possibly that the service itself has a high level of performance.

Services that are specified can also be low- or high-performance. If a service is specified, it does not necessarily mean that service is also high-performance. For example, using our definition of specified service, the telephone network offers this type of service. While at first look this may seem unlikely, consider the nature of the telephone service. In order to support voice conversations, the network must be able to support fairly strict delay and delay variation tolerances, even though the capacity per user session (telephone call) is relatively small, or low-performance. What is well-known from a telephony perspective is somewhat new in the current world of data networking. The support of strict, known delay, and delay variation services is considered a specified service offering in a data network.

The specified service offering is compatible to the specified service requests. In each case, the service performance requirements *reliability*, *delay*, and *capacity* (in the service request) are translated into service performance characteristics (in the service offering).

An example of specified service requests and offerings is shown in a network designed to support real-time streams of telemetry data. A design goal for a network supporting real-time telemetry would be the ability to specify end-to-end delay and have the network satisfy this delay request. A real-time telemetry stream will have end-to-end delay requirements that form the basis for a specified service request. For example, this specified service request may be for an end-to-end delay of 25 ms, with a delay variation of 400 microseconds. This would form the request and the service level (i.e., a QOS level) that needs to be supported by the network. The network would then be designed to provide a specified service offering at a QOS level of 25-ms end-to-end delay and 400-microsecond delay variation. The delay and delay variation would then be measured and verified with service metrics in the network, perhaps using application tools such as *ping* or tcpdump, or with a custom application.

In describing service performance requirements and characteristics within an environment, we will use various performance levels (also known as reference levels)—thresholds, bounds, and guarantees. We will also use general performance levels or set environment-specific levels to distinguish between low- and high-performance.

FIGURE 1-13. **Service Requests and Offerings**

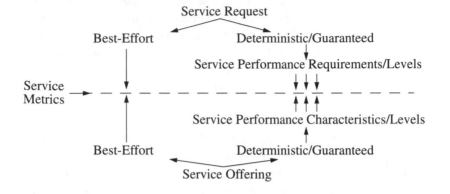

This approach does not mean that best-effort service offerings are inherently low-performance, lossy, or unreliable, or that specified services are necessarily high-performance. What this approach does is signify that predictability in service offerings is also an important characteristic and is separate from performance. There are times when the network is best designed for best-effort service offerings, and other times when both best-effort and specified service offerings are needed. We will see that when specified services requests are made to the network, consideration for these requirements will tend to drive the network design from one perspective, while consideration for best-effort service requests will drive the network design from another perspective. It will be the combination of service requests/ offerings, best-effort and specified, that will make the design complete.

Figure 1-13 shows how service requests and their performance requirements correspond to service offerings and performance characteristics.

1.5.3 Service Performance Requirements

Specified services are now described in greater detail, in terms of the service performance requirements reliability, capacity, and delay. As you will see, these service performance requirements are related.

Reliability

Reliability is a measure of the system's ability to provide deterministic and accurate delivery of information. Reliability consists of determinism and accuracy. Reliability can be deterministic in that a guarantee of delivery of information may need to occur within a well-known time boundary. Such a time boundary is composed of an overall completion time for the task as well as a degree of consistency in the time boundary. These time boundaries are set by the system components, such as in TCP or SMTP time-out values, or by the user's perception of reliability.

For example, the emphasis of the network design may be to bound delay; a system supporting point-of-sale transactions may need to guarantee delivery of customer information and completion of the transaction within 15 seconds (where the network delay is on the order of 200 ms); a Web application can have similar requirements. However, in a compute-intensive application we can usually optimize the system by buffering data during periods of computing. In this case, delay may not be as important as the guarantee of eventual delivery. On the other hand, a system supporting the visualization of real-time banking transactions may require a round-trip delay guarantee of less than 40 ms, with a delay variation guarantee of less than 100 microseconds. If these delay boundaries are exceeded, then the visualization application fails for that transaction, forcing the system to use other, unbounded techniques.

Reliability requires accuracy in that the information received at the destination must usually be guaranteed to be exactly the same as that sent from the source. This also has a delay component, for the guarantee of accuracy will require error checking and retransmission of lost or errored information. It can be argued that reliability is only the guarantee of accuracy with no time constraints. My experience, however, has been that reliability is service-oriented from the user perspective, and user perceptions of service are often time-oriented. In the chapters on requirements analysis, we will discuss some of the typical user tolerances for interactive responses to the system.

Capacity

Capacity is a measure of the system's ability to transfer information. There are several terms that are often used interchangeably with capacity, such as *bandwidth*, *throughput*, and *goodput*. While we will use the generic term *capacity* throughout the book, two well-known types of capacity are described here.

- *Bandwidth* is the theoretical capacity of one or more elements or components in the system. Theoretical, or raw, bandwidth does not take into account overhead from higher-layer protocols or the performance loss due to inefficiencies in the system (i.e., delays in the operating system or peripherals). For example, the theoretical capacity or bandwidth of a SONET OC-3c circuit is 155.52 Mb/s, which is three times the bandwidth of an OC-1 circuit (51.84 Mb/s). This bandwidth does not consider data-link, network-layer, or transport-layer protocol (such as ATM, IP, or TCP/UDP) overhead, or, in the case of wide-area networks, the loss in performance due to the bandwidth*delay product in the network.

- *Throughput* is the realizable capacity of the system or its components or elements. Values for actual capacity will vary, depending on system design, types and configuration of equipment, and where in the protocol stack the measurement for capacity is being taken. When the OC-3c circuit described above is tested, values of actual capacity range from approximately 80 Mb/s to 128 Mb/s (measurements taken at the transport [TCP] layer of the NREN and NAS networks, NASA Ames Research Center, March 1996). Throughput is the more important term when describing the system and its service requirements, as this is what is seen and used by the user and application components.

Delay

Delay is a measure of the time differences in the transmission of information across the system. In its most basic sense, delay is the time difference in transmitting a single unit of information (bit, byte, cell, frame, packet) from source to destination. This will include delays at various layers, such as propagation, transmission, queueing, and processing delays. Both end-to-end and round-trip time measurements are useful, with round-trip times being practical measures of delay, as in the use of the *ping* application.

Another measure of delay incorporates application processing and task completion times. As the size of the task increases, the application processing and task completion times also increase. At some point this overall delay, here termed *latency*, may yield important information about the behavior of the applications and the network. Note that the term *latency* is also used by others to describe the delay through a component of the network, such as the latency through a switch or router. In this book this term is used in a different way, describing the time behavior of application processing. Together, both delay (end-to-end and round-trip) and latency help to describe network behavior. Latency can be thought of as a macroscopic view of network time behavior, while delay is a microscopic view.

Service performance requirements are brought together to describe an overall performance envelope for the system. Figures 1-14 and 1-15 show two such environments. In Figure 1-14, the performance envelope consists of capacity, in terms of data sizes transferred across the network, and end-to-end delay. In Figure 1-15, the service performance envelope is expanded to three dimensions, to include the performance characteristic reliability.

These performance envelopes are useful for visualizing the regions of performance in which the network will be expected to operate. We can also map the service performance requirements from our applications onto these environments, showing each application's relative performance.

FIGURE 1-14. **Example of Service Performance Envelope Describing Capacity and Delay**

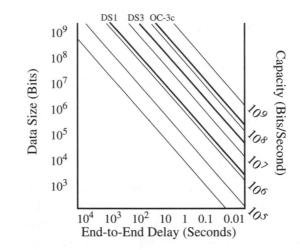

The environment in Figure 1-15 also describes two regions of performance—a low-performance region and a high-performance region—which are functions of reliability, delay, and capacity. We will now expand upon these performance envelopes to show service metrics and reference levels: boundaries and ranges of capacity, reliability, and delay for best-effort, deterministic, and guaranteed services.

FIGURE 1-15. **Example of Service Performance Envelope**

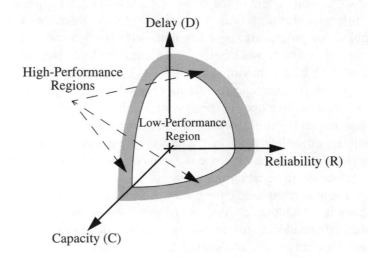

1.5.4 Service Metrics

While service performance requirements are useful in describing service requests, they may not be measurable by the system. Therefore, we will further describe performance requirements in terms of *service metrics*. Service metrics are intended to be measurable, so that we can couple service performance requirements to values that can be used to configure, measure, and verify services.

Since service metrics are meant to be measurable quantities, they can also be used to establish reference levels for service performance. A reference level is a level in service performance (a combination of service metrics for reliability, capacity, and delay) against which the service is compared. Actual measurements of service performance are compared against these reference levels. There are three types of reference levels: *service thresholds*, *service boundaries*, and *service guarantees*.

Service thresholds are discriminators used on applications to distinguish between high-performance and low-performance service. Service boundaries are combinations of low- and/or high-performance levels, used to predict a service level for an application. Service guarantees are strict performance levels. When they are not met, the result may be some type of action from the system (such as policing). Reference levels are described in terms of service metrics for the system (i.e., simple network management protocol (SNMP) management information base (MIB) variables for each network element). For example, we may choose a reference level of the amount of capacity being utilized, a service metric of the number of bytes in or out of each interface of the network elements, and MIB variables of ifInOctets and ifOutOctets.

General reference levels are common to most systems and environments, while environment-specific reference levels apply only to the design environment they were developed for. In establishing reference levels, we will apply the following conditions: first, that reference levels (and service metrics) must be measurable within the system for which they are defined, and second, that when both general and environment-specific reference levels are applied to a system, the more specific reference levels (usually the environment-specific levels) take precedence. Figures 1-16 and 1-17 show some general service thresholds, boundaries, and guarantees.

FIGURE 1-16. Example of Reference Levels—Service Thresholds

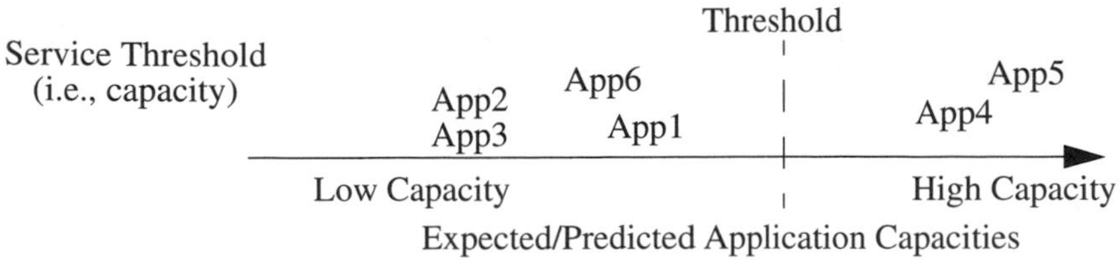

FIGURE 1-17. Example of Reference Levels—Boundaries and Guarantees

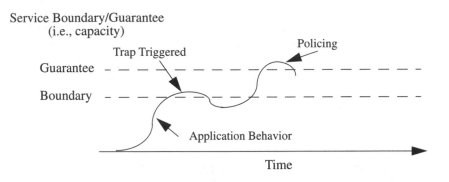

In Figure 1-16, the expected or measured capacities of various applications are plotted on a graph. A service threshold (capacity) is applied to the graph, separating low-capacity and high-capacity applications. Where the threshold is placed depends on the design environment and the relative variation in performance between applications. In some environments there will be a large difference in performance levels between applications (e.g., a medical environment where medical imaging and telemedicine is combined with email and Web browsing), while in other environments all applications will have roughly the same performance characteristics.

Service performance requirements, characteristics, and metrics can also be used to determine service levels. As we proceed through the chapters on requirements and flow analyses, we will see that sets of service performance requirements, characteristics, and metrics can be used to specify a level of service for an application.

1.5.5 Reservations and Deadline Scheduling

We also need to consider applications whose delay requirements may be real-time or interactive, but whose sessions will not be active until some time—minutes to hours—in the future. Some applications can be planned to run at a future time, and the resources needed to run the application can be reserved. One of those resources is the network, and, as applications become more sophisticated, the ability to reserve the network will become a major benefit to those applications and their users. When the application session is active, the service performance requirements are treated the same as for other applications. The big difference here is that we can have prior knowledge about an application session and we can plan for that session in advance. This may be as little as simply keeping tabs on the state of the session and reporting it to the user, or as much as setting up a virtual circuit at session start time with requested capacity, reliability, and/or delay characteristics.

Another type of application with future requirements does not have to start in the future, but has a deadline when all tasks associated with that application session must be completed. Deadline scheduling places increasing degrees of priority on the network resources, which become critical as the deadline approaches. For these applications, we may start with a particular level of performance and increase one or more performance characteristics as timers (times to deadline) expire.

What is important to note from these application types is that there are applications today (and more emerging) that can schedule their resources in advance, and we can take advantage of this in the network design and in the system.

1.6 Concluding Remarks

At this point in the network analysis process, you have learned that networks are not independent entities but are a part of the system, and that network services are one of the goals of the system. Network services are what are offered to the end users and applications, so that they can accomplish their work on the system. In order for you to design the network to support services, you need to know what they are, how they work together, and how to characterize them. Once you do this, you will have a broad view of what we are trying to design for, which you can take to the next levels of detail as you proceed with the network analysis and design.

Taking a systems approach to network design means considering the network as a part of a system instead of an independent entity. The system, composed of users, applications, hosts, and networks, offers services to the end users/customers. Services are sets of functions and features that enable the end users/customers to perform their work within the system.

By describing the system as a set of components, you can develop boundaries and interfaces between the components to help users understand how they interact and recognize the characteristics of the interactions. For the purposes of network design, we choose a boundary between what is offered by the system (the service offering) and what is required from the system by its end users/customers (the service request).

Services can be described in greater detail with service characteristics. We characterize services as

- *Best-effort delivery:* When there are no specific requirements or guarantees associated with the service.
- *Specified delivery:* When the service specifies levels of performance or functionality, or when performance levels or functions are guaranteed by the system.

To go a level deeper in the discussion about services, we must consider the service performance characteristics reliability, capacity, and delay. These characteristics will only be useful if we can measure their values in the system. We discussed these values, service metrics, as well as reference levels (thresholds, boundaries, and guarantees) that help us to specify service levels or to set a service boundary. Service performance characteristics, reference levels, and service metrics are combined in a *service performance envelope*, a diagram that visualizes their relationships and relative values.

Having thought about services and their characteristics, we are now ready to quantify what we want from the network. In order to do this, we first need to gather, analyze, and understand the requirements from the system. This is *requirements analysis*, the next step in the network analysis process.

Suggested Further Reading

There are several excellent requests for comment (RFCs) and Internet-drafts available from the IETF. For the topics of systems design and network services, it is recommended that you read the activities of the IETF Integrated Services Working Group (INT-SERV), Integrated Services Over Specific Link Layers (ISSLL), and Resource Reservation Setup Protocol (RSVP). Other excellent reading:

1. ATM Forum Technical Committee. *Traffic Management Specification v4.0.* April 1996.

2. Braden, R., Clark, D., and Shenker, S. Integrated services in the Internet architecture: An overview. *RFC 1633*, June 1994.

3. Casner, S., Frederick, R., Jacobson, V., and Schulzrinne, H. RTP: A transport protocol for real-time applications. *RFC 1889*, January 1996.

4. Onvural, R.O., *Asynchronous Transfer Mode Networks: Performance Issues.* Artech House, Norwood, MA, 1996.

5. Partridge, C. *Gigabit Networking.* Addison-Wesley, Reading, MA, 1994.

6. Topolcic, C. Experimental Internet Stream Protocol, Version 2 (ST-II). *RFC 1819.*

Exercises

1. Read the relevant RFCs and Internet-drafts from the Integrated Services Working Group (INT-SERV) of the IETF. How do these RFCs and drafts compare and contrast to the discussion of services in this chapter? How do they compare to the concept of services from the ATM Forum, based on the above references?

2. How would services be applied in an Internet environment? Describe three levels of services for this environment. How might these services differ if they were for an intranet environment?

3. RFC 1633 describes a real-time service offering. What does real time mean in the context of this RFC? Name two applications that fall under the description of real time in this RFC.

4. What characterizes a best-effort service? A specified service? Can both types of services coexist on the same network? If so, how? Outline mechanisms to combine both types of services on the network.

5. The performance characteristics reliability, capacity, and delay are related to each other. Redundancy, for example, is a factor in reliability, but is also based on capacity and delay. Show how changes in the capacity and delay in a network can impact its degrees of redundancy and reliability.

CHAPTER 2

Requirements Analysis: Concepts

As you may already have noticed, the network analysis part of this book—consisting of requirements analysis and flow analysis—introduces many new concepts and guidelines and expands upon several existing concepts. Therefore, these two topics are separated into three chapters each, covering concepts, guidelines, and practice, respectively, in order to make this material more readable and useful. The concepts chapters provide the background material for each topic, explaining and defining pertinent concepts. The guidelines chapters expand on these concepts to build a process for you to apply to your designs. The practice chapters bring the concepts and guidelines together with practical examples and case studies, solidifying the process for you. Let's begin with the concepts for requirements analysis.

2.1 Background for Requirements Analysis

We begin the network analysis process with requirements analysis, which is about understanding your design environment. This consists of identifying, gathering, and understanding system requirements and their characteristics, and developing thresholds for performance to distinguish between low- and high-performance services, as well as to determine specified services for the network.

Why do requirements analysis? Requirements analysis is fundamental to the network design process but is often overlooked or ignored. Why is this the case? A major reason that requirements analysis is not given proper consideration is the degree of difficulty of this part of the design process. Gathering requirements means talking to users and network personnel and interpreting the results. Talking to N users may result in $N+1$ different sets of user requirements. Network personnel are often distanced from the users and do not have a clear idea of what users want or need. Additionally, requirements analysis may appear to offer no immediate payoff, for it is part of an overall strategy for intelligently designing and building networks. Finally, requirements analysis means putting thought and time into the design.

A result of not doing proper requirements analysis is that the network design ends up being based on factors other than what the users or applications need. For example, the design may be based on a particular technology, typically one that the designer feels most comfortable with. Another example is a design based on a particular vendor, again one that the designer is comfortable with. An obvious example is having a budget constraint or a deadline for completing the design that forces the designer to make do and apply familiar, easy-to-apply technologies. Problems with these types of designs are that they are not objective, and that familiar technologies, protocols, or vendors may be poor choices for that particular environment.

Requirements analysis helps the designer to better understand the probable behavior of the network being designed. This results in immediate payoffs:

- More objective, informed choices of network technologies and services
- The ability to match interconnection strategies to networks
- Networks and components properly sized to users and applications
- A better understanding of where and how to apply services in the network

As you proceed through the rest of this book, you will see that the requirements analysis process forms the foundation upon which all other components of network design are built.

Through requirements analysis, we will use requirements to distinguish between low- and high-performance applications for our design environment; to identify specific services; to gather performance requirements for use in flow analysis; and to gather other requirements to be used throughout the analysis process. We will see that low- and high-performance is relative to the design environment, and we will use performance thresholds to help us distinguish between them.

In this chapter you will learn to expand upon the service description and to identify or derive network requirements from the system. Network requirements are coupled to services, and we will develop a requirements specification to map out requirements and help determine their dependencies. You will learn how to apply some of the concepts discussed in the last chapter, such as reference levels to distinguish between low- and high-performance, to a variety of customer requirements. The results of the requirements analysis are the *requirements specification* and the *applications map*. The requirements specification is a series of worksheets that list the requirements gathered for your design, and is the start of several worksheets developed to help you through the design process. The applications map shows the location dependencies between applications, which will be used for flow analysis.

2.2 User Requirements

From the model of system components in our generic system, the user component is at the highest layer. Figure 2-1 shows the relationship between these components.

We begin describing requirements at this layer, which will lead to the development of more specific requirements as we work through each of the components.

From the user perspective we can ask, What does it take to get the job done? In general, the system should adapt to the user environment, provide quick and reliable information access and transfer, and offer quality service to the user. This indicates the following general requirements:

- Timeliness
- Interactivity
- Reliability
- Quality
- Adaptability
- Security
- Affordability

FIGURE 2-1. **User Component of the Generic System**

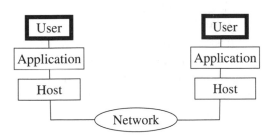

These requirements may change, depending on the user environment. Note that these requirements can be somewhat subjective. Thus, although they are described here, the intent is to use them as the start toward developing more objective requirements in the other components.

Timeliness is a requirement that the user is able to access, transfer, or modify information within a tolerable time frame. What a "tolerable" time frame is, of course, depends on the user's perception of delay in the system. It is this perception that we want to quantify. For example, a user may want to download files from a server, and complete each transfer within 10 minutes. Or the user may need to receive video frames every 30 ms. Each one of these times indicates a delay that the network will need to provide. For timeliness, end-to-end or round-trip delay is an important measurement.

Interactivity is similar to timeliness, but focuses on a response time from the system (and network). In the example above, we could consider the 10 minutes needed to download a file as the response time for the system, and that the file transfer is interacting with the user (which it is), but we want to look at interactivity as an indication of response times that are on the order of human response times. Therefore, interactivity is a measure of the response time of the system when it is required to actively interact with a human. Delay, here the round-trip delay, is a measure of interactivity. Using these descriptions of timeliness and interactivity, timeliness is more likely to be associated with bulk file or image transfer, while interactivity is associated with remote host access (telnet), Web use, or visualization.

Reliability, that is, availability from the user perspective, is a requirement for consistently available service. Not only must the user be able to have access to system resources a very high percentage of the time, but the level of service to the user (in terms of system or network performance) must be consistent. Thus, reliability is closely related to the performance characteristic reliability, but delay and capacity are also important. It is likely that a combination of all three performance characteristics would be used to describe reliability.

Quality refers to the quality of the presentation to the user. This may be the user's perception of the audio, video, and/or data displays. As examples, consider the current Internet capabilities of videoconferencing, video feeds, and telephony. While it is possible to do all of these on the Internet, there are other mechanisms that provide much better presentation quality. It is often not sufficient to provide a capability over a network, but that capability must be as good or better than other mechanisms, or the user will be disappointed. Measures of quality will include all of the performance characteristics.

Adaptability is the ability of the system to adapt to the users' changing needs. Some examples of this are in distance-independence and mobility. As users rely more and more on the network, they are becoming coupled to logical services and decoupled from physical servers. This decoupling means that users don't have to care where servers are located, as long as they can get the services they need. A result of this is distance-independent computing, where the user loses all knowledge of where jobs are being executed. Mobility refers to mobile computing, where the user can access services and resources from any location, using portable computers and dial access to the network. Adaptability to such user needs forces requirements on the system design.

Security from the user perspective is a requirement to guarantee the integrity (accuracy and authenticity) of the user's information and physical resources, as well as access to the user's and system's resources. Security is probably closest to the performance characteristic reliability, but it will impact capacity and delay.

Affordability is the last general user requirement. Although this requirement is not technical, it will impact the network design. What we are looking for in this requirement is what the user or customer can afford to purchase for the network, so that our design does not cost too much to implement. As a user requirement, we are looking for how costs and funding are tied to users or groups of users. We will also discuss funding as a system-wide requirement, from an overall budget perspective.

In addition to these requirements, we will want to know how many users will be expected on the network, and their locations. If possible, estimate what the growth in users will be over the first one to three years after the network is planned to be operational, or for what you expect the life cycle of the network to be. We can now use these requirements as the interface of the user component, as shown in Figure 2-2.

FIGURE 2-2. **User Component Interface to System**

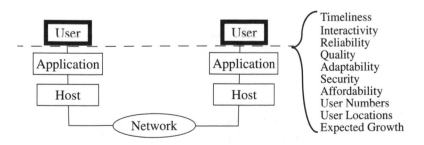

2.3 Application Requirements

The application component interfaces with the user and host components, and is a key part of the requirements analysis. Figure 2-3 shows the relationship of the application component to other components in the system.

Services in the network can be described by the requirements reliability, capacity, and delay. In the previous section, user requirements were shown to be related to these performance requirements, as diagrammed in Figure 2-4. Starting with Figure 2-4, we will map user requirements and performance requirements to applications, and will type applications based on these performance requirements.

2.3.1 Types of Applications

In the system description (user, application, host, network), the application component is pivotal. The application component is where user requirements are translated into performance requirements for the host and network components. It is at the application component where requirements and performance or service levels meet.

In the early days of networking, applications supported basic connectivity and data transfer between hosts. While most applications still have their basis in these two functions, the user requirements (timeliness, interactivity, reliability, quality, adaptability, security, and affordability) and the performance requirements (reliability, capacity, and delay) are now being emphasized. We can use these service and performance requirements to distinguish between applications that need specific service levels and those that do not. Based on service and service performance requirements, we will type applications as:

- *Mission-critical applications* have specified (deterministic and/or guaranteed) reliability
- *Controlled-rate applications* have specified capacity
- *Real-time* (and possibly *interactive*) *applications* have specified delay

FIGURE 2-3. **Application Component of the Generic System**

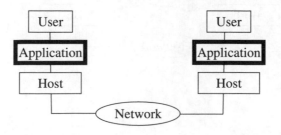

FIGURE 2-4. User Service and Performance Requirements

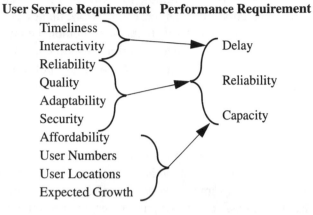

These application types will be described by their requirements and metrics, as well as how they translate to the user requirements.

Descriptions of performance requirements for applications will separate specified services from best-effort services. Since performance requirements are relative, it is important that this information is modified to best suit your environment and design goals.

2.3.2 Reliability

Let's first look at reliability. Reliability is a measure of the system's ability to provide deterministic and accurate delivery of information, but how does that relate to the applications that will use the system?

Reliability can be subjective—many users will argue that their applications require a high degree of reliability (in terms of availability) from the system—but there are some applications that must maintain high reliability in order to function. A loss of reliability in such applications may be serious or disastrous, such as:

- Loss of revenue or customers. For example, an application that handles lots of transactions and money, such as an investment banking or airline reservation application.

- Unrecoverable information or situation. Telemetry processing and teleconferencing applications are good examples here.

- Loss of sensitive data. Examples include customer ID/billing and intelligence-gathering applications.

- Loss of life. Examples include transportation or health-care monitoring applications.

In these situations, either the system is not available to process user/application requests, or the system is not available to complete the transactions that are in progress. For applications such as these, a network that offers only best-effort delivery is not likely to be sufficient, due to its unpredictable behavior. These applications require deterministic or guaranteed reliability, which take the form of predictable or bounded reliability, or a high degree of reliability, or both. Applications that require such reliability are termed here *mission-critical applications*.

2.3.3 Capacity

In terms of capacity, there are applications that require a well-understood amount of capacity. Such applications, termed here *controlled-rate applications*, include voice, nonbuffered video, and some teleservice applications. Controlled-rate applications may require thresholds, bounds, or guarantees on minimum capacity, peak capacity, or sustained capacity.

Note the difference between controlled-rate applications and best-effort applications such as traditional file transfer (where the file transfer application is not written to operate only when a specified service is available). In file transfer (such as in FTP running over TCP, described earlier), the application receives the available capacity from the network, based on the state of the network at that time, as well as interactions between TCP and the lower layers. While at times this will be a high degree of capacity, there is no control over the resources in the network to predict or guarantee a particular level of capacity to the application. Controlled-rate applications require a specific (usually minimum) capacity in order to function properly. This can often also be tied to the end-to-end delay of the network, as capacity will impact delay.

2.3.4 Delay

Increasing interactivity is arguably the driving force behind the evolution of many applications. Consider the evolutionary path of information access, from telnet and FTP to gopher and Archie to Mosaic and Netscape, made even more interactive with the use of JAVA applets and VRML. As we saw in the previous section, interactivity relies on the performance requirement delay.

Delay is a measure of the time differences in the transfer and processing of information. There are many sources of delay, including propagation, transmission, queueing, processing, routing, and so on. This section focuses on end-to-end and round-trip delays, which encompass all of the delay types. From an application service perspective, optimizing the total, end-to-end or round-trip delay is more important than focusing on individual sources of delay. Individual sources of delay become more important as we get into the lower components and elements, as well as in the design optimization process.

Historically, applications used on the Internet did not have strict delay requirements. They relied on best-effort service from the Internet and did not request or expect any service guarantees. Other applications, found primarily on private networks, have had more strict delay requirements. Some private networks have been effective in providing support for service guarantees, either by engineering the network with substantial spare capacity, or at the trade-off of interoperability with other networks. But we now find that applications with delay requirements are migrating to the Internet or IP intranets, and applications previously dedicated to a single user or host are now being used across the Internet and intranets (as well as other networks), forcing a reevaluation of offering services other than best-effort on the Internet.

The term *real-time* has been used to describe the need for strict delay tolerance, but this term is interpreted in many different ways. Often, what real time really means is "as fast as possible," which is difficult to quantify. There are several application delay types defined in this section, including real time, non-real-time, interactive, asynchronous, burst, and bulk.

Real-time applications are those that have the most strict timing relationship between source and destination, with timers set for the receipt of information at the destination. Information received after the timers expire at the destination is considered worthless and is dropped. Thus, this definition of real time does not mean that information has to be transferred within a well-known, established time boundary, but rather that the delay boundary is understood by source and destination, and that the destination does not wait beyond this boundary. Real time could mean end-to-end delays of 30 ms for some applications and 30 seconds for others. An example of this is nonbuffered video playback. If the video stream is delayed beyond the playback timer, the destination will show one or more blank portions of frames (appearing as blips on the screen) and drop the late video. This is done to preserve the time continuity of the video being shown at the playback device.

Non-real-time applications have various end-to-end delay requirements, at times more stringent than real-time applications, but the important factor here is that the destination will wait (within reason) until the information is received. How long the destination will wait is a function of the timers set in the applications and at the hosts. Non-real-time applications include all of the types listed below, interactive and asynchronous, which accounts for the vast majority of applications. Non-real-time applications are further separated into interactive and asynchronous applications.

Interactive applications assume a timing relationship between source and destination while the application session is active. Interactive applications are what many people would consider real time, under the traditional connotation of real time as "as fast as possible." The common interactive applications, such as telnet, FTP, and Web applications, fall under this type.

Asynchronous applications are insensitive to time, either assuming no timing relationship or that the timing is outside the bounds of the application session. A good example of an asynchronous application is email. When email is sent to a recipient, all knowledge of timing (when the email is received at any intermediate stop or at the final destination) is lost to the sender. Only if there is an error in the system or recipient information, or if it is requested, is the sender notified. Applications that process large amounts of data in a bulk or batch fashion may often be considered asynchronous.

Finally, interactive applications may be further subdivided into *burst* and *bulk* types. To distinguish between interactive burst and bulk applications, we need to determine when the processing times of the system components (particularly the application component) overwhelms the end-to-end delay of the system. What we are looking for here is a way to distinguish between when an application will frequently and quickly interact with a user and when a user will have to wait substantial periods of time while the application is processing information.

The relationships between the various delay types, and some application examples, are shown in Figure 2-5.

When we apply general reference thresholds to these application types, we will see that, from a delay perspective, real time is considered high-performance, and asynchronous is considered low-performance. Interactive-burst and interactive-bulk can be either low- or high-performance. This will be discussed in more detail later in the chapter.

FIGURE 2-5. Application Delay Types

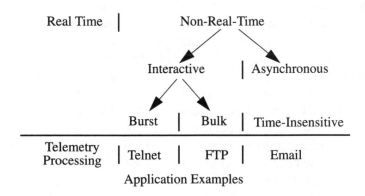

2.3.5 Application Groups

We have so far used various applications as examples to convey application requirements. It is useful to group applications with similar performance characteristics together, as it helps both in the mapping of performance characteristics and in gathering requirements. By developing application groups, often we can more quickly and easily determine general performance characteristics by mapping the application to one of the groups. By using application groups, we have fewer service profiles to consider.

The following application groups are identified by using the requirements analysis process. There is some overlap between these groups, and it is expected that this is a small fraction of the actual number of possible application groups.

- *Command and control/telemetry applications*. While this may seem military in appearance, it really describes applications where data and command information is transmitted between remote objects and one or more control stations for command, control, tracking, and status determination of the remote objects. A remote object may be a commercial aircraft, a submersible remotely piloted vehicle (RPV), a spacecraft, or sensors in a house. Telemetry/command and control applications can be characterized as having high-performance delay and reliability, possibly being mission-critical and/or real-time applications.

- *Visualization applications*. This ranges from two-dimensional viewing of objects to three-dimensional and virtual reality viewing and manipulation of objects. The visualization may be of a numerical simulation or of experimental data. Examples include visualizations of fluid flow fields around various objects (e.g., weather modeling, aeronautics, or medicine), to commercial and military gaming simulations. Visualization applications can be characterized as having high-performance capacity and delay, possibly being real-time and/or controlled-rate applications.

- *Distributed-computing applications*. Applications using this type of computing may range from having the computing engines sharing the same local bus (parallel computing), to being co-located at the same LAN (as in a computing cluster), to being distributed across LAN, MAN, and WAN boundaries. The degree of distribution or parallelism in the computing is also determined by the granularity of the task and the degree of coupling between the computing engines. An example of distributed-computing is in making use of personal computers in the corporate environment late at night, when they are idle, by coupling their computing capability to accomplish large tasks. Distributed-computing applications can be characterized as having high-performance delay, possibly being interactive applications.

- *Applications for Web access, development, and use.* These applications are the current interactive equivalents of the traditional remote host and information-access utilities telnet and FTP. Web access and use involves accessing remote hosts and downloading and/or uploading information. This is done with the aid of graphic interfaces. Typically, Web sessions are interactive, and the amounts of information are small relative to the other application groups. These applications are generally considered delay-sensitive, but not high-performance.

- *Bulk data transport.* When the amounts of information desired are relatively large and the sessions are less interactive (or asynchronous), applications are used that optimize the data transfer rate at the expense of interactivity. The traditional example of this is FTP, and currently more effective applications such as *mftp* and *arcp* are available. For more information on *mftp* and *arcp* see *<www.nas.nasa.gov/>*. These applications are not considered high-performance.

- *Tele*service applications.* This describes the group of applications that provide a subset of voice, video, and data together to be delivered simultaneously to groups of people at various locations. Examples include teleconferencing, tele-medicine, and teleseminars. The multicast backbone (*mbone*) is an example of network support for this application group on the Internet. Tele*service applications can be characterized as having high-performance capacity, delay, and/or reliability, depending on the application.

- *Operations, administration, and maintenance (OAM) applications.* System OAM applications and services are required for the proper functioning and operation of the network. Examples include domain name service (DNS), mail services/SMTP, news services/NNTP, address resolution service, network monitoring and management, network security, and systems accounting. These applications generally require high reliability.

You may be able to apply more application groups to your environment. An exercise that you can perform is to list the top 20 applications that you expect to use in your network (or currently use in the existing network). List the actual or estimated performance characteristics for each application and try to place them into groups. You can then use these groups in the future to help you estimate similar application characteristics.

Application types, their performance requirements, their locations, and application groups form the interface between the application component and the rest of the system. This interface is shown in Figure 2-6.

FIGURE 2-6. Application Component Interface to System

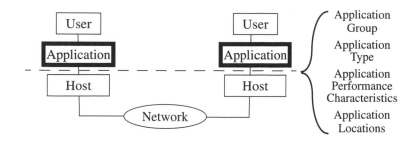

2.4 Host Requirements

We now turn to the requirements of the hosts and equipment that the system will support, particularly the types of host and equipment, as well as their performance characteristics and location information. The relationship of the host component with the rest of the generic system is shown in Figure 2-7.

2.4.1 Types of Hosts and Equipment

The host and equipment can be grouped into three categories: generic computing devices, servers, and specialized equipment.

- *Generic computing devices* are the desktop computers that most users have. Popular examples include various forms of DOS- and Windows-based PCs, Macs, and UNIX workstations and PCs. These are the hosts that form the access points into the network and typically service a single user. Their requirements are important from an end-to-end perspective, as they provide the interface between the applications and the network. They also tend to be overlooked, a form of "black box" that networks are connected to and applications are run on, but are otherwise somewhat untouchable. This has led to what is known as the "last foot" problem in systems performance. (This is a modification of the "last mile" problem, which was the difficulty in getting infrastructure, networking, and services into a campus or building). The "last foot" problem is getting services and performance from the network interface on the host to the applications and users.

FIGURE 2-7. **Host Component of the Generic System**

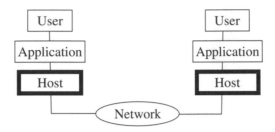

- *Servers* are computing equipment that provide a service to one or more users (or clients). They are typically more powerful, in terms of memory, processing, networking, and peripherals, than users' desktop computers. Examples of servers are computing servers, storage servers (also known as mass storage or archival systems), and application servers. Servers also have requirements for "last foot" performance, as well as having requirements specific to its server role. A server's functions can be streamlined to support this server role, which in turn may impact the system. For example, a server may be designed to support high-performance, deterministic access to a large number of users. The cumulative effect of the users' access of this server on the network needs to be considered. Servers have an impact on the flow of information within the system, which will be examined in the chapters on flow analysis.

- *Specialized equipment* may or may not be hosts or servers. A parallel system supporting a large database search engine may be considered specialized equipment, as well as a server or host. A bank of infrared sensors, however, would be considered just specialized equipment. Specialized equipment typically does not support direct access to user applications, but rather gathers, produces, or processes information to be sent to the user. Examples of specialized equipment include supercomputers, mainframes, parallel or distributed-computing systems, and data gathering and processing systems. A large computer such as a supercomputer or mainframe may be considered either specialized equipment or a computing server.

Specialized equipment tends to be location-dependent. This is significant, for while in most environments generic computing resources and servers are becoming location-independent, specialized equipment still retains its location dependencies. This is primarily due to cost. A wind tunnel that provides flow information for car manufacturers is large, making it difficult to move around, and expensive, making it difficult to replicate. If a network is being designed to

FIGURE 2-8. **Specialized Equipment Tends to be Location-Dependent**

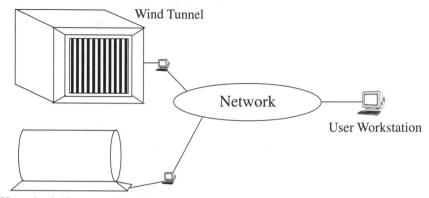

support this wind tunnel facility, and the wind tunnel is in Dearborn, Michigan, then the system has to be designed to provide support to that city, and the characteristics of the network must take the performance and location requirements of the wind tunnel into account. If a network was being designed to provide remote access to hyperbaric chambers (pressurized vessels used to replicate pressure conditions for underwater divers) for doctors, then the locations of these chambers (likely to be near popular diving spots) will become access requirements for the system. This is illustrated in Figure 2-8.

While wind tunnels and pressure chambers are very specialized (and relatively rare) devices, this concept can be expanded to more common devices, such as automated teller machines, a variety of medical equipment, even stoplights. Also consider location-specific information—from libraries, universities, government centers, or medical centers. Much of this information is also closely tied to its location.

2.4.2 Performance Characteristics

The "last foot" problem with hosts focuses on the performance of the various components of the host: the hardware, firmware, and software that provide the glue between users, applications, and the rest of the system.

For many environments, it may be difficult or impossible to determine or measure the performance characteristics of the hosts. Components of the host may be proprietary, with information scarce or unavailable. The software and firmware driving the host (operating system, device drivers, application programming interface, etc.) are complex and may be beyond the capabilities of personnel responsible for host operation and maintenance. When it is not practical to determine or measure the performance of the host, the network designer should be aware that the end-to-end design perspective is being compromised.

A simple, general diagram of a host or server looks like Figure 2-9. The performance of each of these components impacts the overall performance of the host. For example, disk-drive seek times, memory access times, and the effectiveness of driver, OS, or API software will all affect the ability of the host to place/retrieve information on/from the network.

By looking at each of the components as integral to the overall performance of the host (and the system), we are applying the end-to-end perspective within the host—the host in effect becomes a microcosm of the system. What we are looking for in performance characteristics include

- Storage performance, that is, disk drive performance (seek times) or tape performance

- Processor (CPU) performance

- Memory performance (access times)

- Bus performance (bus capacity and arbitration mechanisms)

- OS performance (effectiveness of the protocol stack and APIs, i.e., the number of memory copies in the protocol stack, or the cost of execution of a given OS on a particular processor)

- Device driver performance (effectiveness of driver software)

Information about any of these components can be helpful in estimating the overall performance of a host, or in identifying the limiting factor in host performance. Trying to understand the performance implications of each component of each host in the design environment can be quite time-consuming. A simple and quick use of

FIGURE 2-9. **Host/Server Components**

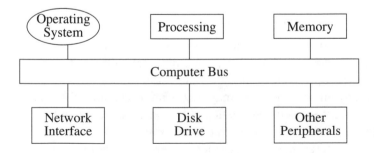

host performance requirements is to ensure that there are not any obvious dramatic performance bottlenecks at the host. Understanding the host component can help you to recognize these bottlenecks early in the analysis process.

2.4.3 Location Information

Knowing the locations of existing or expected hosts, servers, and specialized equipment can be helpful in determining the relationships between users, applications, and networks, as well as the start toward determining flow characteristics for the system.

Location information helps to determine the relationships between components of the system. Coupled with the types and performance levels of hosts, servers, and equipment, this information gives us insight on what the relative concentrations of users and hosts should be, their placement, and the level of networking needed.

Location information also helps to determine the flow characteristics for the system. In Chapter 5 we will discuss flow models that describe flows within the system based on the relationship between users and hosts/servers/specialized equipment, derived partially from location information about these components.

Some design environments where location information is particularly important are in the outsourcing of system components or functions; in the consolidation of organizations, system components, or functions; and in the relocation of system components or functions within an organization.

An example of how this information can be used is in the outsourcing or relocating of computing resources. Outsourcing may be accomplished by having the outsourcing agent operate, administer, and maintain (OAM) the resources at the customer site, or by removing the resources from the customer site and having the outsourcing agent provide the resources as well as the OAM. When the outsourcing agent provides the computing resources, knowing where the resources are to be relocated will be important in determining the flow models and the level of networking needed. The outsourcing agent may choose a location that is optimized toward the administration of the computing resources, yet degrades the overall performance of the system. If a customer's computing resources are accessed via FDDI or 100 Mb/s Ethernet LAN, and are then moved away from the customer into a WAN environment, either the access cost to those resources will rise (through provided high-speed WAN connections) or the performance will degrade. In some cases, by moving the resource from a LAN to a WAN environment may result in some applications being rendered unusable.

FIGURE 2-10. **System Components Can Have Location Dependencies**

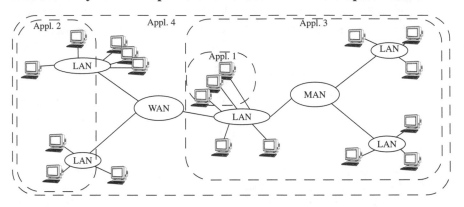

When the locations of system components change, it is important to evaluate or reevaluate the requirements of the system, to determine if service and/or service performance requirements have changed. Figure 2-10 illustrates that there are often location dependencies between applications and hosts, and that these dependencies need to be identified as part of the host requirements.

For example, if a LAN application that has a requirement for 100-ms round-trip delay is applied to a WAN with a round-trip delay characteristic of 200 ms, then either the network design, the application, or users' expectations will have to be modified to support the new environment.

Figure 2-11 shows the interface between the host component and the rest of the system. This interface consists of the types of hosts and equipment, the location dependencies, and host/equipment performance characteristics.

FIGURE 2-11. **Host Component Interface to System**

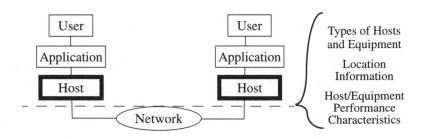

FIGURE 2-12. **Network Component of the Generic System**

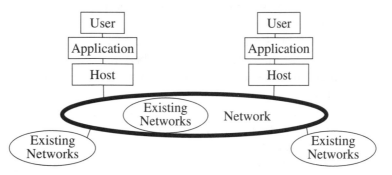

2.5 Network Requirements

Figure 2-12 expands the generic system to show that the network component incorporates any existing networks that will interface to your design.

From the network component perspective, requirements for a network design must consider the requirements, services, and characteristics of any existing networks that will be incorporated into, or interface with, the new network.

2.5.1 Existing Networks and Migration

Most network designs today need to incorporate existing networks. This includes system upgrades—such as adding a new application to the system, migrating to a new or different technology or protocol, or upgrading the network infrastructure—and the expansion or reduction of the system's size or scope.

Sometimes the network design must accommodate constraints imposed by the existing network. Requirements for the users, applications, and hosts of the existing networks must be considered as part of the system being designed, and their requirements analysis done along with the analysis of the new parts of the system. Requirements that are specific to existing networks are the scaling of these networks; the locations and concentrations of their users, applications, and hosts/equipment; interoperability between the existing and expected networks; the overall network and system performance; and existing network-layer and support services.

With the scaling of the existing and expected networks, we need to consider how their sizes will affect each other. How will the addition of the new network(s) to the existing network(s) change the size and scope of the system? Will the change be dramatic, as in growing from a LAN to a WAN, or will the change be within the LAN/MAN/WAN boundaries of the existing network(s)?

Depending on how the new networks interface with or incorporate the existing networks, or how the network modifications are done, the locations and/or concentrations of other components of the system are likely to change. This will show up when we develop flows later in the analysis process.

There will also be interoperability issues between the existing and expected networks. Interoperability between existing and expected networks occurs at boundaries between the networks, usually where different technologies or media are used. In addition, by taking an end-to-end perspective on the design, the boundaries between existing and expected networks are points where service information and performance guarantees need to be translated. Requirements should include the technologies and media of the existing networks, and any service and/or performance guarantees or expectations from existing networks.

The overall performance of the system will be affected by our design for the expected network (or network modification), how it interacts with existing networks, and the performance levels of existing networks. Since the performance of existing networks will impact overall system performance, the performance characteristics should be integrated into the performance of the expected network. Note that this only applies to users and applications that will use the existing portions of the network, or whose information must transit existing networks. Since existing networks are already in place, it is usually possible to measure the performance of these networks. Thus, while the performance of expected networks is based on a best estimate, the performance of existing networks (and potential performance impacts) can be better known and understood.

We must also consider existing network-layer and support services. Network-layer services include addressing strategies, choices, and configurations of routing protocols and naming strategies, while support services include security, accounting, and monitoring and management. The current and planned requirements of each of these services should be considered.

Another aspect in considering existing networks is identifying constraints on the design. All of the requirements listed above can limit the performance of the new system, or constrain the system design. Knowing these limitations and constraints can help to optimize the design against design trade-offs, such as technologies, service offerings/guarantees, and cost. Knowing the limitations and constraints of existing networks can also be useful in making arguments to have them replaced, augmented, or deprecated.

Figure 2-13 shows the interface between the network and the other components of the system, including any existing networks. This interface consists of scaling factors, network and support services, interoperability, location information, and performance characteristics.

FIGURE 2-13. **Network Component Interface to System**

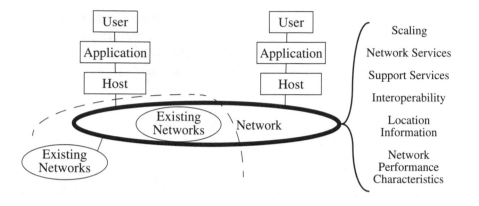

2.5.2 Functional Requirements

Since throughout the design process we will discuss network management and security, it will be useful to briefly outline requirements for network management and security here, as a start toward considering them in the design. It is likely that our analysis of network management and security later in the design process will generate new requirements or modify some that we develop here. At this point in the design process, we want to think in general terms about how we can accomplish network management and security in the design.

Requirements for Network Management and Security

As we will see in the design process, there are four categories of network management tasks:

- Monitoring for event notification
- Monitoring for metrics and planning
- Network configuration
- Troubleshooting

Monitoring is obtaining values for network management parameters from network elements of the system, processing the data, displaying some or all of the data to network operators, and archiving the data. Monitoring for event notification involves taking a frequent snapshot of the network, in order to understand the state of the network, to help in isolating and solving network problems. If the data are collected for a long-term analysis of network performance, the monitoring is for metrics and capacity/reliability/delay engineering. Network configuration and troubleshooting are more specialized tasks that are modifications of event notification and metrics and planning.

In monitoring, we want to develop a set of characteristics that we will use for event notification and metrics and planning. These characteristics may be specific to each type of network element, which will be better understood later in the design process. We will also consider the facilities for accessing these characteristics, which will include network management protocols, end-to-end monitoring tools, and direct access methods.

Some architectural issues with network management include determining the paths that the management data will take, as well as the hierarchy in management data flows. Management data can be in the path of the users' network traffic (*in-band*), or may take a different path (*out-of-band*). For the pros and cons of in-band versus out-of-band management, see Chapter 10. Management data flows can be hierarchical, indicating separate components of and locations for the management system, or flat, indicating that the management system is in a single host.

As with the other components of this chapter, the performance characteristics of network management also need to be considered. At this point, we can list some general network management requirements:

- Monitoring methods
- Instrumentation methods. These include the network management protocols (SNMP, SNMPv2, CMIP, RMON), parameter lists (MIBs), monitoring tools, and direct access
- The characteristics sets for monitoring
- In-band versus out-of-band monitoring
- Centralized versus distributed monitoring
- Performance requirements

Before developing a security plan for our network, we must first determine user requirements, define security policies, and perform risk analysis. At this point in the design process, we will focus on determining the users' requirements for security. This consists of

- Any government-specified security requirements (i.e., from the Department of Defense, Department of Energy, etc.)
- Company- or organization-specified security requirements
- User-specified security requirements

Any of these may be applied to users, user groups, projects, or specific types of data, as well as to how data are generated, transferred across networks, processed, and stored. We will also consider how network resources are accessed, both from within and from outside the company, and what the security requirements are for access.

2.5.3 Financial Requirements

Another system-wide requirement is the level of funding that is available to implement the network design. Funding is often associated with an overall cost limit, with recurring and nonrecurring components. Nonrecurring costs are based on the building of the network and consist of network design, deployment, and all hardware/software components, as well as the initial installation or establishment of any services from service providers. Recurring costs are for tasks and items that are expected to occur or be replaced/upgraded on a periodic basis. This includes network operations, administration, and maintenance, costs from service providers, and provisions for modifications to the network. The time frames for recurring costs vary, driven by customer/end user financial cycles and technology life cycles.

The level of funding is usually a constraint to the design, therefore it is important to know what this level is as early in the analysis process as possible, in order to avoid creating a design that is not economically feasible. The financial requirements gathered here will be combined with the user's affordability requirement, to form a complete financial picture of the design. In the analysis and design processes, we will consider funding constraints to the design, and how these processes work to optimize the design in order to minimize cost.

2.5.4 Enterprise Requirements

There may be times when you will have to consider requirements for the network design that are commonly considered enterprise, such as phone, fax, voice, and video. The integration of these types of requirements over the same transmission infrastructure as data is one way to distinguish an enterprise environment from other design environments.

2.6 Concluding Remarks

The requirements analysis process is about identifying, collecting, and evaluating system requirements for the network. System requirements can be separated into components, where the choice of components is based on your design environment and what you want to accomplish with the network design. In this chapter we considered components based on users, applications, hosts, and networks.

By separating system requirements into components, the set of requirements becomes more workable. As we apply the principles and guidelines of the next chapter to each of these components, you will begin to see how understanding each component helps to build a picture of the overall system.

As you work through the next chapter, keep in mind the requirements we have identified in this chapter for each component of the generic system.

Suggested Further Reading

1. Bostic, K., Karels, M.J., McKusick, M.K., and Quarterman, J.S. *The Design and Implementation of the 4.4 BSD Operating System*. Addison-Wesley, Reading, MA, 1996.

2. Jain, R. *The Art of Computer Systems Performance Analysis: Techniques for Experimental Design, Measurement, Simulation, and Modeling*. John Wiley & Sons, New York, 1991.

3. Peterson, J.L., and Silberschatz, A. *Operating System Concepts*. Addison-Wesley, Reading, MA, 1988.

Also examine Internet-drafts from the IETF Audio/Video Transport (AVT) Working Group.

Exercises

1. The generic system has user, application, host, and network components. In which component(s) does each of the following apply:

    a) Database software

    b) An application server

    c) A printer or print server

2. Interactivity is a user requirement for responsiveness from the system. What order-of-magnitude estimates can you make for the expected response times for:

    a) Access to a Web page

    b) Downloading files from the Web

c) Interactive visualization, for example, in a distributed game-playing environment

d) A database query

3. For each application delay type in Figure 2-5, give an example of an application with that delay behavior.

4. List the top five applications for your environment, according to popularity, use, or amount of traffic on the network. Which application group does each application fit into? Can you think of any new application groups, not listed in this chapter?

5. For a host in your environment, determine its software/hardware configuration, including

   a) Operating system (type and current revision level)

   b) Network interfaces

   c) Amounts of memory and storage

   d) Types of peripherals

6. Specialized equipment includes equipment that is location-dependent or specialized in function, or information that is location-specific. Consider a network that connects a medical library to hospitals and universities, as shown in Figure 2-14. What types of information will be specific to each medical library? What types of information will be common to all medical libraries? List some possible difficulties in transferring medical data across such a network.

7. Your design environment includes several Ethernet networks that will be integrated into the design. List the performance and functional characteristics of Ethernet (10bT).

FIGURE 2-14. Medical Library Network

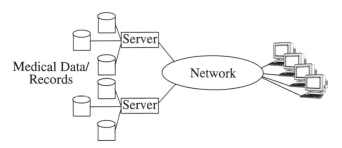

CHAPTER 3

Requirements Analysis: Guidelines

The guidelines for requirements analysis are part of the process model. This model, shown in Figure 3-1, outlines the major steps in gathering and analyzing requirements for your network design.

FIGURE 3-1. The Process Model for Requirements Analysis

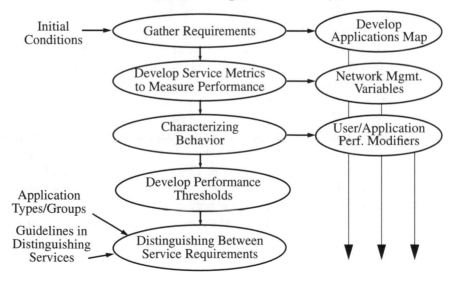

3.1 Gathering and Listing Requirements

Service requirements are gathered and developed with *initial conditions* on the design, with input from end users, customers, and network personnel, and then refined by applying our experience and knowledge about the analysis process. Some guidelines for quantifying requirements and developing thresholds are given here, but first we must communicate with the end users, customers, and network personnel to gather their requirements. We begin with a discussion of the initial conditions on a design.

3.1.1 Determining Initial Conditions

Initial conditions are the basis for the start of the design project. They help to determine what you are designing for, as well as the reasons for the design. Initial conditions will consist of the type of design project (new design, modification of an existing design, analysis of a design, outsourcing), the scope of the design (network size, distance, number of sites), initial design goals, and any outside forces (political, administrative, financial) acting on the design. You will want to understand these initial conditions, as they will influence the network design throughout the analysis and design processes and will often act as constraints on the design.

Before starting the process of gathering and analyzing requirements, you will likely have some notion of the initial conditions for the network project you are undertaking. For example, you will probably know the type of design project, as well as the scope of the project. Initial design goals can be more difficult to determine, and you may not be aware of outside forces unless you are part of the organization that is requesting the design. You are likely to have some, but not all, of the initial conditions for the design.

Knowing the type and scope of the network project will help you to focus your design efforts. For example, designing a new network will minimize the number of constraints placed on the design by the existing network (except for those networks that a new network will interface with), allowing you to focus on achieving design goals for this new network. When the design is a modification of an existing network, you will have more information about the behavior of the network, and what is expected from the changes to the network. The existing network will also constrain the design, as you will have to consider how to connect and interoperate with part or all of the existing network. Thus, the performance and functions of the existing network, along with the reasons for making changes to the network, are important initial conditions.

These conditions also apply when you are doing the analysis of a design. In this case, the network may not be functioning as planned, and you are trying to determine where there are problems in the design, or where the implementation varies from the design. If you are designing a network to allow for outsourcing of resource OAM (operations, administration, and maintenance), then the initial conditions will include where the outsourcing will occur, and the methods used by the outsourcing agent to provide OAM functions.

There are likely to be several constraints on the network design. By examining the initial conditions at the start of the analysis process, you stand a much better chance of understanding and working with these constraints. Common constraints on a network design include funding limitations; working with various organizations or groups within an organization; organizational rules and regulations; and technical constraints from existing users, applications, hosts, and networks.

Funding limitations are critical to the design. As we will see in the design process, design choices are coupled to available funding. Disregarding funding in the design will lead to design choices that will not be implemented, while considering this limitation up front will help you to make the most intelligent use of funding for the design. It is also important to get as good a forecast for future funding as possible.

Organizational constraints, such as who you will be working with or how groups interact, can become problems during the analysis and design processes. Knowing this in advance will allow you to prepare for the problem, usually by buffering yourself and the design effort from problem groups or individuals. Sometimes, but not always, management can help with this type of problem.

Existing components in the system will often act as constraints. Users suffer from inertia, not wanting to accept changes in the ways that they do their work. Applications written to be used locally on a host or for a particular network technology or protocol may have to be modified to function on the new network. Host interfaces and drivers may have to be changed. Existing networks will bring their performance and functional limitations to the design. By knowing early in the process what parts of the existing system you will be incorporating or supporting in the network design, you can determine which design choices will work and, more importantly, which will not work.

Determining the initial conditions for the design will lead you into the requirements analysis process. You will know some of the initial conditions, but will have to learn others. As you start digging for answers, you will be gathering information for the analysis process.

3.1.2 Working with Users

In working with users, your first inclination may be to think "this takes too much time, they're not cooperative, they don't know what they want," and so on, but it is a vital part of the process. By initially spending time with the end users/customers, you will better understand their behavior patterns and environment. For the end users/customers, discussing the network with you will help them to understand what you're trying to accomplish and will build lines of personal communication that will be useful when you're installing, debugging, and operating the network later on.

While it can be challenging to communicate with end users/customers, there are some successful techniques that you can use:

- Develop a survey or questionnaire for the users and send it via fax or email or make it available as a Web page
- Arrange a meeting or whiteboard session to discuss their environment
- Spend time with one or more high-performance users to get immersed in their environment

Working with your users will pay off in another way, in getting them to see that you are taking a systems approach in the network design. In order for the system to work optimally, the users need to be able to communicate their needs to you, the applications need to be designed to work across the network, and hosts need to be chosen with the system in mind. Since the network is central to the system, your role in bringing this systems approach to the users is important. In a sense, you are fostering support for the network and its design.

It is important, therefore, not to take a hit-and-run approach, talking to the users only to get their requirements then not following up with them. By building a relationship with the users of the network, through discussing their requirements, advising them of the results and anticipated actions/designs, and informing them of progress with the network design, installation, and operation, you are developing advocates for your network. This may be vital when you want to upgrade the network in the future.

3.1.3 Listing Requirements and Mapping Applications

As you gather requirements from the users, you will want to compile them into a concise, easy-to-use list. The next chapter presents some templates that we will use to list and compile requirements. In filling out these tables, you will go through the process of gathering the necessary requirements, which should help you to identify what's important for your environment, as well as determine relationships between various requirements.

As a list of what the system needs from the network design, these requirements will be used as the foundation for the rest of this book. The tables can be used as a worksheet, which will make it easier to use when gathering the requirements for your design.

Another purpose of listing requirements is to also list our initial conditions, constraints, and assumptions about the environment we are designing the network for, as well as to determine the system components for which we need to get more information. As part of the analysis process, the application location information will be used to show their relative locations in the design environment.

3.2 Developing Service Metrics to Measure Performance

After gathering requirements for our design, the next step is to analyze these requirements in order to be able to distinguish between various performance and service levels in the network. We will use performance thresholds to distinguish between low- and high-performance for our design environment, while also using service performance characteristics to identify specific service levels. Performance thresholds and service performance characteristics are measured in the system with service metrics.

Service metrics are either actual measurable variables in the network, or are derived from measured variables. These service metrics are important, as they are where "the rubber meets the road"—where requirements from all layers in the system are distilled into configurable and measurable variables.

In order for a performance requirement to be useful, it must be configurable, measurable, and verifiable within the network. This is particularly true when parts of the network are outside the control of the network administrator: for example, when a service provider is used to supply a service such as ATM, SMDS, or Frame Relay in the network, or when parts of the network (or the entire network) are outsourced. In cases such as these, service metrics can be used to ensure that you are getting the service you are requesting (and paying for) from the service provider/outsourcing agent.

Service metrics will depend on your design environment and the types of equipment you implement in the network, but at this point in the analysis process, you can influence or require what will be measured in the network and how it will be measured.

Service metrics for reliability include

* Availability, in terms of percent uptime or downtime
* Recoverability or stability, in terms of mean time between failure (MTBF), mean time between service outage (MTBSO), and mean time to repair (MTTR)
* Error and loss rates at various levels, such as the bit error rate (BER), cell loss ratio (CLR), cell misinsertion ratio (CMR), and frame and packet loss rates

For application services, as with user services, availability is currently the most popular measure of reliability. Recoverability (MTBF/MTBSO and MTTR) is also often used, while error rates are more likely to be seen at the element level in the system.

Service metrics for capacity include

- Data rates, in terms of peak data rate (PDR), sustained data rate (SDR), and minimum data rate
- Data size, including burst size and duration

Service metrics for delay include

- End-to-end, round-trip, or system delay
- Latency
- Delay variation
- Timeliness

As configurable and measurable quantities in the network, service metrics can be described in terms of variables in the network, as well as having mechanisms to configure and measure these variables. Current mechanisms to configure and measure service metrics are with network management platforms that use the simple network management protocol (SNMP) and the common management information protocol (CMIP), which access variables described in management information bases (MIBs). MIBs describe generic and enterprise-specific variables. Some MIBs that are relevant here include the remote monitoring (RMON/RMON 2) and ATM monitoring (AToM) MIBs.

In addition to these management protocols and MIBs, we can use commonly available tools to help us measure service metrics. One such tool is the utility *ping* (available in most TCP/IP sources), which roughly measures round-trip delays between selected sources and destinations in the network. A more recent tool is *pathchar* (available from the Web site *ee.lbl.gov*), which combines round-trip delay and per-link capacity measurements with path traces, such as with the common tool *traceroute*.

For example, one method to monitor reliability in the network is to use *ping* to estimate delay and packet loss (see Figure 3-2). *Ping* tells us the approximate round-trip delay, as well as when ICMP echo packets (*ping* packets) are lost in the network or at the destination. While not an exact method, it is fairly simple to set up and use, and provides an early warning mechanism for reliability problems.

FIGURE 3-2. Using *Ping* and IP Packet Loss as Measurements of Reliability

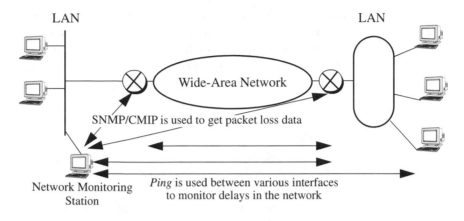

TABLE 3-1. Service Metrics

Service Metric	Where Metric Will Be Measured in System	Measurement Method(s)

When developing service metrics, we want to also try to determine where in the system we want to measure each metric, as well as potential mechanisms for measurement, as in Table 3-1.

3.3 Characterizing Behavior

The goal of characterizing behavior for our design environment is to determine if we can estimate network performance through understanding how users and their applications will function across the network. In this section we will examine some of the characteristics of users and applications that can be used to modify and better estimate network performance requirements. We will then apply these user and application characteristics during the flow analysis process.

3.3.1 Usage Patterns

In conjunction with identifying service metrics for our design environment, it will
be useful to understand how applications will be used in the system. Simple usage
patterns can include for each application the total number of users for each application, the frequency that a user is expected to use the application (number of
sessions/user-day), how long an average application session will last (usually as seconds), and an estimate of the expected number of simultaneous user sessions for the
application.

The logic here is that we can develop a rule of thumb for scaling the expected
performance (capacity) of the network by examining user and application behavior.
Figure 3-3 shows the characteristics of how a user uses an application. In this figure,
an application session is described by some common characteristics. First, the sessions are shown with the times that the session is active (as boxes). The size of each
box indicates the duration of activity, and the number of boxes per unit time indicates the frequency of activity. Also shown in this figure is the number of simultaneous sessions that are active at any point in time.

Estimating the frequency and duration of application sessions and the number
of simultaneous sessions will allow you to apply a modifier to the performance
requirement for each application (or at least those applications that you consider to
be important enough to characterize). For example, if you can estimate the number
of simultaneous sessions for an application, that can be used as a multiplier for that
application's capacity requirement. Similarly, if you know the duration of an application session, you can use that to help estimate the amount of time that a service
will need to be configured within the network.

FIGURE 3-3. Characteristics of User Behavior

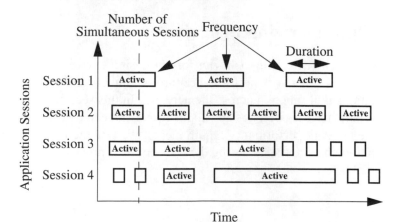

3.3.2 Application Behavior

It will also be useful to determine the behavior of application sessions. Along with usage patterns, application behavior can help you to modify performance requirements to achieve a better estimate of what services and performance levels you will need for your network design.

In characterizing application behavior, you want to consider the data sizes that the application will be processing; the frequency and time duration for data to be passed across the network; the traffic flow characteristics for the application, particularly flow directions (i.e., from client to server); and the degree of multicasting in the communications (one-to-one, one-to-many, many-to-many).

In applying usage patterns and application behavior, you can go from a fairly simple to a very complex model. For example, you can make some simplifying assumptions as to usage patterns and application behavior. One simple model is to assume that there will be only one session of an application active at any time. This assumption cancels out the frequency and duration of an application session with the total number of users for that application. Another model is to apply statistical formulas to the usage pattern and application behavior. This can be quite successful when the application is well understood, such as telephony applications.

While you can attempt to characterize behavior for all users of and applications for your design environment, you will usually get the greatest benefit by applying this analysis to the specified and/or high-performance applications and their users, as their requirements typically drive the design. Characterizing usage patterns and application behavior can be both difficult and time-consuming. You will find that doing so will help your understanding of the requirements and how to apply them, if you can afford the time and effort it will take.

What has been described in this section can be more formally developed into a workload model, using mathematical formulas and/or computational methods to analyze the characteristics and expected behavior of the design environment. Workload models are particularly beneficial for design environments where the input parameters to the model are well understood. For many data networks this is not yet the case, although much work is being done in this area. References for further reading about workload models are presented at the end of this book.

3.4 Developing Performance Thresholds

Now we will expand on the service requirements previously discussed, quantifying requirements when possible. In distinguishing between best-effort, specified, and low/high performance services, we will use the following criteria:

1. A general threshold can be used to separate performance requirements into low-performance and high-performance.

2. An environment-specific threshold can be used to separate performance requirements into low-performance and high-performance.

3. Specified services will have known bounds or guarantees.

Criteria 1 and 2 require establishing and measuring thresholds for application service performance.

3.4.1 Reliability Requirements

For applications with reliability requirements, popular measures of reliability are availability, recoverability, and error rates. The most common measure of reliability is in terms of availability, as percent uptime or downtime. For example, a request for proposal (RFP) from a potential end user/customer may state a guaranteed uptime of 99.99%, but what does that really mean?

Availability

For a system that supports around-the-clock, seven-days-a-week service to its customers, availability can be thought of as the percent uptime or downtime per week, month, or year, based on the total amount of time for that period. Table 3-2 shows some commonly used availability percentages, ranging from 95% to 99.99%, with 99.99% as a current upper limit.

One way to view percent availability is by how much downtime can be expected per time period. The range 95% to 99.99% covers the majority of typically requested availability requirements. At the low end of availability, 95% allows the system to be down quite a bit of time (1.2 hours/day). This may be fine for testbeds

TABLE 3-2. Availability Differences with Time

Availability (% Uptime)	Amount of Allowed Downtime (hours [h], minutes [m], or seconds [s] per time period)			
	Yearly	**Monthly**	**Weekly**	**Daily**
95%	438 h	36.5 h	8.4 h	1.2 h
99.5%	43.8 h	3.7 h	50.5 m	7.2 m
99.95%	4.38 h	21.9 m	5.05 m	43.2 s
99.98%	1.75 h	8.75 m	2.0 m	17.3 s
99.99%	0.88 h	4.4 m	1.0 m	8.7 s

or system prototypes, but is unacceptable for most operational systems. As some commercial network services offer availability levels around 95%, this should be factored into the overall availability requirements for the network.

An availability level of 99.95% is closer to where most systems operate. At this level of availability, about 5 minutes of downtime is allowed per week, which equates to a few transients per week, or one minor interruption per month (where a transient is a short-lived (on the order of several seconds) network event, such as traffic being rerouted, or a period of congestion). Many environments, which have had early availability requirements below 99.95%, are now relying on the network much more.

At 99.98% availability, the system begins to push most operational limits. This level of availability, which indicates a highly relied-upon environment (those that use mission-critical applications), will impact the network design in several areas, as will be discussed in later chapters.

Finally, availability greater than 99.99% approaches the current fringe of reliability, where the effort and costs to support such a high level of uptime can skyrocket. There are even some applications that cannot tolerate any downtime while in session. For these types of applications, the availability is 100% while in session. An example of such an application is the remote control of a vehicle (i.e., remotely piloted airplane, submersible, or spacecraft), where downtime may result in the loss of control of the vehicle. In cases like this, however, the times of high availability are usually well-known in advance and can be planned for.

We should note at this point that many system outages are brief in time and may not impact the user. In some cases the user may not even know that a problem existed. Yet such events (transients) are part of the reliability estimate, especially in environments where there are strict tolerances on reliability. Therefore, while a two-minute weekly downtime (for 99.98% availability) may appear noticeable, it could actually be a distribution of several 15-second transients, each of which results in the applications stalling for several seconds.

With this information and the previous table of availability estimates, we can estimate a general threshold for reliability in terms of availability. A general threshold for reliability (availability) is 99.9%. When using this general threshold, availability requirements less than 99.9% are considered low-performance, while availability requirements greater than 99.9% are considered high-performance.

How can availability be measured? This question may be asked in at least two parts: where should availability be measured, and what service metrics can be used to measure it? Where availability should be measured depends on what the designer or administrator is trying to accomplish. Two guidelines for availability measurement:

1. Availability is measured end-to-end.

2. A loss of availability in any part of the system is counted against any overall availability metrics.

Typically, availability is measured end-to-end, either between users, hosts, or networks. For example, availability may be measured end-to-end between user networks, at network monitoring stations, or at network interfaces. As Figure 3-4 shows, measurement points include the LAN/WAN interface, router entry/exit points, and at monitoring stations distributed throughout the network.

What may be measured at these points to give availability information would be the link-layer or IP information indicating loss of signal on the network, loss of end-to-end connectivity, or packet/frame loss.

Alternatively, availability may be measured selectively between particular users, hosts, or networks. Such selectivity may indicate a higher importance for certain parts of the system. For example, availability to a server farm network from each user network may be more important than the availability between any particular user networks. Figure 3-5 shows availability measured in this fashion.

This is important to the network design—how we decide to measure and verify availability is closely tied to how we design the connectivity to and between "important" hosts, applications, and/or users. Indeed, how we measure availability (as well as the other service performance characteristics) indicates what we consider to be important in the system.

FIGURE 3-4. **Availability as Measured End-to-End Between Networks**

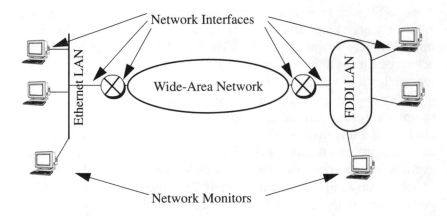

FIGURE 3-5. **Availability as Measured Selectively Between Networks**

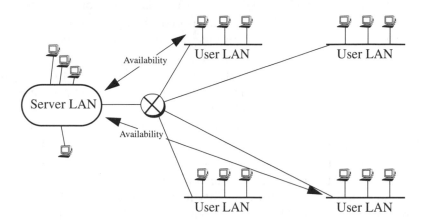

Therefore, an availability of 99.98% may be end-to-end, between any two net-works in the system, or only between selected networks. When availability is between any networks in the system, outages that affect one or more networks should count against the overall availability of the system.

Recoverability

We also estimate reliability in terms of recoverability, using estimates for MTBF/MTBSO and MTTR. These terms are similar to the use of uptime and downtime for availability, but are more specific in how long system outages last and how often they occur. Note that MTBF/MTBSO and MTTR are mean times, so they do not represent absolute failure or repair times.

MTBF and MTBSO estimate the frequency of system outages. For example, an MTBF/MTBSO of 4400 hours (or 2.64E5 minutes) states that failures in the system are expected approximately every 6 months (180 days). MTTR gives an estimate of how long system outages may last. For example, an MTTR of 60 minutes may be expected if on-site expertise is available, an MTTR of 4 hours (240 minutes) may be expected if the location is remote and dial-in access to the system is not available. These terms are usually used together to specify reliability. When we put the examples of MTBF/MTBSO (4400 hours) and MTTR (60 minutes) together, we get a reliability estimate roughly equivalent to an availability of 99.98%.

The difference here is that the combination of MTBF/MTBSO and MTTR also states how long and frequent outages may be, while an availability estimate does not have that level of detail. From Table 3-2, an availability of 99.98% may mean that a 15-minute outage may occur every day, or that a single outage of 1.5 hours may occur within the year, and the availability requirement is still met. With this in mind, a better way to specify availability is to associate a reasonable time span with it. Stating an availability of 99.98%, measured weekly, is more precise than just 99.98% availability. This also provides a better granularity when factoring events beyond control (e.g., fires, floods, etc.).

MTTR is particularly important in that it can be related to the repair time or response time in a service contract. If you want an average response time of N hours, then your MTTR should be higher than or at N hours. Or you may specify an average repair time of M hours, which can coincide with an MTTR of M hours. Common values of average response/repair times are 1, 2, and 4 hours. If we approximate this with MTTR values of 1, 2, and 4 hours, we get the MTBF/MTBSO/availability values described in Figure 3-6.

A general threshold for reliability in terms of recoverability is an MTTR of 1 hour and an MTBF/MTBSO of 4000 hours. Thus, a specified reliability (recoverability) of MTTR less than or equal to 1 hour and an MTBF/MTBSO greater than or equal to 4000 hours is considered high-performance.

FIGURE 3-6. **MTBF/MTBSO and Availability for MTTR of 1, 2, and 4 Hours**

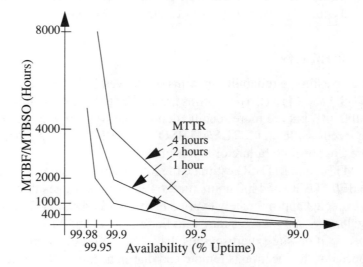

Error and Loss Rates

Estimating reliability in terms of error/loss rates is more complex than the previous estimates. While error/loss rates are more commonly used at the element level, we can also make some general reliability estimates from them. As before, the ability to estimate reliability is strongly based on our ability to measure it within the system. For these rates, this is done

- Per link or circuit, such as bit error rates (BERs)
- Between network equipment, such as cell loss ratio (CLR) or cell misinsertion ratio (CMR) (between ATM equipment) or packet loss rates (between network-layer routers)
- End-to-end, between hosts or applications

Determining what is an acceptable error rate depends on the application's ability to tolerate errors or information loss. This, in turn, implies reliability and dependencies between the various layers in the network. For example, an application that transfers data in the network may rely on the transport layer to provide guaranteed transmission. If the transport layer protocol used is TCP, then reliability of transmission is based on TCP's ability to recover from unsignalled errors in the network, or on notification of transmission failures. If the transport protocol is the user datagram protocol (UDP), however, there is no reliability guarantee from the transport layer and reliability is passed down to the data-link and physical layers, or must be provided by the application itself.

Loss may be measured at the link and network layers, and reported as a percentage of available traffic in the network. Thus, we could establish cell, frame, or packet loss thresholds and time periods, as in Table 3-.

The time periods for each of these loss rates excludes the others. One interesting part of such a loss measurement is that we could use the well-known *ping* application as a possible measurement tool. A *ping* loss rate can be used as an indicator that the network is approaching a loss threshold and that a more accurate measurement (e.g., SNMP polling of router statistics or RMON parameters) is needed.

TABLE 3-3. Example Loss Thresholds

Packet Loss Rate (as % of total network traffic)	Maximum Total Time (per month)
25% to 100%	Up to 2 hours
2% to 24%	Up to 3 hours
< 2%	Remainder of month

While *ping* can be useful in this mode, loss of ICMP packets (of which *ping* is one type) can be affected by how network elements (such as routers) handle them. For example, *ping* packets may be among one of the first packets to be dropped by the router when it gets congested. The important point here is to use applications such as *ping* with an awareness that it (like all applications) is imperfect and may or may not accurately represent the state of the system. That is why it may be better used as a threshold indicator, as it would have less of a direct impact on the accuracy of loss measurements, while still being quite useful.

There are some applications that will tolerate some loss of information. Applications that transfer video and/or voice, such as teleconferencing, will allow some loss in order to preserve continuity of signal. Some telemetry applications also allow for data loss.

Thresholds for Reliability

Reliability estimates may take the form of thresholds or guarantees. Some good methods to estimate availability thresholds for your environment:

- Evaluate the availability requirements of each of the applications that will be used in your environment, from discussions with users of the applications or from documentation for each application.
- Determine low-performance/high-performance thresholds.
- Estimate availability based on the probable end-to-end paths that the applications will use, and what equipment and services exist or may be in those paths.

In addition, check availability guarantees (if any) for services or technologies that exist in your environment or that potentially will be used in the system being designed. For example, Pacific Bell's switched multimegabit data service (SMDS) has a stated availability, in terms of mean time between service outages of greater than or equal to 3500 hours, with a mean time to restore of less than or equal to 3.5 hours. On the other hand, the Bellcore specification for SMDS calls for an availability of 99.9%. From our earlier discussion, we can see that both of these specifications describe similar availability characteristics, with the MTBSO/MTTR specs being more specific.

Some of the estimation techniques above require knowledge of which technologies/services exist or are planned for the system. Since at this point in the process we probably will not know which technologies/services we will be using for our network, these techniques are best if used after the technologies/services are chosen, possibly to check or verify the other techniques.

General thresholds for reliability from the user perspective focus on availability. At a high level, the user normally expects the system to be available as close to

100% of the time as possible. Availability can get close to 100%, within a tenth, hundreth, or thousandth of a percent, but with the trade-off of system complexity and cost. At this point we can describe a general reference threshold for availability, based on experience and observation. In general, a threshold of 99.9% availability can be used to distinguish between low- and high-performance services. In addition, a general threshold of approximately 99.5% can be used to distinguish a particular low-performance availability environment, that of prototypes and testbeds. These thresholds are shown in Figure 3-7. Note that the thresholds described in this section are general thresholds, and will likely be superseded by any environment-specific thresholds that are developed.

To summarize, the application service requirements and thresholds for reliability are availability, recoverability, and error or loss rates. For availability, measured as percentage of uptime or downtime, the general threshold estimates are

- Testbed or prototype reliability (availability): less than 95%
- Low-performance reliability (availability): less than 99.9%
- High-performance reliability (availability): greater than or equal to 99.9%

(*Note*: These availability thresholds are measured monthly.)

For recoverability, measured as MTBF/MTBSO and MTTR, the general threshold estimates are

- Low-performance reliability (recoverability): MTTR greater than 2 hours or an MTBF/MTBSO less than 8000 hours
- High-performance reliability (recoverability): MTTR less than or equal to 2 hours and MTBF/MTBSO greater than or equal to 8000 hours

(*Note*: These recoverability thresholds are chosen to provide a reasonable MTTR. If a smaller MTTR is chosen, then the MTBF /MTBSO will be correspondingly lower.)

FIGURE 3-7. **General Reference Thresholds for User Requirements**

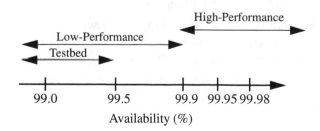

Availability (%)

Finally, for error or loss rates, measured as end-to-end information loss rate and retransmission rate, the thresholds arc highly spccific to cach user/application environment, but in general we can estimate

Low-performance (loss rate): IP packet losses of

$> 25\%$ for < 2 hours/month

$10\% <$ packet loss $< 25\%$ for < 2 hours/month

$1\% <$ packet loss $< 10\%$ for < 5 hours/month

$< 1\%$ for the remainder of the month

In addition to the above, guaranteed service levels for each of these requirements will be specified as application service requirements. Estimating availability requirements will be an iterative process. As user, host, and network service requirements are developed, availability will need to be adjusted.

3.4.2 Delay Requirements

For applications that have delay requirements, we will use the terms *end-to-end delay* and *delay variation* as measures of delay for the system.

Thresholds for Delay

Useful delay thresholds are interaction delay, human response time, and network propagation delay. These thresholds are useful in helping to distinguish low- and high-performance delay levels for your design environment.

- *Interaction delay (INTD)* estimates how long a user is willing to wait for a response from the system during an interactive session. Here a session is the time period during which an application is active. The interaction delay will depend on user behavior, their environment, and the types of applications being used. Interaction delays may range from a few seconds to a minute or more. In general, a useful range is 10 to 30 seconds.

  INTD is important when designing a network for interactive applications. An interaction delay estimate is useful in characterizing applications that are loosely interactive, those where waiting to receive information is expected. This applies to transaction-based applications, such as Web, file transfer, and some database processing. Some delay will be noticed by the user, and INTD is an estimate of how long the user is willing to wait.

- *Human response time (HRT)* estimates the time boundary when users begin to perceive delay in the system. When the system response time is below the HRT, users generally do not perceive delay in the system. Above the HRT, users will notice the system delay and may become frustrated. A good estimate of the HRT is approximately 100 ms. This is an important delay characteristic, as it distinguishes the threshold where the user perceives the system through its delay.

HRT is important for highly interactive applications, where wait times may not or should not be perceived by the user. This is usually the case when the application supports an interactive environment for the user, such as in visualization, virtual reality, and collaborative applications, but may also apply to applications where system delays beyond HRT result in loss of productivity.

- *Network propagation delay* estimates the signal propagation delay in the network. This provides a lower bound to the end-to-end and round-trip network and system delays. Propagation delay is dependent on distance and technology. It is useful as a lower delay bound, for it tells us when an application may not work well across the network, when its delay requirements are more stringent than the propagation delay for the network.

These delay estimates are shown in Figure 3-8. Any of these delay estimates may be used as reference levels for user service. For example, we can use HRT as a threshold for all services, and constrain the system to provide delay characteristics less than the value of HRT for that environment. Or we can choose a value for INTD that defines interactive service. In all cases, propagation delay will provide a lower bound for delay. Any of these delay estimates could also be used as service guarantees.

These delay estimates come from experience and are presented here for you to consider; you may disagree with their values, or find other useful estimates for delay. You are encouraged to develop your own estimates, or improve upon these. Since you know the environments you are designing for, you are in the best position to apply these estimates to your designs. We can use the estimates for HRT and

FIGURE 3-8. Delay Estimates for User Requirements

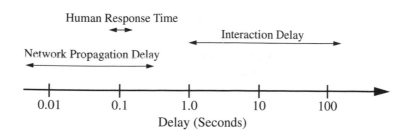

INTD to help us distinguish between *interactive-burst* and *interactive-bulk* applications. When both the responsiveness of the application (how frequently and quickly the application interacts with the user) and the end-to-end or round-trip delay (whichever is available to measure in the system) are bounded by one of these delay characteristics, we estimate that the application is interactive-burst or interactive-bulk.

In Figure 3-9, HRT and INTD are used as boundaries to separate interactive-burst and interactive-bulk applications. Between these two delay estimates, ranging from 100 ms to 10 seconds, is a grey area where the application could be considered either interactive-burst or -bulk.

The use of INTD and HRT is possibly the most straightforward way to distinguish between interactive-burst and interactive-bulk applications, but at times a more detailed analysis is needed. For those times, we can define a task completion time (TCT) for the application, where a task is the amount of time work is being performed by the system before interaction with the user is required. This is a subset of an application session; it can range from a single iteration of a computation to all work performed during an application session. Thus, the TCT is based on how the application performs its work. Tasks and task completion times are defined primarily by our ability to measure them.

FIGURE 3-9. Distinguishing Between Burst and Bulk Applications

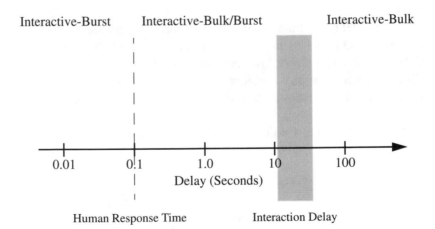

FIGURE 3-10. Task Completion Time (TCT) and Round-Trip Delay

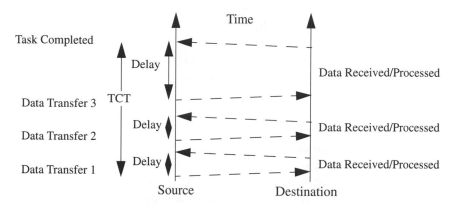

Figure 3-10 describes TCT and its relationship to round-trip time and task iteration. In this figure, an application session is transferring data across the network, but in a series of steps (or iterations). This behavior is consistent with applications that are processing transactions, distributing computations, or are client-server.

One way to distinguish between interactive-burst and -bulk applications is with the TCT, measured in seconds, and end-to-end delay, measured in milliseconds. For ease of measurement, end-to-end delay is measured as the round-trip time (RTT), in milliseconds, which can be measured via ICMP Echo (*ping*). The ratio of HRT to RTT describes the degree of responsiveness inherent in the system, which is dependent on the distance that the application is communicating. A small RTT (relative to the HRT) means that the distance is small enough that system responsiveness would be within the HRT time, while a large RTT means that the delay will impact the system's responsiveness.

System responsiveness is also in part due to the application's TCT. The system's responsiveness can be described by the ratio of HRT, RTT, and TCT (where HRT and RTT are measured in milliseconds, and TCT is measured in seconds):

$$\text{System Responsiveness} = \text{HRT/TCT, when HRT/RTT} > \text{or} = 1$$

and

$$\text{System Responsiveness} = \text{HRT/(RTT*TCT), when HRT/RTT} < 1$$

When the system responsiveness is less than 3 (a low degree of responsiveness), then the application can be considered interactive-bulk, and when it is greater than or equal to 3 (a high degree of responsiveness), it can be considered interactive-burst.

For example, a network that has an RTT (or *ping* time) of 100 milliseconds (an approximate value for a network crossing the continental United States) and a TCT of 30 seconds would have timeliness and system responsiveness of

$$HRT/RTT = 100ms/100ms = 1$$
$$System\ Responsiveness = 100ms/10s = 10$$

This would be considered an interactive-burst application. A Web application, for example, would have a timeliness value similar to this. If the application is file transfer (FTP), then the TCT may be much higher, like 100 or 1000 seconds. Note that when the TCT for a file transfer is relatively small, say a few seconds or so, then the application is considered interactive-burst, which is how it would behave. This would put R in the range of interactive-bulk applications. This approach defaults to the INTD and HRT values we used earlier in this discussion, when TCT is the time to perform the application, but can also allow the application to be separated into tasks and take into account the interactivity before and after each of the tasks.

Two things to note about this characterization of application delay: first, the threshold for system responsiveness that distinguishes interactive-burst and -bulk applications is approximate, and second, since RTT varies with distance, system responsiveness also varies with distance. This means that an application may be considered interactive-burst in an environment with a high RTT, such as a wide-area network, and may be considered interactive-bulk in an environment with a low RTT, such as a local-area network. This has interesting consequences in the network design, as we will see later in the book.

Another way to distinguish between interactive-burst and -bulk applications is with data rates. Burstiness is defined as

$$Burstiness = PDR/SDR$$

where PDR and SDR are peak and sustained data rates, described earlier in this book. We would choose a value for burstiness to distinguish interactive-burst and -bulk applications, much like we did for system responsiveness.

How is this analysis useful in the design process? In distinguishing between applications that have real-time, interactive-burst, interactive-bulk, and asynchronous delays, we will be able to determine

1. Whether there are delay requirements for any of the applications, or whether all applications can use a best-effort service.

2. If there are delay requirements, how strict they are, in terms of:
   – Performance
   – Reference levels (boundaries, thresholds, and guarantees)

This analysis will allow us to develop flow specifications and a logical design that will support applications that fall under number 1 above, number 2, or both.

End-to-End Delay

End-to-end, or system, delay is composed of many delay sources, such as propagation, queueing, transmission, I/O, switching, and processing. While it would be useful to be able to measure and monitor all sources of delay, it is not practical for most environments. Therefore the total, end-to-end delay is used. For many environments, especially IP environments, the round-trip delay is measured, through various versions of the application *ping*. This provides a useful, easily measured, and readily available form of end-to-end delay measurement. In this book, round-trip delay is included as a form of end-to-end delay.

Recall that we used HRT, INTD, propagation delay, and responsiveness as potential thresholds for distinguishing between service levels. All delay thresholds are based on combinations of

- Physical limits of the network—for example, the size of the network and the distances between applications or users
- Host and network element hardware and software performance, including network protocols
- Application behavior at particular delay thresholds
- User interaction with the system at particular delay thresholds

A key guideline in determining delay requirements is to determine the limiting factor between these delay thresholds. The limiting factor will be the ultimate delay bottleneck within the system. As limiting factors are found, they can be reduced or removed, revealing the next limiting factor. This process is repeated until a limiting factor that cannot be reduced or removed is encountered, or until the system is performing at acceptable levels.

Given that physical limits on delay are absolute boundaries (the speeds of electromagnetic radiation through various media are well-known and constant values), they may impact or negate other delay thresholds. For example, if an application requires an end-to-end delay of 40 ms in order to support an interactive VR environment, and the application session is being distributed between Los Angeles and Tokyo, the end-to-end delay of the network (approximately 225 ms) will exceed the application delay requirement, regardless of the network design. Thus, either the application has to take into account the end-to-end delay between Los Angeles and Tokyo, possibly by modifying the code, algorithms, or usage model, or the application sessions cannot be distributed between these sites. Knowing this before the network is designed would allow the application developers or network designers to adapt to the physical limits of the environment.

Now let's say that the distance of the network above is reduced, and the physical limitation on the delay is 10 ms (the network is now between San Francisco and Los Angeles). However, through testing, or summing the delay estimates of all hosts and network elements in the path, an end-to-end delay of 100 ms is expected within the system. What can be done? Hardware and software performance can be quite difficult to understand, identify, and improve upon. In designing a network, we need to consider each piece in the end-to-end path of communications, which may consist of a variety of hosts and network elements. What can we look for that will reduce the likely sources of delay in the system, without an unreasonable amount of analysis and resources? Areas to check for potential sources of delay include computer operating systems, network protocols, and host peripherals, including disk drives and network interface cards/device drivers.

What we can look for in these areas are operating systems that are notoriously slow and poorly written, protocols that are poorly implemented, and hosts and/or peripherals that are mismatched or weakly interoperable. This type of information obviously will not come from the manufacturer, but it can often be found in Internet mailing lists, news groups, independent testing, and academic research, all of which are increasingly available via the Web. By doing some research, you can rapidly learn a lot about performance problems with host and network element hardware/ software. Of course, what you learn through this process may easily apply to other areas of the design process and may affect other performance characteristics. A note of caution: Don't believe everything you read from these sources—including this one! Make your own observations and analyses, and draw your own conclusions. As we will see later in this book, support services—network management and security—will also play a role in the delay of the system.

Delay thresholds based on application behavior and user interaction are generally more flexible than physical or host/network element delays. Recall that values for INTD, HRT, and responsiveness were estimated ranges, and that these ranges can be expanded or contracted to map to the user/application environment. While in the example above the end-to-end physical delay was the ultimate boundary, when the distance of the network was decreased so that the end-to-end delay was on the order of 10 ms (for example, the distance from Los Angeles to San Francisco), if the end-to-end delay is reduced to 40 ms, then the application behavior (interactive VR environment), with its 40-ms end-to-end delay, becomes the limiting factor. If this is acceptable to the user, then the delay characteristics are (from our high-level esti-mates) optimized for that environment.

To determine general thresholds between low- and high-performance delay, we use the delay components described earlier: real-time, interactive-burst, interactive-bulk, and asynchronous.

Real-time application delays are on the high-performance side, although a general threshold between low- and high-performance cannot really be determined, for real time describes a requirement for specified service, not a general level of delay in the system. The reasoning behind real-time delays being high-performance is that, since they are specified service delays, they will also be smaller than other delays. When delays are large, there is less of a need to guarantee them in a service model.

A general threshold between low- and high-performance can be developed for interactive-burst and interactive-bulk applications. Recall that HRT (approximately 100 ms) was the threshold when users begin to perceive a delay in the system. This threshold can also be used as the general threshold to distinguish between low- and high-performance delays for interactive-burst applications.

Likewise, the INTD, approximately 10 to 30 seconds, was the threshold when users become frustrated with their application session. We take the low end of this delay (10 seconds) as the threshold between low- and high-performance delays for interactive-bulk applications.

Finally, the delay characteristics of asynchronous applications are outside the boundaries of what we consider high-performance, thus, asynchronous applications are considered here to be low-performance.

Delay Variation

Delay variation is coupled with high-performance or specified delay to give an overall delay performance requirement for applications that are sensitive to the interarrival time of information. Some examples of such applications are those that produce or use video, audio, and telemetry information. For delay variation coupled with delay, when no information is available about delay variation, a good rule of thumb is approximately 1% to 2% of the end-to-end delay.

For example, an estimate for delay variation in the absence of any other information, when the end-to-end delay of an application is 40 ms, is approximately 400 to 800 microseconds. This would be a rough approximation, however, and should be verified if possible.

3.4.3 Capacity Requirements

For applications with capacity requirements, measures of capacity include data rates and sizes.

Data Rates

In evaluating application capacity requirements, we want to consider applications that require large amounts of capacity and those that require a specific value or range of capacities. When an application requires a large amount of capacity, it is important to know when the application has a real (measurable, verifiable) requirement for high capacity and when it will just attempt to utilize whatever capacity is available.

Applications that use TCP as their transport mechanism, without any additional conditions or modifications from the higher-layer protocols (or from the application itself), will receive performance levels based on the current state of the network. This is done through TCP tuning its transmission parameters throughout the TCP session to react to conditions of apparent congestion in the system.

Estimating Data Rates

Estimating a data (or maybe more appropriately, information) rate is based on how much information you know about the transmission characteristics (and data flow) of the application and how accurate the estimation needs to be. We can estimate a peak data rate (PDR), a minimum data rate, a sustained data rate (SDR), or a combination of these. These data rates may be at the link layer or network layer.

The data rates of all applications are bounded, so the real question is where the bounds are in the system. If the application itself, along with the network protocols, supports a very fast data rate, somewhere in the system some other component is limiting this rate. In every system there is a limiting factor for the data rate (and everything else).

Many applications rely on the transport mechanism, such as TCP, to provide an "as fast as possible" data rate. We have an intuitive feel for some of these applications (e.g., FTP, telnet)—for example, we can be fairly certain that a telnet session will not have a data rate of 100 Mb/s; likewise an FTP session should not run at 50 kb/s, given higher available capacity. What we can do for these types of applications is consider their data sizes and TCTs.

Here the TCT—in this case the overall completion time—and data sizes are based on what the user may want or expect, or what the application will produce.

TABLE 3-4. TCTs and Data Sizes for Sample Applications

Application	Average TCT (Seconds)	Average Data Size (Bytes)
Distributed Computing (Batch Mode)	10^3	10^7
Web Transactions	10	10^4
Database Entries/Queries	2–5	10^3
Payroll Entries	10	10^2
Teleconference (Using Multicast)	10^3	$3*10^5$

Taking an application that has nebulous capacity and delay characteristics, like FTP, we can estimate a data rate from user- and application-provided data sizes and TCTs. We may ask a number of users what size files they expect to transfer, and how long they are willing to wait for the transfers. Likewise, we may be able to check the data sizes and TCTs of the applications, resulting in a table like Table 3-4. From estimates such as those in Table 3-4, we can either estimate upper and lower bounds for the data rate, or an average rate.

For other applications, the characteristics of the data transfers may be better known, such as the sizes of the data sets being transferred as well as the frequency and duration of these transfers. This may apply to transaction-based applications, such as cooperative computing, transaction processing, and some Web applications.

Consider a remote interactive data-processing application that connects to retail stores and processes customer information, such as credit card entries. We can base a task as the processing of a single customer's credit card information. Then, the TCT needs to be on the order of the INTD discussed earlier—approximately 30 seconds, although here it may be expected to be much smaller, say on the order of 5 to 10 seconds, and the data size for each task is fairly small, on the order of 100 to 1000 bytes.

Another example is a computing environment where multiple hosts are sharing the processing for a task. At each iteration of the task, data is transferred between hosts. Here we may know the frequency of data transfer, the size of each transfer (which may also be constant), and how much time is required to process the data (which will indicate how much time a transfer may take). A shared, multiprocessor computing environment is shown in Figure 3-11.

FIGURE 3-11. **Example of Multiprocessor Computing Environment**

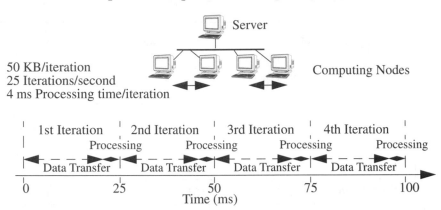

For some applications, the capacity characteristics are well-known, and estimating a data rate can be relatively easy to do. Applications that involve voice and/or video have relatively well understood capacity characteristics. The rates of these applications are likely to be constant, so that their peak and minimum data rates are the same. For example, an MPEG-2 low-level constrained-parameter bitstream (CPB) will have a rate of 4 Mb/s, or a main-level CPB will have a rate between 15 and 20 Mb/s.

There are currently no general thresholds between low- and high-performance capacity. It is not obvious why this should be so, except that reliability and delay characteristics have a direct impact on the user's perception of system performance, while capacity has a secondary impact on performance, through reliability and delay. There will be, however, environment-specific thresholds on capacity. It appears that, of all of the performance characteristics, capacity characteristics have the closest ties to the end users and their applications.

Generic performance thresholds are added to the performance envelope we developed in Chapter 1. These thresholds, as shown in Figure 3-12, are used to separate the envelope into low- and high-performance regions. This gives us a visual interpretation of the performance characteristics.

3.4.4 Environment-Specific Service Thresholds

General thresholds give us some common estimates for low-performance and high-performance characteristics. Such thresholds are useful when there is a lack of information about the users and applications for the network being designed, but often the environment indicates what the performance thresholds should be.

FIGURE 3-12. **Performance Envelope with Generic Thresholds**

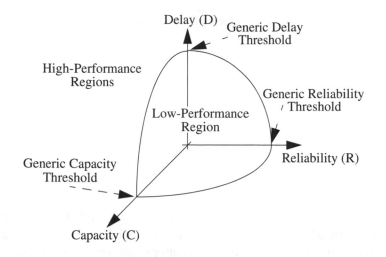

The thresholds that would distinguish between low- and high-performance characteristics for a retail store transaction-processing environment will be quite different from those for a scientific computing environment. What is important is that we are able to distinguish low- and high-performance characteristics for each environment (environment-specific thresholds), and not compare characteristics across environments.

As with general thresholds, the reason for developing environment-specific thresholds is to determine which applications have high-performance characteristics. It is likely that these high-performance applications are what we will design toward, along with those applications that have specified characteristics. We may use the information that we have developed so far in this chapter to develop environment-specific thresholds. There are at least two processes that we can apply here: the comparison of characteristics for all applications, and using an arbitrary service threshold.

Comparing Application Characteristics

When we can group application characteristics, then a comparison can often be made to determine where a threshold can be applied. Consider a plot of delay characteristics for a number of applications, A through M, for a particular environment, such as in Figure 3-13.

FIGURE 3-13. **Delay Characteristics for Sample Applications**

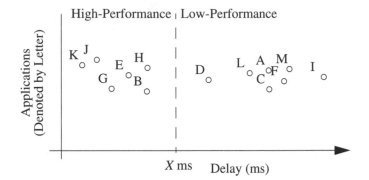

In this diagram, delay characteristics are grouped into two areas. We can use this information to place an environment-specific threshold at a delay of approximately X milliseconds. Those applications that have a delay characteristic of less than X milliseconds are considered high-performance for this environment.

Arbitrary Service Thresholds

There are times when application characteristics cannot be compared, through lack of information about the characteristics, or because when the characteristics are plotted, they form a roughly continuous range of values. Figure 3-14 shows a plot of a characteristic where no threshold is clear. It will be necessary at this point either to use only the general thresholds, use an arbitrary threshold, or forget this part of the process and move on. Arbitrary thresholds may come directly from the customers or end users, and are arbitrary in the sense that they are not founded in measurements or documented in any way. Arbitrary thresholds are the last choice to distinguish between low- and high-performance characteristics.

FIGURE 3-14. **Sample Plot of a Characteristic as a Continuous Range of Values**

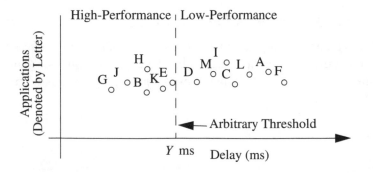

3.4.5 Specified Services

Now we will shift our focus away from performance levels and best-effort services to specified services. As has been discussed earlier, specified services have specific service performance requirements. This makes it more straightforward to compile requirements.

Deterministic Services

Deterministic services have more specific performance characteristics than the best-effort services we have been discussing. In most cases, we will have a good estimate of these performance characteristics, yet we will not be able to guarantee performance. We will use boundaries to approximate where the high- and/or low-performance levels are, which will be used in the design process later in this book for capacity planning and flow specification.

Guaranteed Services

Guaranteed services are a step beyond deterministic services, in that there is some mechanism to enforce the service to the application or user. Thus, in order to develop requirements for guaranteed services, we need to have well-defined performance characteristics.

We use the term *service guarantee* to describe a service performance characteristic. Like a service boundary, it describes what we are trying to achieve in terms of performance, but unlike a service boundary, some action is expected to happen in the system when the performance deviates from the guarantee. Action can be taken in either direction, for performance above the guarantee as well as below it. The action may be to reserve more buffer space, change the path of the flow, or mark the data as available to be dropped by the system. This could be considered policing or enforcing a flow.

In Figure 3-15, an application's performance approaches the service limit (guarantee). No action is taken until the application exceeds its guarantee, where policing occurs. At the network element where policing occurs, this can take the form of marking the packet/frame/cell for downstream network elements to take action on, or dropping the frame/packet/cell at that network element. Policing is often useful to protect traffic flows downstream from a flow that exceeds its service limit and attempts to use more network resources than are contracted.

FIGURE 3-15. **Policing the Performance of a Flow**

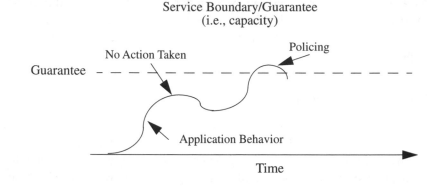

Service guarantees are developed in a similar fashion to service boundaries, except that the need to explicitly request a guarantee is stated. In the resource-allocation example above, we stated that the reliability goal was 99.99%, but that we must meet a reliability of at least 99.97%. This lower boundary for reliability could have been stated as a service guarantee, which would mean that later in the design process we would consider mechanisms to provide and police that service in the system.

In Figure 3-16, service thresholds, boundaries, and guarantees are now all applied to the service performance envelope.

FIGURE 3-16. **Fully Developed Performance Envelope**

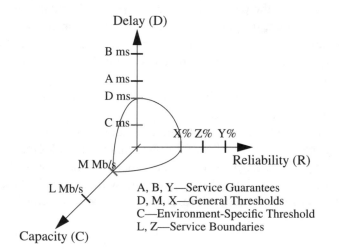

In this figure, low- and high-performance regions are separated by the general thresholds D, M, and X, while an environment-specific delay, C, exists within the low-performance region. Service boundaries and guarantees are shown here in the high-performance region, at various locations in the envelope.

Example 3.1—Telemetry Application

Let's first consider a telemetry application environment, such as that shown in Figure 3-17. In this example, we are receiving and processing a telemetry stream from a helicopter.

Telemetry processing in this environment consists of two components: an automated guidance-control system that will analyze telemetry data from a helicopter and adjust control parameters, and a motion-visualization system used by a controller at a workstation. Both components receive the same telemetry stream.

In an analysis of this environment, we have determined (from discussions with the end users and application developers) that for this application to be useful, data should be received by the guidance-control computer within 20 ms of being generated from the helicopter. We also know that the controller will interact with the helicopter based on the input from the telemetry stream, and that this will be bound by the HRT for the application (100 ms). From this information, we can bound the delay of the telemetry stream, as shown in Figure 3-18.

FIGURE 3-17. **Example of a Telemetry Application Environment**

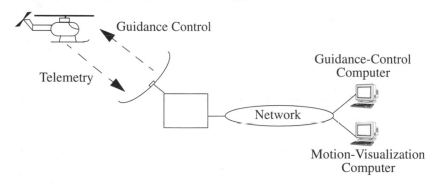

FIGURE 3-18. **Delay Boundaries for Example 3.1**

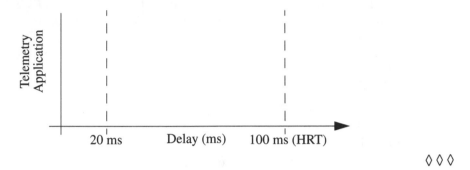

◊ ◊ ◊

Example 3.2—Computing Consolidation

For our second example, consider an organization that is undergoing a consolidation of its computing facilities, as in Figure 3-19.

FIGURE 3-19. **Computing Consolidation Environment**

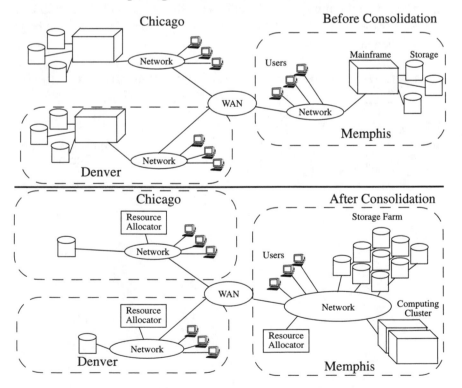

The primary application in this environment is a computing resource allocator, an application that keeps track of the resources within the system and allocates computing jobs to each of the computing servers, based on the requirements of the job.

Allocation is done rapidly, on the order of 250 ms, and the state of each computing server is constantly being checked. Before the consolidation, the reliability of the computing servers to their users was kept above 99.97%, while the reliability goal was only 99.95%. For the consolidated environment, they want to strive for a better degree of reliability, hoping to achieve 99.99%, but will accept a lower degree of reliability, although not below the actual reliability of the previous system (99.97%).

Here we have a high-performance reliability boundary to design toward (99.99%), and a lower-performance boundary that must be kept (99.97%). This lower boundary possibly should be considered as a service guarantee, but here we will treat it as a deterministic boundary. The bounds on the reliability for this resource-allocation application are shown in Figure 3-20.

The deterministic boundaries for all performance characteristics can be applied to a performance envelope for the application. If, for example, we have an application that requires the following specified performance: reliability, 99.8%; capacity, between 14 and 20 Mb/s; and delay, no greater than 80 ms, we can apply them as shown in Figure 3-21.

FIGURE 3-20. **Reliability Boundaries for Resource-Allocation Application**

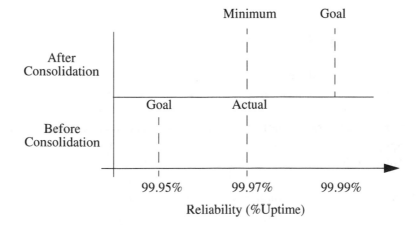

FIGURE 3-21. **Performance Envelope with Specified Service**

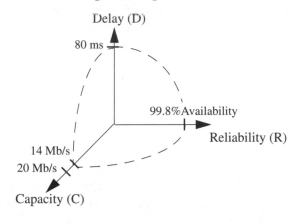

◊ ◊ ◊

In the system design, deterministic service means that there will need to be some mechanism to provide the service performance that is being requested, as well as some way to measure and verify the performance of the system over time, to notify the application, end user, or administrator that the services are (or are not) being supported. Mechanisms to consider for supporting deterministic services include resource allocation via fair queueing and resource reservation via RSVP.

3.5 Distinguishing Between Service Performance Levels

At this point in the process we have descriptions for various service (performance and function) levels, such as best-effort, low-performance, high-performance, and specified services. We have typed applications as mission-critical, real-time, and controlled-rate to distinguish them as needing specific services, and have also developed general and environment-specific thresholds to separate performance requirements into low- and high-performance for your design environment. Now, we will examine some guidelines to help you use these concepts together to distinguish between service performance levels for your designs.

3.5.1 Guidelines in Distinguishing Services

The steps presented below are in our recommended sequence. You should use these steps as you see fit, in part or as a whole, modifying their sequence to best fit your analysis methodology and design environment. In order for you to apply these steps, you need to have a listing of the applications that will likely be used in this network, along with any performance information that you are able to gather, derive, or estimate.

These steps go from the most specific match with an application's requirements to the least specific, so that the last step is the default when none of the other steps apply.

1. The first step is to determine if any of the applications have obvious requirements for specified (deterministic or guaranteed) performance from the system. When an application has requirements for specified performance, the application and its requirements are noted as specified.

2. The second step is to type applications. When applications are not identified as having specified requirements, can they be typed as mission-critical, real-time, or controlled-rate? If so, they may have specified performance requirements, even if they were not recognized in the first step.

3. The third step is to apply application groups to the applications. For those applications that do not have obvious specified requirements, and cannot be typed as mission-critical, real-time, or controlled-rate, assess whether they can be grouped as telemetry/command and control; visualization; distributed computing; Web access, development, and use; bulk data transport; tele*services; or OAM applications. If so, then they may have specified performance requirements as listed earlier in the chapter.

Those applications that cannot be described by Steps 1 through 3 are likely to be best-effort applications.

When you have a design project that has very little time for analysis, you can reverse the sequence of these steps and go as far down in the process as time permits. This will allow you to make some quick generalizations about service levels, and get more specific if you have the time.

Once you have categorized the applications, you will then apply the general and environment-specific service thresholds. This will indicate where low-performance and high-performance regions are located in your design environment. The result is a listing of application types and services, which can also be applied to a performance envelope, such as the one described in Figure 3-16.

3.6 Concluding Remarks

The principles and guidelines for requirements analysis provide you with the means for analyzing your design environment. You will first establish initial conditions for the design, which will lay the foundation for building the set of requirements. Initial conditions vary, depending on the design environment, as well as whether the design is for a new network or an upgrade of an existing network. Armed with the initial conditions, you can gather requirements from the users and map application requirements to determine their location dependencies. (Tables to gather requirements are presented in the next chapter.)

Once you have the requirements listed and mapped, you will need to identify service metrics to help monitor, manage, and verify that your requirements will be met in the network. Your choices of service metrics will lead to defining network management variables that will be used in Chapter 10 (in fact, by choosing SNMP MIB variables, you are also choosing network management variables).

Building on the service metrics, you need to develop performance thresholds in order to distinguish between specified, best-effort, and low/high-performance services in your network. Characterizing the behavior of users and applications (including workload modeling) will often help in this process. You then apply these performance thresholds (generic, environment-specific, and specified) to your design environment, generating a list of services expected for your network.

In the next chapter, we will apply the principles and guidelines of this chapter to examples and case studies. We will also consider the degenerate cases of the requirements analysis process, including ways that we can simplify this process when necessary.

Suggested Further Reading

1. Bell Communications Research. *Generic System Requirements in Support of Switched Multimegabit Data Service*, TR-TSV-000772, Issue 1. May 1991.

2. Gray, J. *The Benchmark Handbook for Database and Transaction Processing Systems*, Morgan Kaufmann, San Francisco, 1991.

3. Jain, R. *The Art of Computer System Performance: Analysis, Techniques for Experimental Design, Measurement, Simulation, and Modeling*. Wiley, New York, 1991.

4. *Pacific Bell/Nevada Bell Switched Multi-Megabit Data Service (SMDS) Network Interface Specification*, Pub L-780090-PB/NB, Issue 1. August 1992.

Exercises

1. The initial conditions for a network design help you to set the groundwork for the design, by establishing a baseline from which your design can develop. What are likely initial conditions for the design of a completely new network? For a new network that will be integrated with existing networks? For the upgrade of an existing network?

2. Consider the design of a network where you cannot talk to the end users. What other resources can you use to gather requirements about the users, applications, hosts, and existing networks? Briefly outline a method for gathering requirements in the absence of end user involvement.

3. Service metrics are used to monitor, measure, and verify services in the network and to determine if requirements are being met. Therefore, service metrics must be meaningful to the network operator, manager, and/or end users. For example, to verify a service level of 40-ms round-trip delay, we could use the utility *ping* and monitor for a threshold of 40 ms:

Service Level	Service Metric	Tool/Variable
40-ms delay	Round-trip delay	*ping*

   For each service level below, describe a service metric that could be used for measuring the service level, and a corresponding tool or variable for the metric.

   a) Availability between two connected networks, A and B.

   b) End-to-end delay between network A and a computing resource on network B.

   c) Average traffic rate to/from server C, measured across all network interfaces on C over 5-minute intervals.

   d) End-to-end path(s) between host X on network A and resource Y on network B.

4. The utility *pathchar* (available at *ee.lbl.gov*) helps to determine the characteristics (delay, capacity, and packet drops) of a path in the network. Here is an example of a *pathchar* trace:

   ```
   roller# ./pathchar www.stanford.edu
   pathchar to www.stanford.edu (36.190.0.136)
     mtu limited to 1500 bytes at local host
     doing 32 probes at each of 64 to 1500 by 44
     0 roller.nas.nasa.gov (129.99.236.14)
     |    10 Mb/s,    319 us (1.81 ms)
     1 test-bin.nas.nasa.gov (129.99.236.254)
     |    11 Mb/s,    603 us (4.12 ms),    +q 1.28 ms (1.75 KB)
     2 nas-bcn1.nas.nasa.gov (129.99.223.254)
   ```

```
|    60 Mb/s,    70 us (4.46 ms)
3 nas-fix1.nas.nasa.gov (129.99.144.236)
|    10 Mb/s,    402 us (6.45 ms)
4 192.92.167.3 (192.92.167.3)
|    ?? b/s,     110 us (5.90 ms)
5 ARC1. NSN.NASA.GOV (192.203.230.5)
|    ?? b/s,     1.43 ms (8.67 ms),   4% dropped
6 sanjose1-br1.bbnplanet.net (198.32.184.19)
|    37 Mb/s,    -18 us (9.73 ms),    +q 5.66 ms (25.9 KB) +2,  3% dropped
9 sunet-gateway.stanford.edu (198.31.10.1)
|    285 Mb/s,  219 us (10.2 ms),    +q 4.24 ms (152 KB) +3,  2% dropped
10 Core-gateway.Stanford.EDU (171.64.1.33)
|    11 Mb/s,    254 us (11.9 ms),    +q 4.41 ms (5.80 KB) +3,  3% dropped
11 ceras-gateway.Stanford.EDU (171.64.1.6)
|    4.8 Mb/s,   -75 us (14.2 ms),    +q 5.98 ms (3.61 KB) +2,  2% dropped
12 www.Stanford.EDU (36.190.0.136)
12 hops, rtt 7.28 ms (14.2 ms), bottleneck 4.8 Mb/s, pipe 14233 bytes
```

Show how this utility can be used to provide rudimentary service metrics for availability, delay, and capacity.

5. What is the difference between specifying an availability of 99.99% and a down-time of 1 minute/week? Give an example where the specification for downtime is more useful than the corresponding specification for availability.

6. Figure 3-8 shows delay estimates for human response time, interaction delay, and network propagation delay. Give an application example for each delay esti-mate. Are there applications that can be bounded by two of these delay esti-mates? List examples.

7. How can delay variation impact a traffic flow? What characteristics of an appli-cation indicate that it is sensitive to delay variation? How can delay variation be measured within the network?

CHAPTER 4

Requirements Analysis: Practice

Having examined the principles and guidelines for each step in the requirements analysis process, we will now apply the process model from Chapter 3 to case studies. In applying this process, we will first look at the templates, tables, and maps that we will be using. We will also consider ways to simplify the process when necessary, what is termed the *degenerate cases* for the process.

4.1 Templates, Tables, and Maps

For the requirements analysis process, there are five tables that you can use to aid in the gathering and listing of user, application, host, network, and functional requirements. These tables are based on the discussions of requirements in the last two chapters, and are intended to be modified as necessary for your design environment.

Table 4-1 is the user component of the specification. This table lists each of the user requirements and expands on the expected growth to include growth after 1, 2, and 3 years.

For the applications requirements in Table 4-2, each application can be typed as mission-critical, controlled-rate, real-time, a combination of these, or as best-effort. For each application, the performance characteristics delay, capacity, and reliability are entered for the application type(s) that apply.

TABLE 4-1. User Requirements

User Requirements	Description of Requirement for Design Environment
Location(s) and Number(s) of Users	
Expected Growth in the Number of Users	
After 1 Year	
After 2 Years	
After 3 Years	
User Expectations	
Timeliness	
Interactivity	
Reliability	
Quality	
Adaptability	
Security	
Cost/Funding	

TABLE 4-2. Application Requirements

Categorizing Applications	Mission-Critical	Controlled-Rate	Real-Time	Best-Effort	Application Locations
Application A					
Application B					
Application C					

Table 4-3 is used to list and describe the hosts, servers, and specialized equipment that you expect to have in the design environment. In this table you would describe any of the host performance characteristics (disk drives, processors, memory, bus, OS, drivers) that you are able to gather or derive and that may impact the network design.

TABLE 4-3. **Host Requirements**

	Type of Host or Equipment	**Performance Characteristics**	**Numbers and Locations**
Host A			
Host B			
Host C			

TABLE 4-4. **Network Requirements**

Existing Networks	**Scaling**	**Inter-operability Issues**	**Overall Performance Issues**	**Network-Layer Issues**	**Support Service Issues**	**Network Locations**
Network A						
Network B						
Network C						

For Table 4-4, you would input the requirements of existing networks for the design. Here is where we describe the requirements for interconnectivity between the existing networks and the network being designed, in particular the constraints that the existing networks place on the design. The functional requirements of Table 4-5 are the initial descriptions of the requirements for network management and security in the design, as well as the level of funding that is available.

4.1.1 Application Maps

The application location information that we have listed can be used to show their relative locations in the design environment. For example, Table 4-6 lists some application locations in a requirements specification. We can map this information to show where applications overlap. This is the applications map, as seen in Figure 4-1. In this example, there are applications that cover the entire design environment (A), that cover one campus (B, C, and D), and those that cover parts of each campus (E, F, G, and H).

At times, an application map will show all applications covering the entire design environment, as in Figure 4-2. When all of the applications cover all areas of the design, then the application map will not be useful. In a degenerate case such as this, user or host locations may be mapped instead of applications. The application map will be used in the next chapters as input to the flow analysis process.

TABLE 4-5. **Functional Requirements**

	Requirements
Network Management Requirements	
Monitoring Methods	
Instrumentation Methods	
Characteristics Sets	
In-Band versus Out-of-Band Monitoring	
Centralized versus Distributed Monitoring	
Performance Characteristics	
Security Requirements	
Government-Specified	
Company- or Organization-Specified	
User-Specified	
Level of Funding for Network	

TABLE 4-6. **Example of Application Locations**

Categorizing Applications	Application Locations
Application A	All locations
Application B	San Francisco
Application C	Oakland
Application D	Oakland
Application E	San Francisco (part) and Oakland (part)
Application F	San Jose and Oakland (part)
Application G	San Francisco (part) and Oakland (part)
Application H	San Jose, San Francisco (part), and Oakland (part)

FIGURE 4-1. **Example of Application Map**

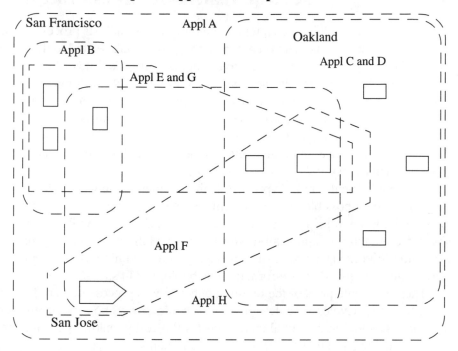

FIGURE 4-2. **Application Map—Degenerate Case**

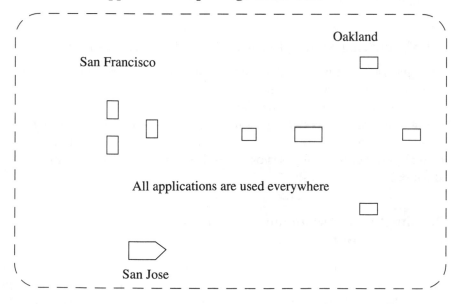

4.2 Simplifying the Requirements Analysis Process

As you have seen in the last chapters, the requirements analysis process can be time-consuming. The benefits that you get from this process are related to the amounts of time and effort you are able to put into it, but there may be times when it is not possible to complete a full requirements analysis. For example, you may be asked to develop a thumbnail sketch of a concept design and have only a few hours to do so. Or you may be working on a proposal response and are required to include a brief sketch of a design in the response. In cases such as these, you likely will not have the time or resources to put much detail in the design. How can you simplify this process when necessary?

The requirements analysis process is about understanding your design environment. Whenever possible, getting information about your end users, their applications, and hosts will help you to understand how the network will be used. In the absence of end user or application information, we fall back to getting requirements from more traditional sources, such as managers and administrators, for example, information systems (IS) or information technology (IT) staffs.

There are some parts of the requirements analysis process that are fundamental to successfully developing a design, and so should always be considered. These parts are: developing the initial conditions for the design, gathering some requirements or making assumptions about the requirements, and typing or grouping applications. To simplify the process, we will focus on those parts that apply to services in the network.

4.2.1 Simplifying Assumption—Only Best-Effort Delivery

One degenerate case is using the simplifying assumption that all applications can use best-effort delivery from the network. This reduces or eliminates the need for specified and/or high-performance services in the design, and (as we will see during the flow analysis process) will allow us to base the design on a capacity plan instead of a (more complicated) service plan. This degenerate case tends to factor out individual requirements and focuses on general requirements, those that impact trends and patterns in network usage.

4.2.2 Simplifying Assumption—Focusing on Highest-Priority Application

Another degenerate case builds on the previous assumption of only best-effort delivery to include one or a few applications that are the highest-priority applications for the design environment. In this case, all of the parts of the requirements analysis process still apply, but they are reduced in complexity. By focusing on only the highest-priority applications, we are effectively categorizing all others as best-effort delivery. Thus, the in-depth requirements gathering, service metrics, behavior characterization, and performance thresholds will apply to only the highest-priority application.

Example 4.1—Small Business

This example is a network design for a small business: we need to provide a quick analysis of the requirements for the customer's environment, as if we were consultants preparing to bid on the design work, or a vendor doing a rough pre-sales design. For this environment, we have the following information, provided during the first meeting with our potential customer:

1. There are no known specific performance requirements for any of the applications that the company plans on using.
2. The company has offices in Austin, Houston, and Dallas/Fort Worth.
3. Applications include database transaction processing, currently based out of Dallas/Fort Worth, and a bursty communications package used in Austin.
4. The goal of this project is to connect these offices with a wide-area service.
5. This project is expected to cost less than $250K.

While there are no specific performance requirements for our applications, the customer was able to provide ballpark estimates of their capacities:

Application A	100 Kb/s	Communications
Application B	70 Kb/s	
Application C	400 Kb/s	
Application D	1.5 Mb/s	Database transaction processing

The customer also provided the numbers of hosts that are at each site:

Austin	25 PCs	10 other
Houston	15 PCs	8 other
Dallas/Fort Worth	17 PCs	10 other

If no specified service is indicated, then the applications are listed as best-effort. This may change as we learn more about the applications, but for now this is as specific as we can get. All of the applications for this example are thus categorized as best-effort.

From discussions with the customer, the communications package (Application A) is determined to be bursty in nature, with small data sizes and frequent transmissions. We can consider this application to be interactive-burst, while the database transaction–processing application (Application D) is described by the customer as transferring large amounts of data (initial estimates are 1 MB/transaction), and we list this application as interactive-bulk.

Table 4-7 begins the requirements specification for our example. For the user service requirements, we know that there are users at the three locations, and we have an upper limit on the amount we can spend on the network. Since this is a quick analysis, we do not have any detailed information about the users.

In this example, there are only best-effort applications. We have indications from the customer that the communications package (Application A) is bursty, and we show this as interactive-burst in the table, while the database transaction–processing application (Application D) is estimated to be interactive-bulk. Now we apply the customer's estimates on application capacities to each application (see Table 4-8).

TABLE 4-7. **User Requirements for Example 4.1**

User Service Requirements	Description of Requirement for Design Environment
Location(s) and Number(s) of Users	Austin, Houston, Dallas/Fort Worth
Cost/Funding	Less than $250K

TABLE 4-8. **Application Requirements for Example 4.1**

Categorizing Applications	Best-Effort	Application Locations
Application A	Interactive-burst (100 Kb/s)	Austin and Houston
Application B	70 Kb/s	All locations
Application C	400 Kb/s	All locations
Application D	Interactive-bulk (1.5 Mb/s)	Austin and Dallas/Fort Worth

TABLE 4-9. Host Service Requirements for Example 4.1

	Type of Host or Equipment	Numbers and Locations
Host A	PC	Austin (25), Houston (15), DFW (17)
Host B	Other	Austin (10), Houston (8), DFW (10)
Host C	Database server (S_D)	DFW
Host D	Teleconferencing server (S_A)	Austin
Host E	Application C server (S_C)	Austin

◊ ◊ ◊

In Table 4-8, we also show the locations where each application is expected to be used. The only other information available about this customer's environment are the host numbers and locations, which are entered into Table 4-9. There are no network or system-wide requirements identified for this environment at this stage in the design process. This is an example of a quick and dirty, minimal listing of customer requirements. For this type of quick analysis, the requirements specification can help you to collect and organize your customer's requirements, and help you to ask the right questions to get more requirements.

In this case, Table 4-8 showed that there were no specified requirements, which makes the rest of the process much easier. This table allowed us to easily indicate a threshold (HRT) for Application B, while also showing where each of the applications will be used. Table 4-9 shows that we have not found any important host-specific requirements, but did find out where the hosts are concentrated.

A requirements specification such as this is useful to qualify a customer's environment and needs rapidly—to estimate how much work will be involved, as well as potential cost, and to eliminate or identify any show-stopping requirements. As the requirements become more sophisticated, however, more work needs to be done to understand the customer's environment.

4.3 Case Study

Our case study is for a large manufacturing company. This company has a test and development center (the TDC), where they test new designs and modify old ones. This type of company could be found in many industries, such as automotive or aerospace.

4.3.1 Background Information

The TDC currently consists of a single building in Oakland, California, which contains five testing centers (see Figure 4-3). Each testing center has a test platform, where models are mounted and tested; a variety of test equipment, using acoustics, infrared, microwave, and other mechanisms for testing; several workstations for technicians; and a network to connect them to each other and to the other areas of the building. There are also two visualization rooms, one for local workers and another for visiting technicians. Each room has a workstation and network connection. Finally, there is a computing center, which is in the process of deploying a cluster of high-end graphics workstations, along with about 10 terabytes (TB) of storage.

FIGURE 4-3. **Layout of the Current TDC**

Oakland Facility (Building 1013)

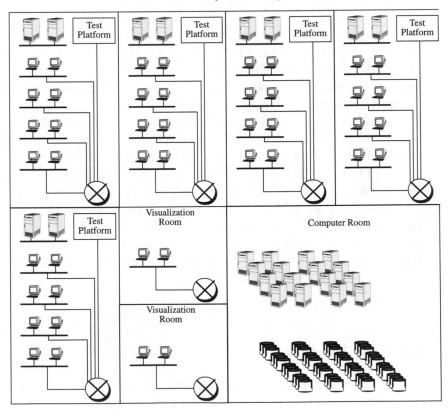

The functions of the TDC are to

1. Test models and generate experimental data from these tests.

2. Simulate models using the computing cluster and generate computational data from these simulations.

3. Refine models using a series of tests and modify each model from the tests.

The model of operations for the TDC is that when a design concept is developed, this concept is first tested by generating a simulation of the design. If this simulation looks promising, then a model is developed based on the simulation. This model is tested in the TDC, and the results of the tests are compared to the simulation. The model is refined, as necessary, until the model either shows that the design should be developed into a new or existing product, or that the design is flawed and should be scrapped.

Currently, in order to use the TDC, technicians from other parts of the Bay Area need to come to the TDC in Oakland with their models, run tests on these models (which may take up to 4 weeks), collect their data, and evaluate their data either at the TDC (in one of the visualization rooms) or at their home location. Unfortunately, there are problems with this process. First, the technicians are often at the TDC, away from their home locations, which is expensive and inefficient. Second, they cannot effectively analyze their data without specialized equipment from their home locations. Third, the Oakland TDC is running out of space.

Management has decided that the TDC will be expanded and that some of the functions of the TDC will be done remotely, at other sites in the Bay Area. They are planning to increase the size of the Oakland facility, to expand the testing and evaluation functions to San Francisco, and to move the model fabrication lab to San Jose. They have asked us to design a network to allow the expansion to occur with the least amount of interference to the users, as well as to improve their performance on the network.

4.3.2 Project Definition

The project we are tasked with is to design metropolitan-area networks (MANs) and campus networks to connect remote campuses to their existing networks at the TDC, which consist of shared Ethernets and FDDIs, connected by routers, so that their technicians will be able to access the TDC remotely. This MAN will connect the technicians to the TDC, to the computing cluster, to the visualization and testing areas, as well as to connect to local (metropolitan-area) model-building facilities. The applications, existing networks, and goals are listed in this document.

The company's plans for the TDC are to allow outside access to the TDC for remote technicians, to have model-building facilities close by (within the metropolitan area), and to provide remote access to not only experimental data, but also to computational data from their computer systems and storage facilities. They also want to expand the number of concurrent tests from two to four. To accommodate remote access, the company plans to separate computing, model fabrication, testing, and visualization, and to connect these functions via campus- and metropolitan-area networks. The planned system will look like Figure 4-4.

4.3.3 Requirements Analysis

Step 1   Determining Initial Conditions. For this project, we know that we will be designing a MAN to allow this organization to expand to San Francisco and San Jose, and a LAN to expand within the Oakland facility. We will be connecting to the LAN at the 1013 building, to their existing Ethernet and FDDI networks.

FIGURE 4-4. Layout of the Planned TDC

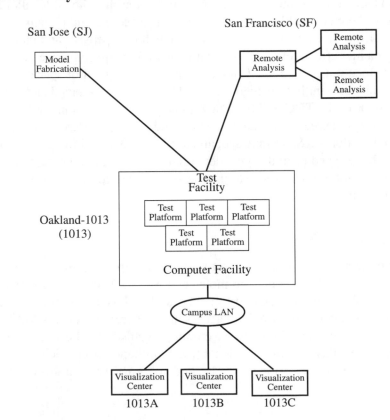

The scope of this project is a Bay Area MAN and campus LANs. It incorporates three sites, San Jose (one building), San Francisco (three buildings), and Oakland (five buildings), with about 250 users. The number of users is expected to grow by 50% over the next year, to about 370 users. We are limited to a $2 million budget for the year. This will include infrastructure, network hardware/software, installation, operations, and maintenance for the year.

Step 2   Working with the Users. Most of the information in the requirements analysis was provided by the information technology (IT) staff for this project. We were able to arrange a meeting with the users in the 1013 building, and conducted a whiteboard session where they outlined what they expect from the new system.

Step 3   Listing Requirements. All of the requirements gathered in Step 2 are shown in Tables 4-10 through 4-14.

TABLE 4-10. User Requirements

User Service Requirements	Description of Requirement for Design Environment
Location(s) and Number(s) of Users	Test and computing facilities (Oakland 1013), 60 users
	Model fabrication (San Jose), 30 users
	Visualization (1013A), 10 users
	Visualization (1013B), 25 users
	Visualization (1013C), 40 users
	Analysis (San Francisco), 80 users
Expected Growth in the Number of Users	
After 1 Year	50% increase
User Expectations	
Interactivity	Users expect remote control to behave as if they were at the model's location
Reliability	For some applications, reliability must be 100% during the application session
Adaptability	Network must adapt to user additions, deletions, changes
Security	Each test must be kept separate from other concurrent tests
Cost/Funding	$2 million/year

The applications for this environment are

- Application A: Demand access to experimental and computational data sets
- Application B: Distributed database
- Applications C and E: Remote control of test equipment at the testing facility
- Applications D and G: Interactive, collaborative visualization of experimental and computational data sets
- Application F: Access to model fabrication database

Application A consists of pushing data from the test and computational facilities to data storage, pulling data from storage to the visualization areas, and sending small initialization files to the computational and test facilities. Application B is a distributed database for the newly formed analysis group. This database will contain the results of historical and current analyses of tests done at the Oakland facility. Applications C and E consist of receiving audio and video from the testing facility, receiving data (telemetry) from experiments, transmitting control information to audio, video, monitoring, and test equipment, and interaction with operators at the test facility. Applications D and G consist of collaborations of technicians at the visualization, test, and computational facilities, synchronization of data between each of these sites, and providing an interactive, VR-type environment. Application F is an on-demand pull of data from the Oakland facility to the San Jose facility. This data will be the structural data sets for each model to be built at the San Jose facility.

Applications C and E may be the same application (it is not known at this time). Likewise, Applications D and G may be the same application. For the purposes of this design, we will treat them as separate applications.

The performance requirements of each of these applications are listed in Table 4-11.

In Table 4-11 we have the current best estimates of the performance requirements for each application. Application A, the demand access to data sets, operates everywhere in the design environment. It is similar to the application FTP, but manages, queues, and guarantees transfer of the data. Its requirements are given in Note 1.

Note 1. Application A has the following characteristics: average data size, 100 MB; number of simultaneous users, 2; expected transfer time, up to 10 minutes. Application A is client-server.

TABLE 4-11. **Application Requirements**

Categorizing Applications	Mission-Critical	Real-Time	Best-Effort	Application Locations
Application A			Note 1	All
Application B			Note 2	SF
Applications C and E	40 ms RT, 1.69 Mb/s, 100% Reliability			C(Oak) E(SF, 1013)
Applications D and G		80 ms RT, 5 Mb/s-group		D(Oak) G(SF,1013)
Application F			400 Kb/s	SJ, 1013

Application B, the distributed database, operates within the SF campus. Its performance requirements are given in Note 2.

Note 2. Application B has the following characteristics: average transaction size, 10 MB; average number of transactions/minute, 40.

Applications C and E are the bread and butter for this organization, and thus have been placed in the mission-critical category. Their performance requirements are: capacity, 1.69 Mb/s (this is a combination of audio and video (800 Kb/s), telemetry (640 Kb/s), control information (50 Kb/s), and interaction between technicians (200 Kb/s); reliability, 100% during application sessions; and delay, 40 ms round-trip (RT). We also know that the number of concurrent sessions of this application will be 4.

Applications D and G are important to the organization, but were not considered to be mission-critical. These applications do have strict timing requirements due to the collaborative environment. Their performance requirements are: capacity, 5 Mb/s per group; delay, 80 ms round-trip. In talking with the customer, we expect there to be a maximum of two groups active at any given time. The applications C, E, D, and G all operate within the Oakland facility and between SF and the Oakland-1013 building. Applications D and G are client-server.

Application F is access to the model database. In discussion with the model builders, they estimate that they will need about 400 Kb/s sustained transfer rate in order to get the model databases. This application operates between SJ and the 1013 building. Application F is client-server.

TABLE 4-12. **Host Requirements**

Type of Host or Equipment	Numbers and Locations
Graphics Workstations	All
Application A Server	1013
Application D/G Server	1013
Application F Server	SJ
Application B Database Server	SF (B1)
Computing Cluster	1013
Storage	1013

TABLE 4-13. **Network Requirements**

Existing Networks	Network Locations
Shared Ethernet (10bT), connected by IP routers	1013
Shared FDDI, connected by IP routers	1013

From the host perspective, we need to determine where any specialized equipment may be located. Many of the applications (A, D, G, and F) are client-server, and B is a distributed database. We also have computing and storage at the Oakland facility. The host requirements are shown in Table 4-12. As we can see from this table, most of the specialized equipment will be kept in the main building in Oakland, the 1013 building, except for the database server in SF building B1 and the model server at the SJ facility.

The graphics workstations all currently have Ethernet interfaces, which will be upgraded to whatever interface the design requires. The routers, along with the computing and storage clusters in the 1013 building, all have FDDI interfaces. These interfaces may be upgraded if necessary.

For the project's network requirements, they currently have shared Ethernet (10bT) and FDDI networks connected by IP routers in the 1013 building. All of the other buildings (SJ, SF, and Oakland 1013A/B/C) are all new and have no installed networks. There is no planned Internet connectivity for this project. Table 4-13 shows these requirements.

TABLE 4-14. **Functional Requirements**

	Requirements
Security Requirements	
Company- or Organization-Specified	All data are protected from outside access
Funding	$2 million/year

For the functional requirements for this project, we have some early expectations in terms of security and funding. For security, they want to make sure that each group's access and data are protected from outside access. Funding for this project has been set at $2 million/year. This includes network infrastructure, hardware/software, installation, and operations for the first year. These requirements are shown in Table 4-14.

Step 4   Developing an Applications Map. With the requirements above, an applications map can now be generated for this project. From the location information provided in the application requirements, we can place the applications where we expect them to be used. This applications map is shown in Figure 4-5. Note that the gateway building (gw) on the Oakland campus is shown with the applications, although no mention of this building was made in the application requirements. The gateway building is where all outside telecommunications services are terminated for that campus, so we have included it, expecting it to be in the path of our MAN communications.

Step 5   Developing Service Metrics to Measure Performance. The applications that were requested to be measured were C/E and D/G, the mission-critical and real-time applications. For C/E, we recommended that they be able to measure and verify that the users were getting to their experiments, and we recommended the following metrics for availability:

IP Packet Loss Rate	**Availability**
< 2%	100%
2% or greater	0%

For D/G, the real-time applications, as well as for C/E, we recommended that we measure the round-trip times between users and end systems. This may be done via *ping* or some other mechanism.

FIGURE 4-5. **Applications Map for Case Study**

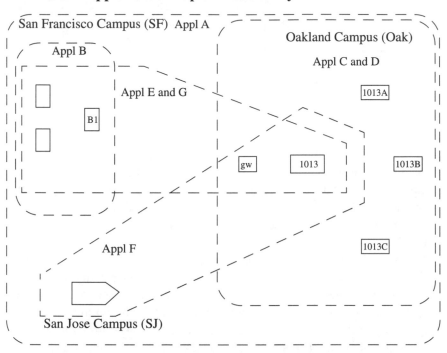

Step 6   Characterizing Behavior. Recall from the application requirements the two notes that accompanied Applications A and B.

- *Note 1.* Application A has the following characteristics: average data size, 100 MB; number of simultaneous users, 2; expected transfer time, up to 10 minutes. Application A is client-server.

- *Note 2.* Application B has the following characteristics: average transaction size, 10 MB, average number of transactions/minute, 40.

We can use these application and user characteristics to estimate performance requirements. For A, we can make estimates based on average data size. A data rate based on the average size would be (100 MB)(2 users)/(10 minutes) = 20 MB/minute = 2.7 Mb/s. For B, the estimated rate will be (10 MB/transaction)(40 transactions/minute) = 400 MB/minute = 53 Mb/s.

For Applications D/G, we have a capacity of 5 Mb/s per group. In discussions with the customer, they expect a maximum of two groups to be using these applications at any time, and they may be anywhere in the SF or Oakland campuses. Thus, we will use 10 Mb/s as the expected rate for D/G.

TABLE 4-15. **Summary of Application Performance Characteristics**

Application	Delay	Capacity	Reliability
A	100 ms HRT	2.7 Mb/s	99.5%
B	25 ms TCT	53 Mb/s	99.5%
C/E	40 ms RT	1.69 Mb/s	100%
D/G	80 ms RT	10 Mb/s	99.5%
F	100 ms HRT	400 Kb/s	99.5%

These rate estimates will be used in the flow analysis process, as well as to determine which network management variables we will need in order to monitor these rates.

Step 7   Developing Performance Thresholds. Summarizing the performance characteristics for all of our applications, we have Table 4-15. When asked about the reliability characteristics, the customer stated that Applications C/E, their mission-critical applications, must be up 100% of the time that they are needed. All other applications are secondary, and a reliability of 99.5% should be sufficient for them.

For the delay characteristics, we have delays of 40 ms and 80 ms (RT) for C/E and D/G, and we estimate that the other applications, A and F, are all interactive-burst or -bulk, and we apply the 100-ms HRT to these applications. For B, we know that they expect 40 transactions/second, from which we can estimate that each transaction will be processed in about 25 ms. This is the TCT for this application. We can now generate a performance envelope for this application (see Figure 4-6). We now use the results of this requirements analysis to proceed with the flow analysis for this project.

FIGURE 4-6. **Performance Envelope**

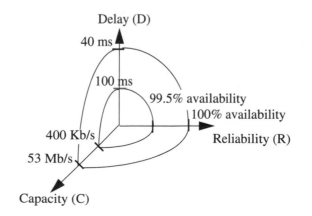

CHAPTER 5 — *Flow Analysis: Concepts*

As with requirements analysis, flow analysis is separated into three chapters, covering concepts, guidelines, and practice. We will begin with the concepts of flow analysis.

5.1 Background for Flow Analysis

Now that we have the user, application, host, and network requirements developed and listed in the requirements specification, we will further analyze these requirements based on their end-to-end characteristics. We will use the concept of a *flow*, which, for an end-to-end connection, has constant addressing and service requirements, to combine service performance characteristics in a useful way. These characteristics will be analyzed and combined, per flow, into a *flow specification*, or *flowspec*. This will be used, with best-effort services, for capacity planning, and with specified services, for service planning.

This chapter introduces flow concepts—consisting of data sources and sinks, flow models, and flow distributions—that will help us to identify, size, and choose flows. We will also develop cumulative performance specifications for each flow.

5.2 Flows

A flow is a set of application and protocol information that has some common attributes, such as source address, destination address, information type, options, routing, or other end-to-end information, and is transmitted during a single session of an application. Flows are end-to-end, between source and destination applications/hosts. Since they can be identified by its end-to-end information, they can be directly linked to an application, host, or network, or associated with an end user. We can also examine flows on a link-by-link or network-by-network basis. This is useful in combining flow characteristics at the network or network-element levels.

Flow analysis is an integral part of the overall analysis process. Flows are where services and performance characteristics are transformed into specifications that can be directly applied to technology and protocol choices. Flow analysis provides an end-to-end perspective on requirements, and shows where requirements combine and interact. It also provides some insight into the degrees of hierarchy and redundancy needed in the network design. In addition, as we will see in the design of the logical network, this analysis also provides information that can be useful in choosing an interconnection strategy, such as switching, routing, or hybrid mechanisms.

There are three types of flows that we will examine: individual, composite, and backbone. We will see that the aggregation of composite flows due to hierarchy in the network will allow us to identify backbone flows, and that these flows will receive additional attention in the network design.

- An *individual flow* is the flow for a single session of an application. An individual flow is the basic unit of traffic flows in this book; they are either considered individually or are combined into a composite flow. When an individual flow has specified characteristics, those characteristics are usually left as part of the individual flow and are not consolidated with other flows into a composite flow. This is done so that the flow's specified characteristics can be treated separately from the rest of the flows. Individual flows are derived directly from the requirements specification, or are estimated from our best knowledge about the applications and users.

- A *composite flow* is the combination of individual (best-effort delivery) flows that share the same path, link, or network. Composite flows are used in the capacity planning for the network. Figure 5-1 shows individual and composite flows in the network.

FIGURE 5-1. **Individual and Composite Flows**

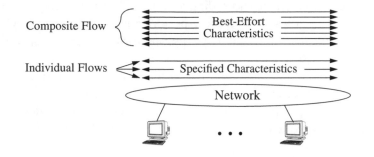

• A *backbone flow* is formed by composite flows when the network achieves a certain degree of hierarchy (see Figure 5-2). A backbone flow is useful in that it indicates locations in the network where special consideration is needed in capacity planning. This is primarily due to the effect of network hierarchy on composite flows. By indicating hierarchy in the network, backbone flows will be useful when developing the routing and addressing plans later in this book. (The following chapter shows how backbone flows are based on flow hierarchy, and establishes rules of thumb for identifying backbone flows.)

Flows are described in this fashion in order to make it easier to combine flow characteristics. Backbone flows combine the characteristics of their composite flows, while individual flows show the guaranteed characteristics that need to be considered throughout the end-to-end path of the flow. All of these flows are important in the design of the logical network. The descriptions of the types of flows that we develop in the flowspec will help us to choose the technologies and services that best fit the customer's needs.

FIGURE 5-2. **Backbone Flow**

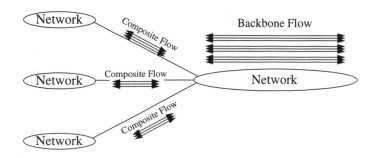

Throughout this chapter, we will analyze flow characteristics to determine if they contribute to composite and backbone flows, and, if so, how to combine their performance characteristics accordingly. In many network designs, most of the requirements and flows will have low-performance and/or best-effort characteristics, while only a few flows will have high-performance and/or specified performance characteristics.

We will see that the few flows that require specified performance will drive the design from a service perspective, while all flows will drive the design from a capacity-planning perspective. This design process accommodates both of these perspectives to provide capacity and service planning for your design.

5.3 Data Sources and Sinks

In the degenerate case for an applications map, all applications will apply to all parts of the system, and we will not have any idea where flows will occur in the network. Even in an applications map that shows applications in different areas of the system, we still do not know what the flows will look like within an application's area.

For example, regarding Applications A and B in Figure 5-3, how do we know if the flows for those applications are between each of the buildings or consolidated to one building? Figure 5-4 shows the potential flows in these two cases.

FIGURE 5-3. **Example of an Applications Map**

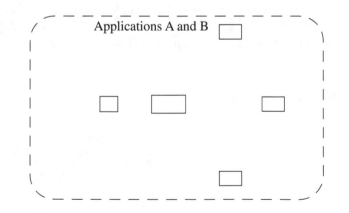

FIGURE 5-4. **Potential Flows in Sample Applications Map**

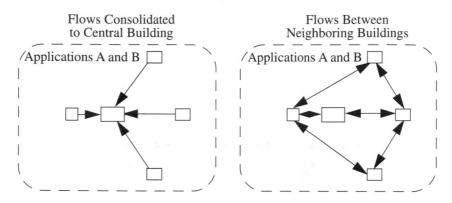

A method to help us identify flows in the network is to determine where data sources and sinks are likely to be in the design. A *data source* is a device or group of devices that primarily produces data that the network will carry, and a *data sink* primarily accepts data from the network, acting as a data repository. While almost all devices on the network will both produce and accept data, there will be some devices that will typically act as either sources or sinks.

Some examples of data sources are devices that do a lot of computing and will generate large amounts of data, like computing servers, mainframes, parallel systems, or computing clusters. Other devices, like cameras, video production equipment, application servers, and medical instruments, do not necessarily do a lot of computing (in the traditional sense), but can generate a lot of data, video, and audio that will be transmitted on the network.

A traditional example of a data sink is data storage, which may be groups of disks or tape devices. Devices that manipulate or display large quantities of data, like video editing or display devices, also act as data sinks.

Data sources and sinks give us an indication about where flows are consolidated and generated. Figure 5-5 shows how data sources and sinks indicate flows in the design. In this figure and throughout the book, a data source is represented by a circle with a dot in the center, and a data sink is represented by a circle with a cross in the center. The dot or cross indicates an arrow passing through the plane of the circle. A dot represents an arrow coming out of the plane, indicating that data is leaving the device (a data source), and a cross represents an arrow going into the plane, indicating that data is entering the device (a data sink). By using these symbols, we can show data sources and sinks on a two-dimensional map, without the need for arrows.

FIGURE 5-5. **Data Sources and Sinks Indicate Flows in the Design**

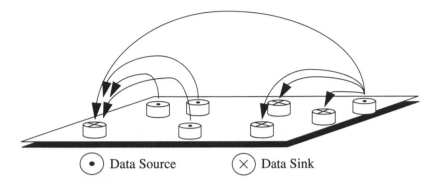

By identifying data sources and sinks in the design environment, we can reduce the number of potential flows in the design and begin to see some direction in the flows. In the example of Figure 5-3, we can look for potential data sources and sinks for the applications on the map, such as servers, server farms, mass storage, large computing systems, and other large devices, and plot them with the applications. The map may then look like Figure 5-6.

What we can expect from an applications map like Figure 5-6 is that there will be flows from the application server to both primary and secondary storage. What may not be as obvious, however, is that there will likely be flows from the server to each of the buildings in the application's area. These buildings, even though they do not show any data sources and sinks, will have users in them (as they are covered by the application's area), which will be accessing the server for data. The result is that, for this applications map, we will likely have flows outward from the server to each of the buildings in the area, as shown in Figure 5-7.

FIGURE 5-6. **Example of an Applications Map with Data Sources and Sinks**

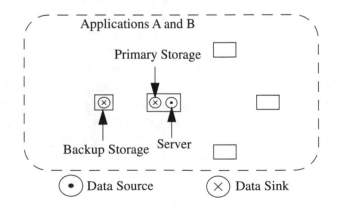

FIGURE 5-7. **Example of an Applications Map with Flows**

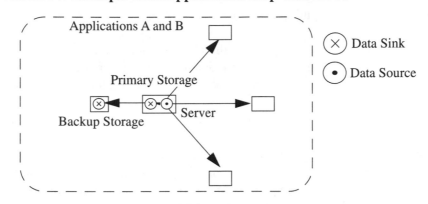

In this figure, we show the flows from the server to the storage systems and buildings where the clients work. This is based on the client-server flow model, one of the flow models discussed next.

5.4 Flow Models

Another method to help in identifying flows in the network is to try to map them to general, well-known flow models. Flow models are characterized primarily by their directionality and hierarchy. Directionality describes the preference (or lack thereof) of a flow to have higher-performance or more deterministic requirements in one direction. While network designs typically treat traffic flows as having equal requirements in each direction, we are finding that many flows (typically from newer applications) have different requirements in each direction. Most flows are asymmetrical, and some of the newer access and transmission technologies (such as the many versions of Digital Subscriber Loop [xDSL], ATM, or broadcast mechanisms) can be optimized for asymmetrical flows.

For the flow analysis process, hierarchy describes the degree of concentration of flows. Hierarchy is one of the most important factors in the network design process, as it is a result of the logical grouping of users, hosts, network, names, addresses, and so on, and determines where we handle these groupings and concentrations of flows.

We will consider the following flow models:

- Peer-to-peer
- Client-server

- Cooperative computing
- Distributed computing

For each, we will examine the directionality and hierarchy of its flows. We will also identify which flows in each model are the most important in determining where backbone flows are likely to be found. These are termed the *critical flows* for the model.

Our first flow model, peer-to-peer, is one where the users and applications are roughly similar in their communications requirements. They are, in effect, peers. There is no obvious directionality or hierarchy in peer-to-peer flows, nor are there any obvious critical flows. As in Figure 5-8, the flows are equally likely between any of the hosts. An example of the peer-to-peer flow model is the early Internet, where users primarily used FTP and telnet to access other computers and transfer information.

The peer-to-peer model is our default model when we do not have any other information about the flows in our design environment. In a sense, it is part of the degenerate case of the applications map. This model also describes flows when all users in a group need equal access to each other for an application. This could be, for example, a tele*services application (e.g., teleseminars or teleconferencing), where any of the participants can act as a data source or sink. While a teleconference is usually considered to be a one-to-many conversation, we can expand that concept to be many one-to-many conversations, possibly simultaneously, within the application's area. The result is an any-to-any conversation, or peer-to-peer model.

This flow model is useful, even though it does not specify any hierarchy or directionality. Peer-to-peer flows are the most likely to be best-effort and will be used in the capacity planning of the design.

FIGURE 5-8. **Peer-to-Peer Flow Model**

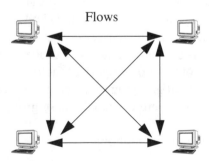

Flows

The client-server flow model is currently the most generally applicable model. This model has flow directionality and hierarchy. While flows in the model occur in both directions between client and server in the form of requests and responses, requests tend to be small relative to responses. Thus, client-server flows tend to be asymmetric, favoring the direction toward the clients. Depending on the type of application in the client-server model, the flow may be considered almost unidirectional, from the server to the client. Client-server flows are also hierarchical. Figure 5-9 shows the flow directionality of a client-server model.

When the flows in the client-server model are asymmetric in the direction from the server to the client(s), the server can be considered a data source. It would then be shown on the applications map, with flows generated from it to the other areas of the map, as was shown in Figure 5-7. The critical flows in a client-server model are those from the server to the clients. When there is a requirement to serve multiple clients with the same information at the same time, multicasting at some layer in the network should be considered to optimize the flows for this model.

While the Internet started with peer-to-peer flows with FTP and telnet, this usage evolved to become client-server-like with the use of FTP servers, followed by applications such as gopher and Archie. Now, with the growing use of Web applications, flows are from Web servers to end users, and between Web servers. As TCP/IP assumes more network operating system (NOS) roles, print and file services will make the Internet and enterprise networks based on TCP/IP more client-server oriented. For example, a person who wanted to access information from a company would have used the application FTP to a known site to download information. This changed into accessing an FTP or gopher server, then to accessing a Web server. Today, a person may access large quantities of information about a company without ever entering that company's network, through accessing an external Web server.

FIGURE 5-9. Client-Server Flow Model

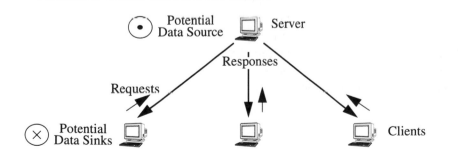

FIGURE 5-10. **Cooperative Computing Flow Model**

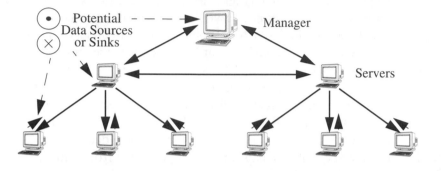

As flows become more hierarchical, they change into a cooperative-computing flow model, as in Figure 5-10. In this flow model, there may be additional hierarchies from flows between servers, or from flows from servers to the support server or management system. These flows—server-to-server and server-to-manager—are considered critical, as well as the flows from the server to its clients. With the additional layer of hierarchy in this model, it is harder to determine if the servers are data sources or sinks. We will need more information about the application in order to make this determination.

A cooperative-computing model is indicated when multiple applications work together and share information to accomplish a task, or when multiple client-server applications are managed by a higher-level application. In a cooperative-computing model, flows are between clients and one or more servers (similar to the client-server model), and also between servers and from servers to managers. Critical flows for this model are dependent on the application behavior; if the applications are client-server, but the servers communicate with each other, then the critical flows may be the server-server flows. If the applications are cooperative, and most of the communications are between servers (or are server-manager), then the critical flows are server-server and server-manager.

This model is often found in use with the visualization application group described in Chapter 2. An example of this model is in scientific computation and visualization. Consider the simulation of a multipart problem, such as the climate modeling, atmospheric/land/ocean model shown in Figure 5-11.

FIGURE 5-11. **Components of a Climate Modeling Problem**

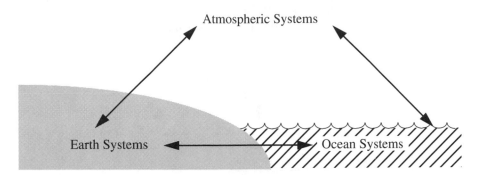

Each component in this figure may be developed on a separate computer, probably at different locations (based on where the computing, visualization resources, and scientists are located). Since each component affects the others (at the boundaries between atmosphere, earth, and ocean), data must be passed between the computing/visualization servers for each component. The flows would look like those in Figure 5-12.

In this figure, if the models are being solved at different locations, then the server-server flows will cross boundaries termed *flow boundaries* (discussed in the next section) and they will be considered for backbone flows in the design.

Another example of a cooperative-computing model is the Internet. Some of the client-server flows associated with Web activities are becoming cooperative-computing flows as servers communicate with each other, caching and mirroring information.

FIGURE 5-12. **Cooperative-Computing Model for Scientific Visualization**

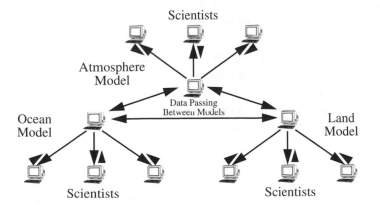

FIGURE 5-13. **Distributed-Computing Flow Model**

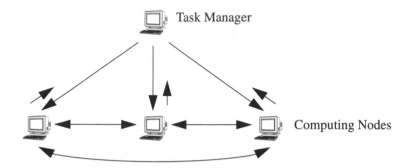

The distributed-computing flow model, shown in Figure 5-13, is the most specialized of the flow models. In a distributed-computing model, flows may be primarily between a task manager and its computing nodes (similar to a client-server model), or between the computing nodes. This depends on how the distributed computing is done.

We can make distinctions in the distributed-computing model based on the relationship between the task manager and the computing nodes and what the task is. The relationship between the task manager and the computing nodes can result in the computing nodes being closely coupled, where there are frequent transfers of information between computing nodes, or loosely coupled, where there may be little or no transfer of information between computing nodes. Tasks may range from having a coarse granularity, where each task is dedicated to a single computing node, to having a fine granularity, where a task is subdivided between several nodes and the computing is done concurrently.

When the task has a coarse granularity and the computing node relationship is loosely coupled, then the distributed-computing model takes the form of computing cluster or computing resource management system, where tasks are allocated to each computing node based on resource availability. Thus, each computing node communicates with the cluster server or resource manager. Figure 5-14 shows the flows for a sample computing cluster.

The flows in this type of distributed-computing model are similar to the client-server model, where communications are primarily between each client and the server. A difference here is that the direction of the flow is not necessarily from the computing server to the computing nodes. In fact, the size of the task initialization file sent from the server to the computing node may be much smaller than the size of the results from the computation, which is sent from the computing node to the server. In this model, the flow directionality is often asymmetric, but in the opposite

FIGURE 5-14. **Distributed-Computing Model for a Computing Cluster**

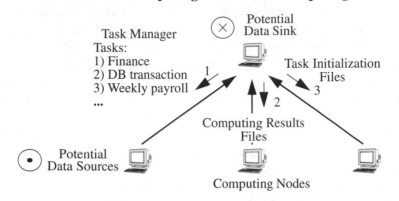

direction of the client-server model. Also, each of the flows between the computing nodes and their computing server is independent of the other flows. There is little to no synchronization between individual flows. The critical flows for this model are from the computing nodes to the computing server. When the flows for this model are asymmetric, in the direction from the computing nodes to the task manager, then the task manager acts as a data sink.

When the task has a fine granularity and the computing node relationship is closely coupled, then the distributed-computing model behaves like a simplified parallel processing system, where each task is subdivided—based on degree of parallelism in the application and topology of the problem—between several computing nodes. The computing nodes work concurrently on the problem, exchanging information with neighbor nodes and expecting (and waiting for) updated information. The task manager sets up the computing nodes and starts the task with an initialization file, as in Figure 5-15.

FIGURE 5-15. **Distributed-Computing Model for Parallel Processing**

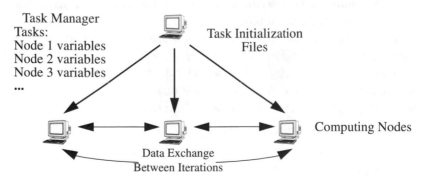

The flows in this type of distributed-computing model can have the most stringent performance characteristics of any of the models. Since computing nodes may block (halt their computations) while waiting for information from neighbor nodes, the timing of information transfer between computing nodes becomes critical. This has a direct impact on the delay tolerance and possibly the delay variation tolerance for the network. Individual flows in the parallel computing model have little to no directionality, as data transfers between computing nodes are similar in size and frequency. Individual flows in this model can be grouped to indicate which computed node will communicate for a given problem or topology. For example, a problem may be configured such that a computing node will communicate with two, four, or six of its closest neighbors.

For this model, the critical flows are between computing nodes. When a computing node will transfer the same information to several neighbor nodes simultaneously, multicasting should be considered to optimize flow performance. There are no clear data sources or sinks for this model. The climate modeling example given in Figure 5-11 could also be considered with a distributed-computing model, depending on the task granularity and degree of coupling of the system.

Flow characteristics will vary between the computing cluster and parallel system models, depending on the degrees of coupling and granularity in the task. Depending on the application and the amount of analysis you want to put into the model, you can use the computing cluster and parallel system models as they are, or modify the task granularity and degree of coupling to your needs.

5.5 Flow Boundaries

The existence of one or more of the flow models, along with the data sinks, sources, and information about the locations of computing nodes, clients, and servers, gives us insight into where individual, composite, and backbone flows may exist. For backbone flows, we are looking for hierarchy in the network. To aid in determining hierarchy, we establish flow boundaries in the system. Flow boundaries are separations between large portions of the system, used to indicate where flow consolidation and hierarchies occur. Flow boundaries can be applied anywhere in the design where they will help indicate flow consolidation but are most commonly used to separate geographic areas of the design environment, for example, between

- Local- and wide-area networks (LAN/WAN)
- Local- and metropolitan-area networks (LAN/MAN)
- Metropolitan- and wide-area networks (MAN/WAN)
- Multiple campuses (Campus/Campus)

- Multiple buildings within a campus (Building/Building)
- Multiple floors within a building (Floor/Floor)

In this context, Campus, Building, and Floor are all subsets of a LAN environment. These are locations in the design where flow consolidations are likely to occur. Flow boundaries can be arbitrary, depending on the size of the network and how detailed you want the flow information to be—and how much work you want to put into it. In general, the LAN/WAN, Campus/Campus, and Building/Building boundaries are the most frequently used.

Another type of flow boundary provides a logical separation of the design environment, instead of a geographic one. These flow boundaries are based on where user traffic (flows) are consolidated or are likely to have specified requirements. They are used to separate between

- Backbones, where several flows transit an area of the design environment
- Flow concentration points, where several flows converge to one area (in the Internet, this would be a network access point, or NAP)
- WANs, where service providers are likely to be used
- Specialized areas, those that have specific service requirements

5.6 Flow Distributions

We also use flow distributions to determine where backbone flows are located in the design. Flow distributions show when flows stay in one region of the network, or transit one or more regions of the network (indicated by crossing one or more flow boundaries). The simplest descriptions of regions for flow distributions are local-, metropolitan-, and wide-area networks (LANs, MANs, and WANs). Therefore, flow distributions usually show when flows travel within a LAN or between LANs, transiting one or more MANs or WANs in the process.

A traditional flow distribution is the *80/20 rule*, shown in Figure 5-16, where 80% of the flow of traffic stays within a LAN and 20% is across the WAN. This distribution implies that the capacity required across the WAN is approximately a quarter of the capacity required across the LAN, and is estimated based on traditional usage patterns across the LAN and WAN environments. This type of approximation could be extended to applications as well, to develop a modifier for the application's performance requirements.

The 80/20 rule was a good rule of thumb for sizing WANs in relation to the numbers and sizes of the LANs in the network. It also worked well with the available capacities of the time. Connecting 10-Mb/s Ethernet LANs with a 1.544-Mb/s T1 circuit mapped well to the 80/20 rule. However, as networks, applications, and services have evolved, the 80/20 rule has become less applicable, though not obsolete.

Flow distributions today can range from 80/20 (LAN/WAN) to 50/50 or even 20/80. This is due, in part, to the increase in distance-independent computing and the decoupling of physical and logical networks.

In the traditional view of networking, where the 80/20 rule generally applies, users are logically (and physically) close to their resources. An application's area usually did not extend beyond the LAN environment. Data sources and sinks, such as computing, printing, storage, and other devices, are likely to be on their directly connected network or within their LAN environment. In many of today's application environments, however, users may not know (or care) where their resources are, and may be just as likely to access a resource that is thousands of miles away as they are to use their local resources. The Web is a good example of this. When following a thread of Web accesses, the user may not be aware that accesses are occurring at various places around the world.

Distance-independent computing or resource use, as in Figure 5-17, is insulating users from knowledge of where resources are located and the distances between themselves and the resources. This results in using resources based on factors other than distance—such as cost, performance, or availability—and leads to flows that are as likely to be in the WAN environment as they are to be in the LAN environment. This modifies an 80/20 flow distribution to be higher in the WAN environment.

FIGURE 5-16. **80/20 Flow Distribution**

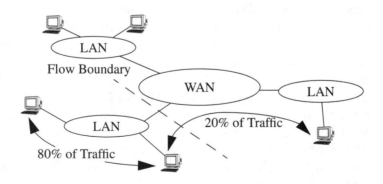

FIGURE 5-17. **Distance-Independent Computing Modifies Flow Distributions**

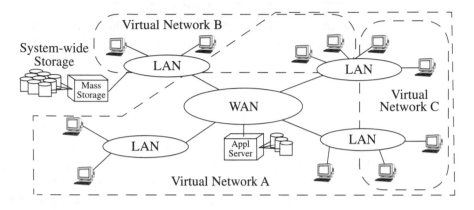

A factor related to distance-independent computing is the decoupling of physical and logical networks. Networks that used to be designed to connect users to resources directly or closely are now designed to provide an infrastructure for overall connectivity, and the grouping of users with resources can now be done as logical networks. As physical and logical networks are decoupled, there is more freedom to place resources where they can be supported more easily or cost-effectively, and to design the logical connectivity accordingly. Of course, logical networks may easily cross flow boundaries (e.g., LAN/WAN), modifying an 80/20 flow distribution to be higher in the WAN environment.

It is important to remember, however, that there are still cases where the 80/20 rule applies. When the network design follows traditional methods of connectivity, when the applications do not consider the network or system, or when distance-independent computing is not important and logical networks map directly to physical networks, then the 80/20 rule will likely still apply. When systems support users in the traditional fashion, traditional flows and flow patterns apply.

5.7 The Flow Specification

When we have the flows identified and each application's requirements listed, we can then determine how to combine the requirements for each flow. The flow specification (flowspec) can have one or more of three forms:

1. A one-part (unitary) flowspec, used for capacity planning of best-effort flows when there are no specified flows.

2. A two-part flowspec containing both best-effort and specified flows. The two-part flowspec builds on the information in a unitary flowspec.

3. A multipart flowspec, providing more detail on individual components of the specified flows. A multipart flowspec builds on the information in a two-part flowspec.

These flowspecs range in difficulty from relatively straightforward (unitary flowspec) to highly complex (multipart flowspec). The two-part flowspec is a good balance between ease of development and amount of detail. Many designs can be adequately represented with a unitary flowspec, when requirements and flows are not well described or understood. As networks become truly integrated into the rest of the system, however, requirements and flows will incorporate more service performance characteristics, and the two-part and multipart flowspecs will better represent the design. That is already the case for many current applications and environments. In developing the flowspec, we will use the information in the requirements specification as the basis for flows, then apply the flow models and distributions to determine where backbone flows are located.

5.7.1 The Flowspec Algorithm

In developing the flowspec, we will first list the characteristics of each of the flows, then apply an algorithm to bring these characteristics together into a specification for the combined flows. This algorithm combines reliability, capacity, and delay characteristics for each of the flows in such a way as to describe the expected overall performance required from the design. The flowspec algorithm applies the following conditions:

1. Since best-effort flows are not capable of specified reliability or delay, only capacity requirements are used in best-effort calculations.

2. For specified flows, we will use all characteristics (if available) in the calculations. These performance requirements will be combined for each characteristic so as to maximize the overall performance of the flow.

3. When guaranteed delay and/or reliability requirements are indicated, they will be used individually in the calculations for the flowspec.

4. Capacities generated by the unitary, two-part, and multipart flowspecs are baseline capacities, and do not reflect any performance modifiers.

FIGURE 5-18. **Unitary Flowspec**

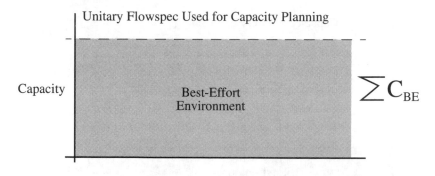

When a flowspec is developed for best-effort flows (a unitary flowspec), then only the capacities of the flows are used. The capacities are added together, and the result is an overall baseline capacity for the flow. Figure 5-18 shows this capacity-planning diagram.

When a flowspec is developed for both best-effort and specified flows (a two-part flowspec), the best-effort flows are calculated the same way as in the unitary flowspec. Then the capacities for the specified flows are added together, forming a total baseline capacity for specified flows. For the reliability and delay characteristics, however, we will take the maximum and minimum values, respectively. Thus, for specified flows, there will be an overall minimum delay value and an overall maximum reliability value, as in Figure 5-19.

A multipart flowspec is used when there are requirements for guaranteed performance in the flows. When this occurs, the calculations for best-effort and specified flows are the same as for the two-part flowspec, except that now those flows that have guaranteed capacity characteristics are listed separately in the flowspec and are not part of the capacity summations for best-effort or specified flows.

FIGURE 5-19. **Two-Part Flowspec**

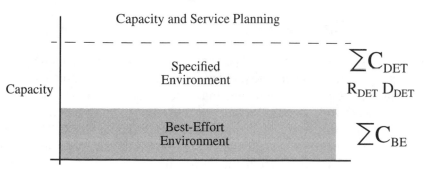

FIGURE 5-20. **Multipart Flowspec**

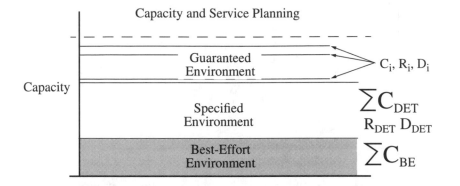

In Figure 5-20, each of the guaranteed requirements for capacity, reliability, and delay are listed separately. They are separated to show that they will be supported differently, and a service plan will be generated to describe how they will be supported. For the two-part and multipart flowspecs, the specified and best-effort capacities are usually combined into a total capacity for nonguaranteed flows.

5.7.2 Performance Modifiers

The capacity requirements for the unitary, two-part, and multipart flowspecs are based on adding the capacities for each application, where there is only one session of each application active at the same time. This is a simple and reasonable estimate of capacity when no other information is available, but when more information on the user and application behavior is available, we can use this information to modify the expected capacities of the flows.

5.8 Concluding Remarks

Flow analysis takes an end-to-end perspective of network service and performance requirements, combining capacity, delay, and reliability requirements into a specification that will be used in evaluating and selecting access and transmission technologies for our network. In building this specification (the flowspec), we use various techniques to identify individual, composite, and backbone flows. These techniques include locating data sources and sinks in the network, and applying flow models, boundaries, and distributions to the identified flows.

The result of flow analysis is the flowspec, which combines flow capacity, delay, and reliability requirements based on the flowspec algorithm. This flowspec will be used as input to the design of the logical network, covered later in this book.

Suggested Further Reading

To better understand the characteristics of the flow models, reading about client-server, parallel processing, distributed processing, and collaborative computing will be useful. Suggested reading material includes:

1. Almasi, G., and Gottlieb, A. *Highly Parallel Computing*. Benjamin/Cummings, Redwood City, CA, 1989.

2. Brownlee, E.N., Mills, C., and Ruth, G. Traffic flow measurement: Architecture. *RFC 2063*. January 1997.

3. Morse, H.S. *Practical Parallel Computing*. Academic Press, San Diego, 1994.

4. Partridge, C. A proposed flow specification. *RFC 1363*, September 1992.

5. Partridge, C. Using the flow label field in IPv6. *RFC 1809*, June 1995.

6. Sinha, A. Client-server computing. *Communications of the ACM*, vol. 35, no. 7, 77–98. July 1992.

Also examine the Internet-drafts from the IETF Realtime Traffic Flow Measurement (RTFM) Working Group.

Exercises

1. Devices can act as both data sources and sinks, depending on the application and flow. Which of the following would be data sources, and which would be data sinks? Why?

    a) A storage device receiving streaming video from a camera

    b) A video editing unit, using video from the above storage device

    c) A Web server and its clients

    d) A storage disk farm

2. Apply the appropriate flow model (peer-to-peer, client-server, distributed computing, cooperative computing) to each example below.

a) Users on the Internet accessing a single Web server

b) Forty workstations processing batch jobs overnight, managed by a central mainframe

c) Electronic mail use across the Internet

d) A transaction-processing application, authorizing credit card transactions between a company's retail stores and its headquarters

3. For each of the examples of Exercise 3, give the most likely direction(s) for the flows described by the flow model.

4. The 80/20 (local/remote) rule describes flow distributions for traditional environments where a user's resources were typically local to the user. Show how the flow distribution for a flow model (you choose which model to use) will change from 80/20 to 50/50 to 20/80 as the flows cross flow boundaries (i.e., LAN/WAN). Which characteristics of the flow model, devices, or design environment indicate that the flow distribution will change?

5. Give an example of a client-server flow model that has both 80/20 (LAN/WAN) and 50/50 or 20/80 flow distributions in the same design environment.

6. Show what the unitary flowspec would look like for the following best-effort flows (all flows are in the same end-to-end path):

Application	Capacity
A	10 Kb/s
B	70 Kb/s
C	1.1 Mb/s
D	250 Kb/s

7. The flowspec can be viewed as a multitiered network service hierarchy, where the capacity plan is the most basic service level, and the service plan describes individual and combined service requirements and guarantees. How does the flowspec relate to the discussion on network services in Chapter 1? Show how a flowspec could be used to describe a three-tier network service hierarchy for a design.

CHAPTER 6

Flow Analysis: Guidelines

The flow analysis process model, shown in Figure 6-1, outlines the major steps in identifying flows for your network design.

FIGURE 6-1. Process Model for Flow Analysis

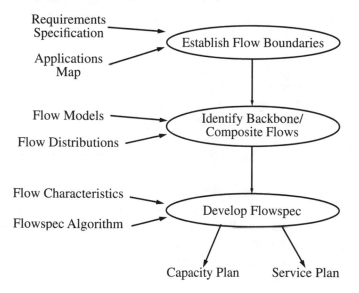

6.1 Applying the Flow Models

How will flow models help in the design and analysis of our design environment? They can provide us with a rapid assessment of the likely flows in the environment. When we can determine that an application will behave in a peer-to-peer, client-server, cooperative-computing, or distributed-computing fashion, we can make some generalizations about that application's flows by applying the appropriate flow model.

Identifying where the data sources and sinks are located in the design environment complements the flow model by determining the directions of the flows within the model. For example, in applying the client-server flow model to an application, we can estimate that there will be flows between the server and each of its clients. If we know where the application will be applied in the design environment (i.e., from the applications map), we can further estimate where these flows will be located. By determining if the server will act as a data source (supplying data to the clients) or data sink (accepting data from the clients), we can apply a direction to the client-server flows.

Example 6.1—Data Mining Environment

Earlier we showed a server and storage applied to an applications map, and flows from the server to storage and to all of the sites within the application's area. This is an example of applying a client-server flow model. Let's now consider another sample design environment, in this case a data mining application. In this example, we have a group that gathers, compiles, and organizes data. This could be data for insurance purposes, for statistics on families (such as a census application or for advertising), or for large medical databases. When data sizes become large, it is useful to be able to search through data rapidly to find a particular piece of information, or to do general searches to find information that is similar to the search topic. One way to bring hierarchy into such searches is with *metadata*, which is data that represents other data.

Our sample design environment includes large amounts of storage and a number of servers that will cache metadata and the results of data searches. The applications for this environment are a Web-based search engine (Application A), a data storage and archival application (Application B), and a data migration tool (Application C). Figure 6-2 shows the applications map for this environment, along with the buildings within each application's area.

FIGURE 6-2. **Example of a Data Mining Environment**

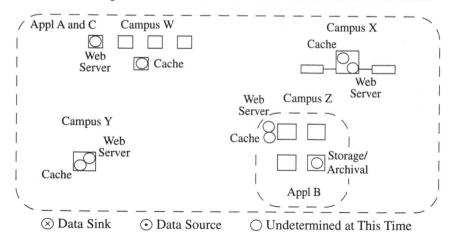

Building(s) shown for each campus

From the applications map, we can see that Applications A and C are applied throughout the environment, and Application B is local to one area. When we look at the data sources and sinks for this environment, we find that there is storage located at each campus, a large storage and archival system in Application B's area, and caching servers in all areas. Placing these devices on the map yields Figure 6-3. In this figure, the potential data sources and sinks are shown as empty circles, indicating that their states (as sources and/or sinks) are undetermined at this time.

FIGURE 6-3. **Example of an Environment with Data Sources and Sinks**

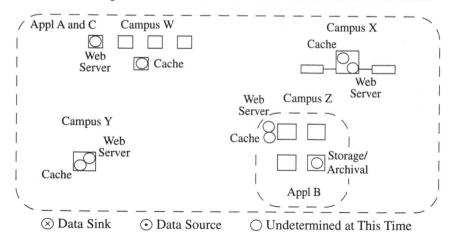

FIGURE 6-4. **Data Movement for Example**

Now we will determine where the data sources and sinks apply in this design environment and begin to build a model of potential flows. We can expect that the Web servers will service requests from users for data queries and download data to their local sites. The requests and their data can then be cached locally, and it is possible that the caches will coordinate their data movements, migrating data from the storage/archival device to the user. The model for data movement in this environment is seen in Figure 6-4.

All of the devices in this environment will act as both data sources and sinks, depending on the application. The storage/archival system in Campus Z will act as a data sink when accepting data from the outside and will act as a data source for the caches. The caches that are located at each campus will receive data from the storage device (thus acting as data sinks), but will also provide data to the local Web server (thus acting as data sources). In order to simplify these perspectives, we can couple the devices to each application. As we will see, the devices will behave differently for each of the applications A, B, and C.

In this model, the Web servers act in a client-server fashion toward their users and coordinate with the caches to migrate data from storage/archival. This is closest to the cooperative-computing model, with flows from the storage/archival device to the caches, between the caches, and to the Web servers, then to the users.

We now separate Applications A, B, and C, showing each in its own map. Each device can be represented as a data source or sink, depending on the application. Application A (the Web-search engine) would have each Web server as a data source, acting in a client-server fashion with the users, and getting data from the caches, which in turn get their data from other caches or the storage/archival device. The flows would look like that in Figure 6-5. When a device behaves as both a data source and sink for the same application, we will use the representation shown in Figure 6-5.

For Application A, each cache is shown as a data source, as that is its primary purpose for this application. Each cache feeds its local server. The server in turn acts as a data source for its users. There will also be flows between each Web server and its clients at the campus, although they are not shown in this figure.

FIGURE 6-5. **Flows for Application A in the Data Mining Environment**

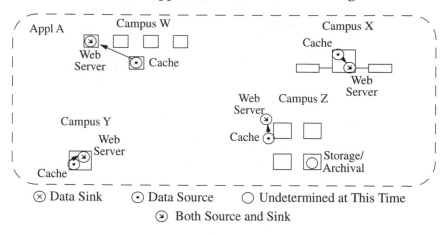

The second application, B, is the storage and archival application (see Figure 6-6). This application supports the movement of data into the storage/ archival device from outside the environment. In this case, the storage/archival device acts as a data sink.

When Application C (the data-migration tool) is shown, in Figure 6-7, the likely flows are from the storage/archival device to each of the caches, and possibly also between the caches. For this application, the caches are primarily data sinks, receiving data from the storage/archival device, which is the data source for this application.

FIGURE 6-6. **Flows for Application B in the Data Mining Environment**

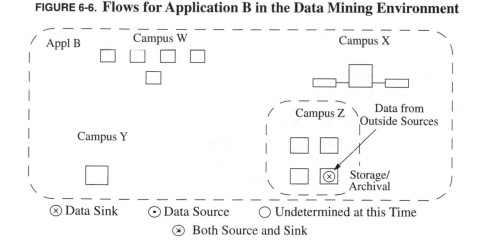

FIGURE 6-7. Flows for Application C in the Data Mining Environment

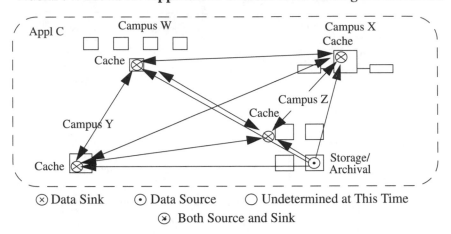

So we see that each device acts as a data source or sink, depending on the application that is using it. The combination of client-server flows and cache-cache flows, along with the hierarchy of data migration, indicate that this environment is cooperative-computing. Putting all of these applications together will result in flows that are bidirectional and asymmetric, which will be important in our flow analysis.

◊ ◊ ◊

6.2 Establishing Flow Boundaries

Flow boundaries are a tool for us to use to assess when a flow is crossing multiple areas in the design environment. Boundaries act like thresholds, highlighting a flow that may need special consideration. Let's take the application of data sources/sinks and flow models one step further, by determining when flows travel between well-defined areas in the design environment. We will use flow boundaries to mark the areas, and note when flows from flow models cross these boundaries. In establishing boundaries, what we are looking for are flow models that cross the boundaries, especially when they do so for critical flows in the model. Therefore, in applying the flow models and boundaries, we will take the following steps:

1. Identify data sources and sinks for the design environment.
2. Determine if any of the flow models apply to the network we will be designing. If one of the applicable models is distributed-computing, then we will need to determine if the model is a computing cluster or parallel system.
3. Place the flow boundaries on the models. You will need to know or estimate the locations of applications and possibly users/hosts to do this. Flow boundaries are applied at the locations described in Section 5.5.

   - Local- and wide-area networks (LAN/WAN)
   - Local- and metropolitan-area networks (LAN/MAN)
   - Metropolitan- and wide-area networks (MAN/WAN)
   - Multiple campuses (Campus/Campus)
   - Multiple buildings within a campus (Building/Building)
   - Multiple floors within a building (Floor/Floor)
   - Backbones, where several flows transit an area of the design environment
   - Flow concentration points, where several flows converge to one area (in the Internet, this would be a network access point, or NAP)
   - WANs, where service providers are likely to be used
   - Specialized areas, those that have specific service requirements

4. For each of the flow models used in the design, determine if the elements of the model (computing nodes, clients, servers) have flows that cross flow boundaries. Identify and note these flows.
5. For flows that cross flow boundaries, determine if they are critical flows in the model.
6. If there are critical flows that cross flow boundaries, then they may require special consideration in the backbone.

For example, if a client-server model is indicated for one or more applications in a network, and the clients will be communicating with the server(s) over a WAN environment, as in Figure 6-8, this will indicate special consideration in the backbone.

FIGURE 6-8. **Client-Server Model Crossing Flow Boundaries**

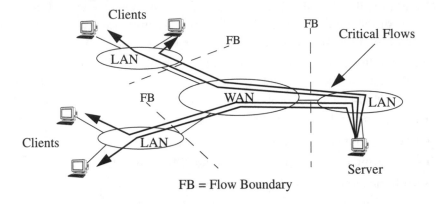

Another example is using a distributed-computing model. If the model is of the parallel processing type, then the flows between computing nodes are critical. Depending on the type of parallel processing, separating the task manager from the computing nodes by a WAN will not affect the flows between the computing nodes as much as separating the computing nodes by a WAN. In Figure 6-9, the computing nodes and task manager are placed in three separate locations.

FIGURE 6-9. **Distributed-Computing Model Crossing Flow Boundaries**

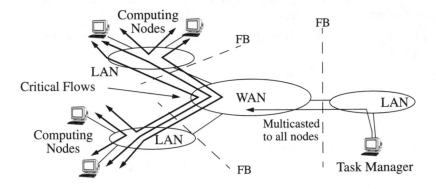

6.3 Applying Flow Distributions

6.3.1 Guidelines for Flow Distributions

Flow distributions tell us the expected relative traffic volumes of a flow when it crosses flow boundaries. Flow distributions that are 50/50 and 20/80 (local/remote) will indicate that these flows contribute to a backbone flow, as well as how application performance requirements are modified and combined in the flowspec. Given that flow distributions may range from 80/20 to 20/80, how and when do different distributions apply? We can base flow distributions on the flow models and flow boundaries described earlier, as well as on individual applications and performance requirements.

The flow models we examined were peer-to-peer, client-server, cooperative-computing, and distributed-computing. Of these, the peer-to-peer model does not indicate any particular flow distribution. The client-server and cooperative-computing models will modify the 80/20 distribution when clients must cross a flow boundary to get to the server(s), or when traffic from different servers in a cooperative-computing model must cross a flow boundary. As a general rule of thumb, when either of these conditions occur, a 50/50 (local/remote) flow distribution is a good starting point for these models.

Distributed-computing flows may range from a cluster computing–type model (for a loosely coupled, coarse granularity task) to a parallel computing–type model (for a tightly coupled, fine granularity task). When the distributed computing behaves like a computing cluster model and the computing nodes are remote from the task manager (when traffic flows between the computing nodes and the task manager are across flow boundaries), then the flows can be estimated with a 50/50 flow distribution. When the distributed-computing behaves more like a parallel computing model and the traffic between computing nodes is across flow boundaries, then the flows can be estimated with a 20/80 flow distribution.

These guidelines are intended to be starting points in determining flow distributions for the network, and will be modified by the applications' requirements, the distributions of users across the network, and user behavior patterns. For example, a client-server environment, which may initially indicate a 50/50 flow distribution, may actually have a 20/80 distribution when the distribution of users is taken into account. For example, consider the client-server model in Figure 6-10.

FIGURE 6-10. **Client-Server Environment with 20/80 Flow Distribution**

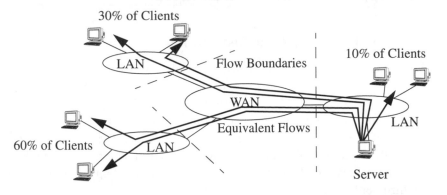

When the client-server flows cross flow boundaries, as in this example, a 50/50 flow distribution is a good first estimate. When the clients are mapped onto this model, however, the number of clients that are on the other side of the WAN from the server is large: 90%. This means that not only do the critical flows cross a flow boundary, but also that they cross a WAN. This is sufficient to increase the flow distribution from 50/50 to 20/80.

Flow distributions of 50/50 and 20/80 indicate that the application and/or flow model is using flows that cross one or more flow boundaries and that we need to consider these applications and/or flow models more closely. For example, we can use these flow distributions to indicate when a flow is part of a backbone flow. We can also use them to develop modifiers for performance. If a 50/50 flow distribution tells us that the same amount of traffic is crossing the flow boundary as is staying local, then we can estimate that the capacity requirement of that application is the same on both sides of the flow boundary. If the flow distribution is 80/20 or 20/80, then the amounts of traffic on each side of the flow boundary are not the same, and we can modify our capacity requirement accordingly.

How should these rules be used? If the flow distribution is 50/50 or 20/80, this indicates that most or all of the flow is remote, and that the capacity requirement of the application applies across the remote network. Therefore, if we have a capacity requirement of 10 Mb/s for an application, and the flow distribution in 80/20 (local/ remote), then we may estimate that the capacity requirement for the remote network is about 2 Mb/s. If the flow distribution is 50/50, then that requirement becomes 5 Mb/s, and if the distribution is 80/20, the remote requirement becomes 8 Mb/s. We can generalize this by stating that if the flow distribution is 50/50 or 20/80, there is sufficient reason to believe that a significant portion of the flow is remote and that the capacity requirement for the remote network is the same as for the local network.

6.3.2 Using the Flow Distributions

Flow distributions indicate when a model may put as much or more traffic across a flow boundary as it would keep local. In doing so, flow distributions are useful in showing where an application will generate a backbone flow in the network. This depends, however, on whether or not the elements of the model are distributed across flow boundaries. For example, if the clients and servers in a cooperative-computing model are all located on the same LAN, it is less likely that there will be flows from this model transiting a WAN, and the 50/50 flow distribution would not apply. When either the servers and/or clients are distributed across LAN/WAN environments, however, the 50/50 flow distribution for cooperative computing becomes relevant.

6.4 Combining Flow Models, Boundaries, and Distributions

Flow models, boundaries, and distributions are used to indicate the possibility of backbone flows in the network and where they may be located. Let's now look at how they are applied.

Backbone flows are where traffic from multiple composite flows are consolidated, and imply hierarchy in the network. Backbone flows are also indicated when one or more of the following occur:

- Clients and servers in a client-server, cooperative-computing, or distributed-computing environment are in different areas, separated by a flow boundary.

- Servers in a cooperative-computing environment are in different areas, separated by a flow boundary.

- Computing nodes in a parallel processing–type distributed-computing environment are in different areas, separated by a flow boundary.

- Multiple models merge, usually at a flow (LAN/MAN or LAN/WAN) boundary.

In applying flow patterns, we will need to identify if any flow models exist in our network. Then, if one or more flow models exist, we will determine if their elements (computing nodes, clients, servers) are distributed across flow boundaries. If so, then the flow distributions may apply. When elements are distributed across flow boundaries, we then examine the flows between elements to determine if the flow affected by the flow boundary is critical.

Starting with the information from the requirements specification, we will determine where the flows are in the network, whether the flows are individual or backbone, and develop the performance characteristics for each flow. To illustrate this procedure, we will go through the following example.

Example 6.2—Application Mapping

Application	Locations
Appl A	Boston
Appl B	New York City
Appl C	New York City and Philadelphia
Appl D	All locations
Appl E	Boston and New York City

These applications are mapped out in Figure 6-11 to show their common locations. Boundaries are then applied to this diagram. There are LAN/WAN boundaries between each of the cities, crossing the WAN environment. There may also be boundaries between campuses, buildings, and/or floors. More information is needed about the environment of each city before more detailed boundaries can be applied. In applying the LAN/WAN boundaries, we see that Applications C, D, and E cross these boundaries and may indicate backbone flows.

At this point, we would see if there are any data sources and/or sinks for our design environment, and if Applications C, D, or E follow any of the flow models or distributions. If some or all of them do, then we would determine the numbers of elements (computing nodes, clients, servers) that are on each side of the boundary. This will help us to determine which flows will contribute to backbone flows.

FIGURE 6-11. **Example of an Application Environment**

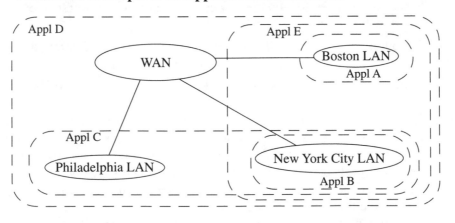

◊ ◊ ◊

Example 6.3—Flow Patterns

In this example, we take a look at a university that is designing a MAN to interconnect existing campus LANs. There are three applications that we need to consider:

Application	Model	Locations
Appl A	Peer-to-peer	All
Appl B	Client-server	North and South campuses
Appl C	Distributed-computing	West and South campuses

The existing LANs, applications, and distances are shown in Figure 6-12. Application A follows a peer-to-peer model that uses the general 80/20 rule, which we can apply between all three campuses. Applications B and C have models that imply more traffic across the MAN and will be used between campuses. At this point, we need to know more about potential data sources and sinks, and the distributions of elements between the campuses. Upon further questioning of university personnel, we find the distributions for Applications B and C:

Application	Distribution
Appl B	Server located at North Campus; 10% of clients at North Campus, 90% at South Campus
Appl C	Computing cluster type; task manager located at South Campus; all computing nodes located at West Campus

FIGURE 6-12. **MAN Environment for University Example**

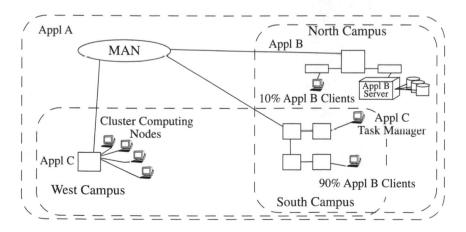

For Application B, the critical flow will be between the clients and the server. The server at North Campus will act as a data source for clients at the North and South campuses. Since most of the clients are separated from the server by a flow boundary, we can estimate that the client-server model will have a flow distribution of 20/80, and that there will be a backbone flow between the North and South campuses. For Application A, the task manager at South Campus will act as a data sink for the computing nodes at West Campus, and the critical flows for a computing cluster type of distributed-computing model are between the task manager and the computing nodes. In this environment, these flows are across the flow boundary, between the South and West campuses. This indicates a flow distribution of 20/80 (LAN/MAN) and a backbone flow between the South and West campuses. The resulting diagram now looks like Figure 6-13.

At this point, we are ready to combine flow performance characteristics for capacity and service planning for our design.

FIGURE 6-13. Flows for University Example

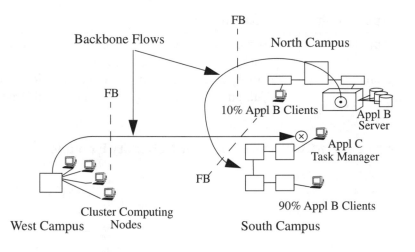

◊ ◊ ◊

6.5 Developing the Flow Specification

Flow specifications (*flowspecs*) are devices to help us in combining application performance requirements into flows, which will be used as the basis for making technology choices in the network design process. We can also consider flowspecs to be templates for requesting, configuring, and verifying services in a services-based network.

In combining application performance requirements, the flowspec provides capacity and service plans for the network. A capacity plan is generated when the flowspec is used to combine capacities for best-effort applications. Capacity plans do not have delay or reliability requirements associated with them, and they are used to estimate the required capacity of the network. A service plan is generated when the flowspec is used to combine capacity, delay, and reliability requirements for best-effort and specified applications. In addition to estimating capacity for the network, service plans help us to determine how to meet delay and reliability requirements for the network.

In developing the flowspec, we will be identifying the flows for our design, using the information from the requirements specification and applications map, along with the flow information from this chapter. All of this information will be the input to the flowspec. At this point in the process we should have the following for our design environment:

- A listing of the applications and their requirements
- Each application's category, as low- or high-performance, specified, or best-effort
- The applications map
- Potential user and application modifiers for performance
- Flow models, boundaries, distributions, and data sources and sinks for our environment

6.5.1 Identifying Flows in the Design Environment

The first step in developing the flowspec is to identify the flows for our design environment. We start with the initial assumptions that all applications are best-effort, and that all flows are peer-to-peer. The requirements specification and applications map will provide more specific information to build on the initial assumption, which, along with the flow analysis, should identify many of the potential flows in the network.

Let's take the earlier example of a data mining environment and add information from a likely requirements specification for such an environment. Recall that there were three applications for this environment, a Web-based search engine (Application A), a data storage and archival application (Application B), and a data-migration tool (Application C). Figure 6-2 is the applications map for this environment, and the requirements specification may look like the following:

Application	Reliability	Capacity	Delay
A (Web Search)	TBD	TBD	TBD
B (Storage)	TBD	TBD	TBD
C (Data Migration)	TBD	TBD	TBD

At this point, we know where the applications will be applied in the design environment, but know nothing about each application's requirements. We can estimate that Application A will be interactive, as it will likely be interfacing with the users, who will be querying the data stores. Applications B and C appear to be in the bulk data transfer application group from Chapter 2, which indicates that they will be best-effort.

Using the application and user behavior characteristics from Chapter 3, the customer was questioned further. From their answers, we have the following information about the data that will be used with these applications:

Application	Characteristics
A (Web Search)	Number of simultaneous sessions, 100; number of queries/session, 25; average duration of sessions, 15 minutes
B (Storage)	Storage size, 10 TB; average file size to cache, 100 MB; expected data input per day, 100 GB
C (Data Migration)	Average file size between caches, 10 MB; average file size to server, 2 MB; percentage of cache hits, 75%

This information can be used to estimate some performance characteristics for our applications. For Application A, we can expect 100 sessions to be active at any given time, with (25/15 = approximately 1.7 queries/minute), for 1700 queries/minute total. Each query will result in data migrating from the cache to the server, and possibly from storage to the cache, or movement between caches. Seventy-five percent of the time, these queries will result in movement of data from the local cache to the server, with an average file size of 2 MB, while 25% of the time, queries will result in data migrating between caches (average file size 10 MB) or from storage to cache (100 MB). Putting this together, we get

(1700 queries/minute)(0.75)(2 MB) = 2550 MB/minute = 340 Mb/s

This is the total rate of queries from the users. For data migration between the caches and from the storage, we will have to estimate the percentage of each type of transfer. Without any other knowledge about the applications, I estimate that about 90% will be between caches and 10% will be from storage to cache. This gives us

(1700 queries/minute)(0.25)(10 MB)(0.9) = 3825 MB/minute = 510 Mb/s
and
(1700 queries/minute)(0.25)(100 MB)(0.1) = 4250 MB/minute = 567 Mb/s

These rates are equally distributed between all of the flows for our applications. Figure 6-14 combines the flows from Figures 6-5, 6-6, and 6-7. These flows are labelled f_a, f_b, and f_c to indicate which application is generating the flow. There are also flows from each of the Web servers to the users. These flows would be identified when we look at each server's area in more detail.

In order to apply the flow boundaries to this example, we need to know the locations of each area in the design environment, as well as the distances between locations. In this example, all locations are within a MAN environment, and each site is a campus LAN with one or more buildings. We can apply flow boundaries to separate the LAN/MAN areas. The dashes in the figure above show where the flow boundaries can be applied. Note that there is an additional boundary at the storage/ archival device. This is to show that the flow from Application B also crosses a flow boundary in accepting data from outside sources.

FIGURE 6-14. **Flows for Data Mining Environment**

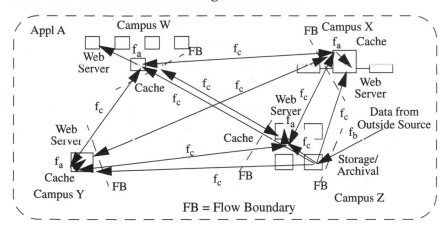

FIGURE 6-15. Cooperative-Computing Flow Model for Data Mining Environment

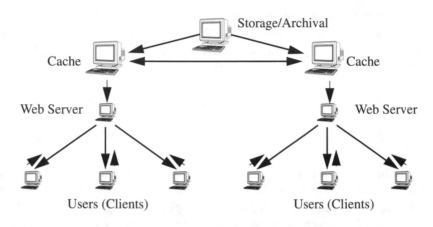

The applications in this design environment are similar to a cooperative-computing flow model. For the data mining environment example, the model would look like Figure 6-15.

The flows from storage to cache and between caches cross flow boundaries, and we will consider them in the backbone flows for the design. At this point we can use composite flows to show where multiple flows are consolidated at a flow boundary (i.e., at the entry point into each campus LAN), and backbone flows between the flow boundaries. Figure 6-16 shows the simplified environment.

FIGURE 6-16. Backbone and Composite Flows for Data Mining Environment

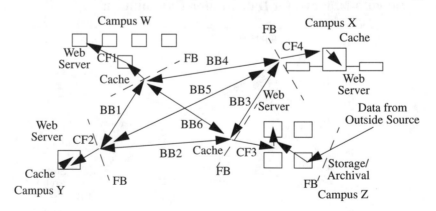

In this figure, each of the composite (CF) and backbone (BB) flows represent a consolidation of several flows. To determine the capacity requirements of each flow, we will use the information from the application behavior analysis. We have estimated that the total capacity required from the servers to the users is 340 Mb/s, from the caches to the servers is 510 Mb/s, and from the storage to the caches is 567 Mb/s. We also know that the flow of data from the outside to storage is 100 GB/day. Without more information about the user concentrations at each campus, we will estimate that the flows to each campus are equivalent. There are four flows from cache to server (f_a), and each flow will have an estimated capacity of (340/4 = 85 Mb/s). There are six cache-to-cache flows, each with an estimated capacity of (510/6 = 85 Mb/s), and four storage-to-cache flows, each with an estimated capacity of (567/4 = 142 Mb/s). The flow from the outside to storage can be estimated, based on 8-hour work day, as (100 GB/day)(day/8 hours) = 125 GB/hour = 28 Mb/s.

Each flow's characteristics are now summarized:

Flow	Capacity
f_a	85 Mb/s
f_b	28 Mb/s
f_c	85 Mb/s
f_{c1}	142 Mb/s

6.6 Prioritizing Flows

Part of the reason for developing a flowspec is to be able to prioritize flows. Such a prioritization may be necessary in order to determine where to start implementing the network, develop implementation schedules, or determine where to reduce network cost. Flows may be prioritized in any one of several parameters, including the number of users affected by each flow, the performance characteristics of each flow, as well as their distances and locations.

One or more of the flow performance characteristics is the most common parameter used for prioritization. Take as an example the following flows in the network, where the total number of users is 2100:

Flow	Reliability	Capacity	Delay	Users
f1	99.95%	50 Kb/s	40 ms	150
f2	N/A	800 Kb/s	80 ms	750
f3	99.0%	120 Kb/s	N/A	400
f4	N/A	100 Kb/s	100 ms	1200
f5	N/A	1.0 Mb/s	25 ms	100

Composite Flows

F1 (f1, f2)	99.95%	850 Kb/s	40 ms	900
F2 (f4)	N/A	100 Kb/s	100 ms	1200
F3 (f3, f4)	99.0%	220 Kb/s	100 ms	1600
F4 (f1, f5)	99.95%	1.05 Mb/s	25 ms	250

Backbone Flows

BB1 (f2, f3, f5)	99.0%	1.92 Mb/s	25 ms	1250
BB2 (f2, f4)	N/A	1.8 Mb/s	80 ms	1950

We may want to optimize this network to ensure that the largest numbers of users get prioritized service. In this case, composite and backbone flows that service the largest numbers of users would have higher priority than other flows. The prioritized list would be as follows:

Flow	Reliability	Capacity	Delay	Users
BB2 (f2, f4)	N/A	1.8 Mb/s	80 ms	1950
F3 (f3, f4)	99.0%	220 Kb/s	100 ms	1600
BB1 (f2, f3, f5)	99.0%	1.92 Mb/s	25 ms	1250
F2 (f4)	N/A	100 Kb/s	100 ms	1200
F1 (f1, f2)	99.95%	850 Kb/s	40 ms	900
F4 (f1, f5)	99.95%	1.05 Mb/s	25 ms	250

Notice that BB2 is prioritized first, even though its reliability and delay characteristics are lower in performance than other backbone and composite flows.

6.6.1 Applying Cost Information to Flows

Once flows are prioritized, we can allocate network costs to each flow. This will help us in choosing technologies, services, and interconnection strategies in Chapters 8 and 9. Taking the example above, if we had a budget of $1.2 million for network design, hardware, implementation, testing, and acceptance, we could estimate percentages based on the number of users serviced per flow. The budget allocations would be as follows:

Flow	Reliability	Capacity	Delay	Users	Budget
BB2		1.8 Mb/s	80 ms	1950	$330K
F3	99.0%	220 Kb/s	100 ms	1600	$270K
BB1	99.0%	1.92 Mb/s	25 ms	1250	$210K
F2		100 Kb/s	100 ms	1200	$200K
F1	99.95%	850 Kb/s	40 ms	900	$150K
F4	99.95%	1.05 Mb/s	25 ms	250	$40K

Each budget allocation is based on the ratio of users per flow/total users for all flows. This breakdown of the budget would allow higher-performance technologies and services to be purchased and placed where they would affect the most users. A trade-off is that smaller numbers of users may not get the network performance they need, even though it may be clearly stated in the flowspec.

Another mechanism for applying cost information is to base cost on the offered service to the user. If we prioritized the flows and allocated the network budget based on capacity, we would get the following:

Flow	Reliability	Capacity	Delay	Users	Budget
BB1	99.0%	1.92 Mb/s	25 ms	1250	$390K
BB2		1.8 Mb/s	80 ms	1950	$360K
F4	99.95%	1.05 Mb/s	25 ms	250	$210K
F1	99.95%	850 Kb/s	40 ms	900	$170K
F3	99.0%	220 Kb/s	100 ms	1600	$45K
F2		100 Kb/s	100 ms	1200	$20K

This type of budget allocation places the money where the capacity is needed.

6.7 Concluding Remarks

At this point in the analysis process, we have a set of tools that we can use to identify and evaluate expected traffic flows in our design environment. The flows originate from the requirements analysis process and are evaluated using data sources and sinks, as well as flow models, boundaries, and distributions. Any or all of these tools may be used to identify where individual, composite, and/or backbone flows may exist in the network.

Once we have determined where the flows are in the design environment, we use the flowspec to build a capacity and/or service plan for the design. The flowspec will be used as input into the design process, beginning with the design of the logical network. Now let's continue the flow analysis process by applying the analysis tools to some examples and case studies.

Exercises

Exercises 1 through 3 reference the data mining environment (Example 6-1) discussed in Section 6-1.

1. How would the data sources and sinks for each application in the data mining environment change if

   a) There were no caches in the environment.

   b) Data flows were directly between the storage/archival device and the Web servers for each data request, and the Web servers updated the caches after each request was completed.

   c) There was only one Web server for the environment, located at Campus Z.

2. Place flow boundaries in this environment. Try both Campus/Campus and Building/Building boundaries. What does each tell us about the client-server and/or cooperative-computing flows in this environment?

3. For this example, we estimate that the flow between a server and a client is approximately 8 Mb/s. Apply performance modifiers for 80/20, 50/50, and 20/80 flow distributions to this flow capacity, and estimate the required capacities for this flow for each flow distribution. What could you recommend if the design environment was based on 10bT? On FDDI? On ATM at T3 rate (using 34 Mb/s as this rate)?

4. You are designing a network for an on-line transaction processing (OLTP) environment (e.g., a retail sales network). Their current environment is a mainframe that has several terminals connected to it, either directly or through a terminal server, as in Figure 6-17.

   They are moving to a cooperative-computing environment, where there will be multiple regional database servers acting in a client-server fashion and updating each other's regions via a database manager, as in Figure 6-18.

   Show the probable data sources and sinks for both environments. How does migrating from the mainframe environment to the cooperative-computing environment modify the traffic flows in the system? In what ways does the new environment improve the traffic flows? What are some of the trade-offs between the two environments—for example, in security, management, simplicity, ease of use, performance, cost?

FIGURE 6-17. Mainframe Environment for OLTP Application

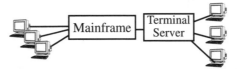

FIGURE 6-18. Cooperative-Computing Environment for OLTP Application

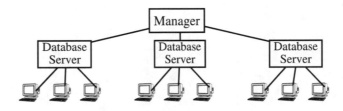

CHAPTER 7

Flow Analysis: Practice

7.1 Simplifying the Flow Analysis Process

The flow analysis process can sometimes be time-consuming, and when the design environment is large, the number of flows in the design can become unwieldy. Here are some suggestions for simplifying this process when necessary.

7.1.1 Simplifying Assumption 1: Showing Only Flow-Model-Based Flows

This assumption is that only the flows that can be modeled by one or more of the flow models are important. We may use this assumption to state that we will consider only client-server flows in the design environment, or consider only distributed-computing and cooperative-computing flows. This assumption makes the flow analysis easier in that we are working with flows that have well-understood models associated with them.

7.1.2 Simplifying Assumption 2: Showing Only Backbone Flows

Another simplifying assumption is that the backbone flows are the most important flows in the design environment and thus are the ones that are shown in the flow analysis. This assumption can be used when you are focusing on the backbone part of the design, such as in designing a backbone WAN to connect existing LANs. In a case like this, we are not focusing on the LAN environments, and it may not be necessary to show the LAN flows. In order for this assumption to apply, the flows can only be a part of a capacity plan from the flowspec and must not be from the service plan.

7.1.3 Simplifying Assumption 3: Standardizing Flows

In order to apply this assumption, the design environment should have flows that are somewhat equivalent between locations. For example, the flows from each of the clients to the server in a client-server flow model may be modeled as a standardized flow, as shown in Figure 7-1.

The result of using this simplifying assumption is that one flow may be used to represent several flows that have the same characteristics, like all of the flows in the above model. In order to be able to use this assumption, you should be sure that all of the flows that will be represented by the standard indeed all have the same performance and service characteristics.

7.2 Examples of Applying Flowspecs

From the requirements specification of Chapter 2 and the listing of flows, including backbone flows, we now apply the flowspec to obtain the overall performance characteristics expected in our network design. As examples, we will develop flowspecs for best-effort flows, a combination of best-effort and specified flows, and best-effort, specified, and guaranteed flows.

FIGURE 7-1. Standardizing a Client-Server Flow

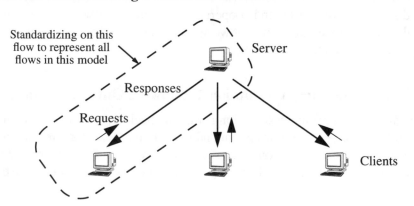

The requirements specification gives us a listing of the applications that will produce flows in our design, as well as the requirements for the user, application, host, and network components. Of particular importance are the application performance requirements and location information for all components. Also at this point, we should be able to apply the flow models, boundaries, and distributions to our design, identifying any composite and backbone flows.

Example 7.1—Multipart Flowspec

A multipart flowspec can contain best-effort, specified, and guaranteed flows. In the following example, some of the performance characteristics for Application D (flow 4) are guaranteed. Mechanisms for guaranteeing characteristics are discussed in Chapters 8 and 9.

This example is a design for a campus network to support an architectural company, whose applications include architectural design, design visualization (in three-dimensional virtual reality), composite video and photographs, and engineering development. There are five applications that we need to consider, Applications A through E. Application A is a best-effort general-purpose application; Application B is an architectural design package; Application C allows for remote access to a database of architectural designs, photographs, and videos; Application D is an engineering visualization application; and Application E is a manufacturing package that takes data from the engineering and architectural applications and generates a scale model of the design.

The applications map for this example is shown in Figure 7-2. From the requirements specification, we first categorize each application. In this example, we have applications with best-effort, specified, and guaranteed characteristics. For Application D, both the capacity and delay are guaranteed, but it is placed in only one category, real-time. (It could have also been categorized as controlled-rate). The

FIGURE 7-2. Application Locations for Example 7.1

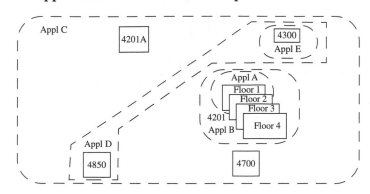

TABLE 7-1. Application Service Requirements for Example 7.1

Categorizing Applications	Controlled-Rate	Real-Time	Best-Effort	Application Locations
Application A			225 Kb/s	4201, Floor 1
Application B	Specified (98.0% R, 900 Kb/s, 100-ms D)			4201
Application C	Specified (240 Kb/s, 80-ms D)			All locations
Application D		Specified (99.9% R, 3.2 Mb/s, 45-ms D)		4300, 4850
Application E		Specified (640 Kb/s, 60-ms D)		4300

Note: R = Reliability, D = Delay

requirements specification for this example is shown in Tables 7-1 and 7-2. Applications B and C are related. Application B is an architectural design package, distributed throughout Building 4201, with a server located on the first floor of that building, and Application C allows for remote access to a database of architectural designs, photographs, and videos. The designs developed with Application B are automatically stored in the database of Application C. Both of these applications are client-server.

TABLE 7-2. Host Service Requirements for Example 7.1

Type of Host or Equipment	Numbers and Locations
Application A Server (S_A)	4201, Floor 1
Application B Server (S_B)	4201, Floor 1
Application C Server (S_C)	4201, Floor 1
Application D Server (S_D)	4300

TABLE 7-3. Flowspec Worksheet for Example 7.1

Application	Flow ID	Flow Models	Flow Distributions	Backbone/ Composite Flows Indicated
Appl A	f1	NI	NI	No
Appl B	f2	Client-Server	50/50	Backbone
Appl C	f3	Client-Server	50/50	Backbone
Appl D	f4	Distributed Processing	20/80	Backbone
Appl E	f5	NI (Point-to-Point)	NI	No

Note: NI = None Indicated

Application D is an engineering visualization application. This application has the most stringent performance requirements for capacity and delay, which is indicated by a guaranteed service request in the requirements analysis. Application D behaves somewhat like a distributed-computing model, and has a server in Building 4300.

Application E is a manufacturing package that takes data from the engineering and architectural applications and generates a scale model of the design. This application is used only in Building 4300, between a workstation and model generator.

Now we examine the flows for this system:

Application	Reliability	Capacity	Delay	Flow
Application A		225 Kb/s		f1
Application B	98.0%	900 Kb/s	100 ms	f2
Application C		240 Kb/s	80 ms	f3
Application D	99.9%	3.2 Mb/s (g)	45 ms (g)	f4 (g)
Application E		640 Kb/s	60 ms	f5

Note: (g) represents a guaranteed service characteristic or flow

The flowspec worksheet in Table 7-3 and the initial flow diagram in Figure 7-3 show all of the composite and backbone flows for the system, but further inspection shows that some of the composite flows are not really composites, but consist of only one flow. For these flows, we will replace the composite flow with the individual flow. We leave the backbone flows, however, even if they consist of only one flow, when they are a result of extending one of the flow models across a flow boundary. The composite flows for this system are listed below.

FIGURE 7-3. **Initial Flow Diagram for Example 7.1**

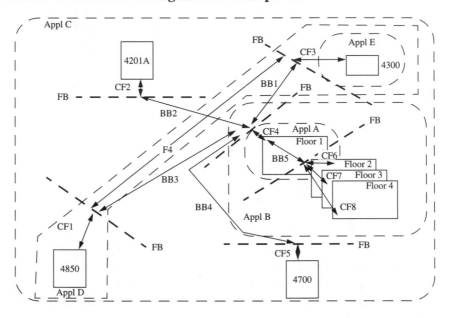

Composite Flows: CF1 (4850) consists of f3, f4 (g)
                   CF2 (4201A) consists of f3   (CF2 replaced with f3)
                   CF3 (4300) consists of f3, f4 (g)
                   CF4 (4201) consists of f3   (CF4 replaced with f3)
                   CF5 (4201) consists of f3   (CF5 replaced with f3)
                   CF6 (4201) consists of f2, f3
                   CF7 (4201) consists of f2, f3
                   CF8 (4201) consists of f2, f3

Backbone Flows: BB1 (4201–4300) consists of f3
                   BB2 (4201–4201A) consists of f3
                   BB3 (4201–4850) consists of f3
                   BB4 (4201–4700) consists of f3
                   BB5 (4201) consists of f1, f2, f3

Individual Flows: F4 (4300–4850)

Composite Flow	Reliability	Capacity	Delay	Flow
CF1		240 Kb/s	80 ms	f3
	99.9%	3.2 Mb/s (g)	45 ms (g)	f4
Total for CF1:				
Best-Effort Capacity		None		
Specified Service	99.9%	240 Kb/s	80 ms	
Guaranteed Service		3.2 Mb/s	45 ms	
CF3		240 Kb/s	80 ms	f3
	99.9%	3.2 Mb/s (g)	45 ms (g)	f4
Total for CF3:				
Best-Effort Capacity		None		
Specified Service	99.9%	240 Kb/s	80 ms	
Guaranteed Service		3.2 Mb/s	45 ms	
CF6	98.0%	900 Kb/s	100 ms	f2
		240 Kb/s	80 ms	f3
Total for CF6:				
Best-Effort Capacity		None		
Specified Service	98.0%	1.14 Mb/s	80 ms	
CF7	98.0%	900 Kb/s	100 ms	f2
		240 Kb/s	80 ms	f3
Total for CF7:				
Best-Effort Capacity		None		
Specified Service	98.0%	1.14 Mb/s	80 ms	
CF8	98.0%	900 Kb/s	100 ms	f2
		240 Kb/s	80 ms	f3
Total for CF8:				
Best-Effort Capacity		None		
Specified Service	98.0%	1.14 Mb/s	80 ms	

Backbone Flow	Reliability	Capacity	Delay	Flow
BB1		240 Kb/s	80 ms	f3
Total for BB1:				
Best-Effort Capacity		None		
Specified Service		240 Kb/s	80 ms	

Backbone Flow	Reliability	Capacity	Delay	Flow
BB2		240 Kb/s	80 ms	f3
Total for BB2:				
Best-Effort Capacity		None		
Specified Service		240 Kb/s	80 ms	
BB3		240 Kb/s	80 ms	f3
Total for BB3:				
Best-Effort Capacity		None		
Specified Service		240 Kb/s	80 ms	
BB4		240 Kb/s	80 ms	f3
Total for BB4:				
Best-Effort Capacity		None		
Specified Service		240 Kb/s	80 ms	
BB5		225 Kb/s		f1
	98.0%	900 Kb/s	100 ms	f2
		240 Kb/s	80 ms	f3
Total for BB5:				
Best-Effort Capacity		225 Kb/s		
Specified Service	98.0%	1.14 Mb/s	80 ms	

Individual Flow	Reliability	Capacity	Delay	Flow
F4	99.9%	3.2 Mb/s	45 ms	f4
Total for BB1:				
Best-Effort Capacity		None		
Specified Service	99.9%			
Guaranteed Service		3.2 Mb/s	45 ms	

Multipart Flowspec for Example 7.1

Flows	Reliability	Capacity	Delay
f1		225 Kb/s	
f2	98.0%	900 Kb/s	100 ms
f3		240 Kb/s	80 ms
f4 (g)	99.9%	3.2 Mb/s (g)	45 ms (g)
f5		640 Kb/s	60 ms

Composite Flows

CF1	99.9%	240 Kb/s	80 ms
Guaranteed Service		3.2 Mb/s	45 ms
CF3	98.0%	240 Kb/s	80 ms
Guaranteed Service		3.2 Mb/s	45 ms
CF6	98.0%	1.14 Mb/s	80 ms
CF7	98.0%	1.14 Mb/s	80 ms
CF8	98.0%	1.14 Mb/s	80 ms

Backbone Flows

BB1		240 Kb/s	80 ms
BB2		240 Kb/s	80 ms
BB3		240 Kb/s	80 ms
BB4		240 Kb/s	80 ms
BB5	98.0%	1.14 Mb/s	80 ms

Individual Flows

F4	99.9%		
Guaranteed Service		3.2 Mb/s	45 ms

The resulting capacity- and service-planning diagram is presented in Figure 7-4. The most important feature of the multipart flowspec is that it identifies guaranteed service requirements for the network. Without this flowspec, it is likely that the guaranteed service requirements would be combined with the other requirements, and we would lose the requirement that the service be guaranteed. For our example,

FIGURE 7-4. Capacity- and Service-Planning Diagram for Example 7.1

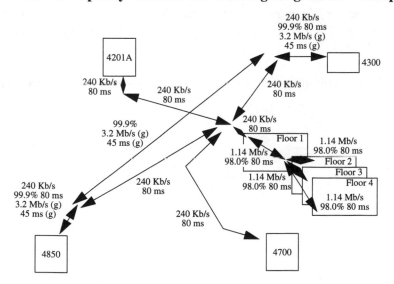

the flow between Buildings 4300 and 4850 will be treated differently in the design process, and we will choose technologies that support (as possible) guaranteed requirements. In this example, the guarantee of 45-ms end-to-end delay should not be a problem, since we are in a campus environment. It is the guaranteed capacity of 3.2 Mb/s that will drive the design for that flow.

$$\Diamond \ \Diamond \ \Diamond$$

7.3 Case Study

We apply the results of the requirements analysis done in Chapter 4 to a flow analysis for our project.

Step 1   Identify Data Sources and Sinks. In our requirements analysis for this case study, we estimated that four of the applications—A, D, G, and F—were client-server, and that B was a distributed database. We also stated that there was a computing center and storage in the 1013 building in Oakland. Let's see where we can apply data sources and sinks for each of these applications.

Application A has a server in 1013 and supports all users in the design environment. This application supports demand access to data sets, so we expect the clients to pull data from the server, and the server (S_a) to be a data source for this application (see Figure 7-5). Note that no flow is shown within Building 1013, although there may be clients in the building. (For simplicity, these figures assume that there will be client-server flows within the building where the server is located, unless otherwise noted.)

Likewise, Applications D and G operate in a client-server fashion, serving users in Oakland and San Francisco (see Figure 7-6). This server ($S_{d/g}$) is a data source for these applications.

The last client-server application, F, has a server at the San Jose campus, and serves the 1013 building in Oakland. Figure 7-7 shows the server (S_f) data source.

FIGURE 7-5. Data Sources/Sinks for Application A

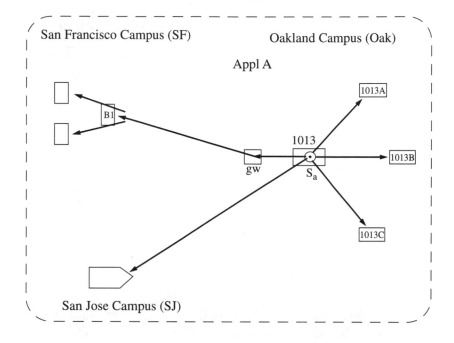

FIGURE 7-6. Data Sources/Sinks for Applications D and G

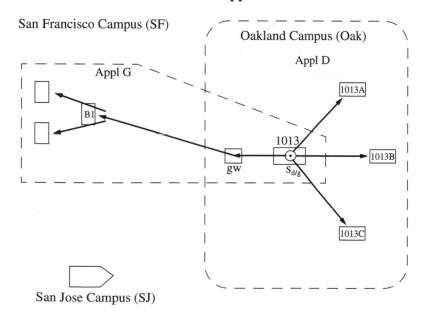

FIGURE 7-7. **Data Sources/Sinks for Application F**

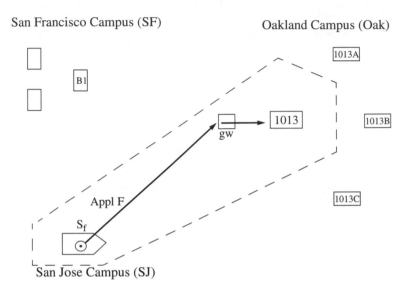

The distributed database application, B, has a server in Building 1 (B1) in San Francisco (SF). This server (S_b) serves the SF campus. In Figure 7-8, flows are shown to the other buildings on the SF campus.

FIGURE 7-8. **Data Sources/Sinks for Application B**

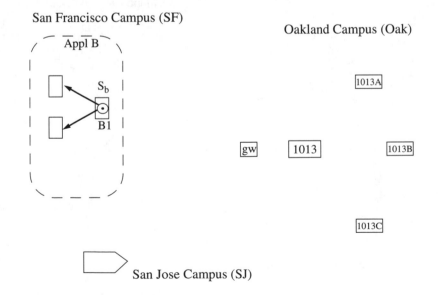

FIGURE 7-9. **Data Sources/Sinks for Applications C and E**

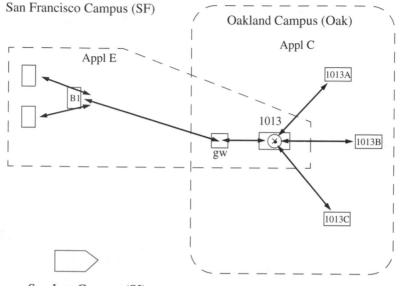

Applications C and E provide remote-control access to the experiment areas in Building 1013. This access is for users in the SF and Oakland areas. Recall from the requirements analysis that these applications consist of audio/video and telemetry feeds to the users, sending control information to the experiment and interacting with the technicians in the experiment area. This means that there are no clear data sources or sinks. Figure 7-9 reflects this by showing the experiment area as both a source and a sink, with flows going in both directions.

The final data source/sink analysis is for the computing and storage clusters in Building 1013. The computing cluster feeds all of the applications (except C and E), as well as the data storage cluster in 1013. Putting all of the servers along with the computing and storage clusters, we get Figure 7-10.

Step 2   Applying Flow Boundaries. For this design environment, we will use flow boundaries at the interfaces to the MAN, and between buildings at each campus. At this time, we should label each of the flows so that we can recognize them in the figure:

FIGURE 7-10. **Data Sources/Sinks for Computing and Storage Clusters**

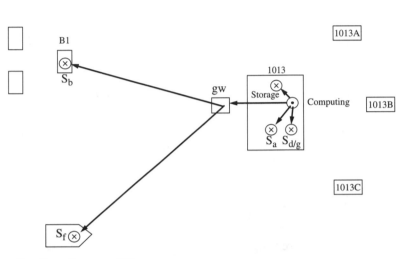

Building 1013 expanded to show all servers

Application	Flow Label
A	f_a
B	f_b
C/E	$f_{c/e}$
D/G	$f_{d/g}$
F	f_f
Computing	f_{comp}

The flows from the computing cluster to the servers are labelled f_{comp}. Now we bring the flows and flow boundaries together in Figure 7-11. In this figure, we estimate flow f_{comp} as a client-server flow with performance equal to f_a.

FIGURE 7-11. Flow Boundaries

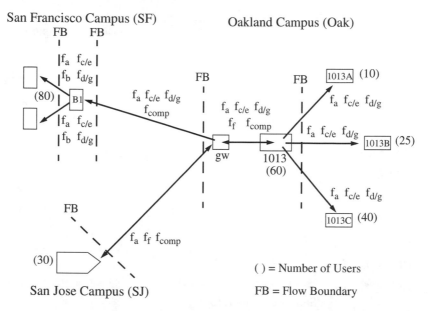

Step 3 Applying Flow Models. We already have the flow models identified for each flow, so at this point we will use the models and flow boundaries to estimate where the backbone and composite flows are. From Figure 7-11, we see that we have flows that are composites of individual flows at the SF and Oakland campuses, and that these flows are combined into backbone flows between Building 1013 and the gateway building, and between Oakland and SF. The flow between SJ and Oakland does not combine any composite flows, but is itself a composite flow. In this figure, we also show the numbers of users at each building (shown in parentheses), based on the user requirements. Each of the backbone and composite flows are labelled in Figure 7-12.

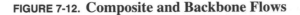

FIGURE 7-12. **Composite and Backbone Flows**

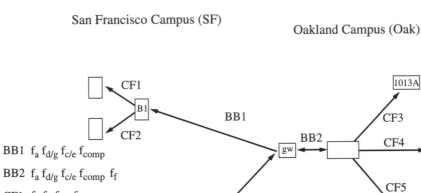

San Francisco Campus (SF)

Oakland Campus (Oak)

BB1 f_a $f_{d/g}$ $f_{c/e}$ f_{comp}

BB2 f_a $f_{d/g}$ $f_{c/e}$ f_{comp} f_f

CF1 f_a f_b $f_{c/e}$ $f_{d/g}$

CF2 f_a f_b $f_{c/e}$ $f_{d/g}$

CF3 f_a $f_{d/g}$ $f_{c/e}$

CF4 f_a $f_{d/g}$ $f_{c/e}$

CF5 f_a $f_{d/g}$ $f_{c/e}$

CF6 f_a f_f f_{comp}

Step 4   Estimating Flow Distributions. From the flow models, flow boundaries, and numbers of users at each site, we estimate the following flow distributions for this design.

Flow	Flow Model	Flow Boundaries	Flow Distribution
f_a	Client-Server	Oak, SF, SJ	20/80 (local/remote)
f_b	Client-Server	SF	50/50 (local/remote)
$f_{c/e}$	Peer-Peer	Oak, SF	20/80 (local/remote)
$f_{d/g}$	Client-Server	Oak, SF	20/80 (local/remote)
f_f	Client-Server	Oak, SJ	50/50 (local/remote)
f_{comp}	Client-Server	Oak, SF, SJ	20/80 (local/remote)

Since all of these flows have flow distributions of 50/50 or 20/80, we will expect the same capacity requirements both remote and local to the application.

FIGURE 7-13. **Two-Part Flowspec**

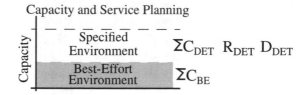

Step 5   Developing the Flowspec. In this project, we have applications that are mission-critical, real-time, and best-effort. We will use the two-part flowspec to determine the performance characteristics of our flows. Recall that the two-part flowspec combines the capacities of the flows and takes their highest-performance delay and reliability characteristics, as in Figure 7-13. We apply this flowspec to our flows to get the performance characteristics of the composite and backbone flows.

Individual Flows	Reliability	Capacity	Delay
f_a	99.5%	2.7 Mb/s	100 ms
f_b	99.5%	53 Mb/s	25 ms
$f_{c/e}$	100%	1.69 Mb/s	40 ms
$f_{d/g}$	99.5%	10 Mb/s	80 ms
f_f	99.5%	400 Kb/s	100 ms
f_{comp}	99.5%	2.7 Mb/s	100 ms

Calculating CF1 (which equals CF2), we apply the capacity modifiers, getting

$$CF1 = CF2 = (2.7) + (53) + (1.69) + (10) = 67.39 \text{ Mb/s}$$

or approximately 67 Mb/s. For CF3 (which equals CF4 and CF5), we get

$$CF3 = CF4 = CF5 = (2.7) + (1.69) + (10) = 14.39 \text{ Mb/s}$$

or approximately 14 Mb/s. For CF6, we get

$$CF6 = (2.7) + (0.4) + (2.7) = 5.8 \text{ Mb/s}$$

or approximately 6 Mb/s.

Composite Flows	Reliability	Capacity	Delay
CF1	100%	67 Mb/s	25 ms
CF2	100%	67 Mb/s	25 ms
CF3	100%	14 Mb/s	40 ms
CF4	100%	14 Mb/s	40 ms
CF5	100%	14 Mb/s	40 ms
CF6	99.5%	6 Mb/s	100 ms

The backbone flows are slightly more complex, in that we need to consider the combinations of consolidated flows. BB1 is a consolidation of the MAN flows for CF1, CF2, and f_{comp}, which is

$$2((2.7) + (10) + (1.69)) + (2.7) = 31.48 \text{ Mb/s}$$

or 31 Mb/s. BB2 is a consolidation of BB1 and CF6, which is

$$(31) + (6) = 37 \text{ Mb/s}.$$

Backbone Flows	Reliability	Capacity	Delay
BB1	100%	31 Mb/s	40 ms
BB2	100%	37 Mb/s	40 ms

These performance characteristics will next be used in developing the logical design.

CHAPTER 8

Logical Design: Technology Choices

8.1 Background for Logical Design

In order to make the design process more straightforward, the design of the network is separated into two components: the logical network and the physical network. The design of the logical network (the logical design) builds upon the flow information to help us to make technology selections and develop an interconnectivity plan, which will be useful in developing network-layer routing and addressing strategies in Chapter 12. The logical design will also be the basis for applying location-dependent information to the design, resulting in the design of the physical network, covered in Chapter 11.

At this point in the design process, we have the requirements specification with application, user, and host requirements, and the capacity and service plans of the flowspec, with its performance characteristics for individual, composite, and back-bone flows. We will use all of this information as input into the logical design.

The logical design consists of determining your design goals for the network, and translating these goals into evaluation criteria for making technology choices for the design. The design environment is then segmented into small, workable areas, and technology choices are made based on the evaluation criteria. After making our technology choices, we then determine how to interconnect areas of the design. We will look at various interconnection mechanisms and where they may apply in the design. We will also look at how to integrate security and network management into the design.

It is important to note that the technologies that will be discussed in this chapter may be at different stages of development, testing, or deployment, based on when this material is applied to the design. *When evaluating and selecting technologies for your design, check the current (or expected) state of each candidate technology before applying it to the design, in order to ensure that your technology choices can be implemented.*

Figure 8-1 shows the process model for the logical design. This chapter focuses on making the technology choices, the interconnection mechanisms are covered in Chapter 9, and network management and security are covered in Chapter 10.

One of the results of the design process will be one or more diagrams describing the logical design. These diagrams will be combined with diagrams describing the physical design to form a complete description of network connectivity, infrastructure, and applicable technologies. The complete set of diagrams are used to prepare the environment for the network, including ordering equipment, deploying cable, and writing the transition plan for any existing networks.

FIGURE 8-1. Process for Design of the Logical Network

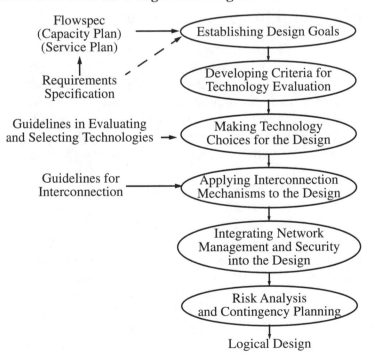

8.2 Establishing Design Goals

When choosing candidate technologies for our design, applying them to the design, and determining how to connect them, we need to have clear-cut goals that the network design will accomplish. Establishing design goals is part of understanding the roles of the network for our design.

You may be able to identify a single primary or driving design goal for your system. For example, a common design goal is minimizing the cost of the network. Another goal may be to maximize the performance of the network, in general or for a specific application or user group. In doing the requirements and flow analyses for your system, the design goals may already be clear.

Common design goals include

- Minimizing network deployment or operations costs (including circuit costs)
- Maximizing one or more network performance characteristics
- Ease of use and manageability
- Optimizing security—which can mean maximizing security, mapping security to a particular group's requirements, or providing multiple security models in the network
- Adaptability to new and changing user needs

One thing to keep in mind is that there are trade-offs to each of these design goals. For example, a design goal of minimizing cost will lead to choices that will trade off performance, ease of use, or adaptability for cost. Alternatively, a design goal of high-performance is likely to lead to choices that are expensive and/or difficult to use. These trade-offs are not a problem as long as you understand what they are, establish your goals for the design, and relate them to your customer/end user.

The design environment that you will be working on can indicate what your design goals will be. If you are designing a brand-new network for an environment that currently does not have any networking, then you will be free from the requirements and constraints of existing networks. Your design may call for the building of a scalable infrastructure, a high-performance backbone, or specialized work groups. If you are designing a network upgrade, adding to an existing network, or adapting a network to a new application, then you are faced with the existing networks, along with their infrastructures, technologies, and protocols, as well as users who are familiar with working on those networks. For these types of environments, you may be guided by making the network transition as easy as possible, minimizing disruption to the existing networks, and may trade off other goals to meet these.

The requirements and flow analyses can also indicate design goals for the network. For example, requirements for specified performance are an indication of high-performance, relatively sophisticated solutions. Backbone and composite flows indicate traffic consolidation, where capacity sharing and cost management can be applied. In the previous chapter, the flowspecs (unitary, two-part, and multi-part) provided flow information for service and capacity planning. Both service and capacity planning directly correlate to the goals listed above. Service planning incorporates maximizing performance characteristics as well as providing ease of use, security, and adaptability to user environments. Capacity planning, on the other hand, can be used to optimize the available capacity of the network, which, in turn, will optimize the network costs.

Another consideration is that design goals may change in priority from one part of the network to another. You may have a user group that requires high-performance in one area (like a work group or computing cluster), which will require a high-cost solution, while the rest of the network is optimized to reduce costs.

It is quite possible that, in trying to establish your goals, you will find that the customer/users want everything: a solution that is low-cost, high-performance, easy to use, and adaptable. At this point you can: 1) pull your hair out (if you have any left by now); 2) arbitrarily choose one or more goals; 3) attempt to show the trade-offs to your customers/end users, or 4) let the customers/end users prioritize their goals for the system. You can develop an argument for or against a design goal by developing a list of trade-offs associated with the design goal and presenting them to the customers/end users. One often-used argument is the trade-off between cost and performance. A graph showing the relative costs of technologies, listed for each area of the network, allows those who make funding decisions to pick the level(s) of performance and to understand the costs associated with each level.

Figure 8-2 shows a graph comparing cost and performance for candidate tech-nologies. A graph like this can be used to show that, for extra funding, a different technology can be used that will bring better performance or function to the users and applications.

FIGURE 8-2. **Cost/Performance Graph**

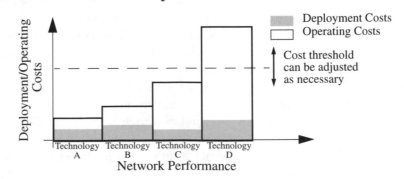

The result of determining your design goals is a set of prioritized goals, based on a primary design goal and one or more secondary goals. The primary design goal will override the other goals when considering trade-offs between the goals and will drive the design. When the primary goal is met, the secondary goals will be used to finish the design. There are times when the design goal will also be a constraint on the design. Constraints are thresholds that we will not be allowed to cross, or that we will have to pay a penalty to cross. Examples of constraints are overall deployment or operations budgets, strict network performance requirements, physical factors (e.g., the distances, delays, and propagation speed of electromagnetic radiation), or deployment time schedules.

For example, let's consider a design environment where we are going to build a local work group network. For this design, we have been budgeted $2 million to be used to purchase PCs and the network. This budget does not include installation, operation, or maintenance for the PCs or network. Each PC will cost about $2500, and we are required to have between 300 and 600 PCs in the network, depending on how much we spend on the network. However, we cannot have less than 300 PCs in the network. These PCs will be working together in work groups of 32 to 64 to compute solutions, and their performance requirements are estimated as: capacity, 80 Mb/s; delay (between any two PCs in a work group), 100 microseconds.

For this design environment, we are constrained by cost, the minimum number of PCs in the network, and by performance, particularly delay within the work group. A graph of budget allocations for PCs and the network—including NIC cards, LAN/work group hardware and software, and cable infrastructure if necessary—would look like Figure 8-3.

FIGURE 8-3. **Budget Allocations for Example**

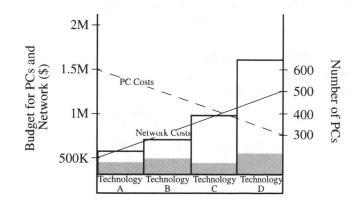

Figure 8-3 shows the range of network and PC costs, which will total $2 million, and provide between 300 and 600 PCs for the network. This graph also shows the available technologies within allowable network costs. If we have a primary design goal of minimizing the overall budget for this environment, we could choose to minimize the number of PCs, which will give us more funds for the network (possibly giving us better network performance), while reducing the overall budget. If the design goal was to maximize network performance, we could reduce the number of PCs and use the remaining funds for the network, which does not reduce the overall budget but will maximize the funds available for the network. Another possible design goal for this environment could be to make this work group network available to as many users as possible. This would drive us to maximize the number of PCs on the network, reducing both funding for the network and probably the network performance.

Thus, the choices that we make for primary and secondary design goals will affect our evaluation of the network design. It is important that you understand your design goals as you begin the design process.

8.3 Developing Criteria for Technology Evaluation

In preparation for making technology choices for our network design, we will examine the characteristics of technologies that are important from a design perspective. We start by analyzing the design goals for this environment, along with the service-planning and capacity-planning information from the flowspec, and translate this information into evaluation criteria.

Design goals can often be used as evaluation criteria themselves, or can easily be translated into evaluation criteria. Minimizing network deployment and operations costs, and maximizing ease of use for users and network personnel, lead to choosing technologies based on the criteria that are relatively simple and intuitive (that is, if any network technology can be thought of as intuitive). This also leads to choosing technologies that are standards-based and commonly available, and are well documented. Commercial off-the-shelf (COTS) network products come to mind here.

Maximizing performance leads to choosing technologies that meet or exceed expected capacity, delay, and/or reliability requirements. Maximizing reliability will also indicate a need for redundancy in the network, either through the choice of technology, how the technology is applied, redundancy in the routing protocols, or a combination of all of these. Technologies that maximize performance are likely to be more complex solutions, trading off the criteria of simplicity and cost. Performance may also indicate a need for specified (deterministic and/or guaranteed) services in the design, which will require a mechanism to provide specified service, and technology and protocol choices that can support services.

Adaptability is acknowledging that the design environment will be dynamic, and that your technology choices will need to support dynamic behavior, such as rapid reconfiguration of user groups, address assignments, routing, and location adds/drops to/from the network. An example of adaptability in the WAN would be to choose a network service from a service provider instead of building a private WAN infrastructure. Many of these are parts of the virtual network concept. Adaptability may also be applied to traffic flows, where we will want to distinguish between flows and handle (switch or route) each flow independently.

From the flowspec, we can do service and capacity planning. With service planning, we expect some level of specified performance from the network. This indicates that one of the important design goals will be to maximize one or more network performance characteristics. Some of the other service design goals—such as ease of use and manageability, optimizing security, or adaptability—may also be important to your design. Basically, when looking at network performance characteristics in the design, you should automatically also consider the other service-oriented goals.

In contrast, capacity planning means that we expect to combine multiple capacity requirements over a common technology. This is one of the considerations when trying to optimize cost for the network. Thus, the design goal of minimizing network deployment or operations costs is part of capacity planning. This does not mean that service planning excludes cost optimization, or that capacity planning excludes services. They help to indicate what the primary design goal(s) may be. Figure 8-4 illustrates the relationships between capacity and service plans (from the flow analysis) with our design goals.

FIGURE 8-4. **Design Goals, Capacity and Service Plans**

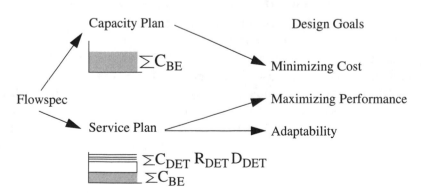

Once we have decided what the design goals of the network are, we look at the characteristics of technologies that will help us to achieve our design goals. Some of the characteristics that we consider are *nonbroadcast multiple access* (NBMA) and *broadcast capabilities*, service support, performance upgrade paths, and flow considerations.

8.3.1 NBMA and Broadcast Technologies

In developing criteria to evaluate and choose network technologies for your design, we want to look beyond their traditional characteristics—their capacities—to find other characteristics that are important from a design perspective. In addition to the capacities of technologies, we can find differences in the design characteristics of NBMA and broadcast technologies, in the types of services that they can support, their upgrade paths, and how they can meet the capacity and service plans of the flowspec.

In developing evaluation criteria, there are two important distinguishing characteristics between NBMA and broadcast technologies: *native broadcast support* and *connection support*.

Broadcast Support

Broadcast technologies support the ability of a host to communicate with or transmit to all other hosts on the directly attached network simultaneously, through using a well-known broadcast address. This means that every host on the directly attached network can find and access every other host on that network. Traditional LAN technologies—such as Ethernet, Token Ring, and FDDI—are broadcast technologies. In order for networks to provide direct access between all computers, address resolution needs access to all computers. This is often done through use of broadcast. For example, the IP address resolution protocols ARP and RARP make use of this capability to resolve IP and link-layer addresses.

NBMA technologies do not inherently have a broadcast mechanism. This is not necessarily a problem, but it does mean that we will need to consider how IP address resolution will be supported in the NBMA environment. Depending on the technology and how it is used in the network, there are a number of mechanisms for supporting address resolution, including hardwiring network-to-link-layer address bindings in hosts, using vendor-specific broadcast support mechanisms, or using one of the evolving, standards-based mechanisms. NBMA technologies include ATM, Frame Relay, SMDS, and HiPPI. When a network design incorporates an NBMA technology, the design will need to ensure that multicast is provided for those services on the network that need it.

The lack of an inherent broadcast mechanism means that we have some flexibility in how we provide broadcast in the network. Since broadcast can be considered a mechanism for local, directly connected access, it has been one of the factors coupling logical networks with physical networks. Some NBMA networks can be flexible in their handling of broadcasts, so we can create logical subnetworks that are not coupled to any physical topology. This is a powerful design option, which we will see many times throughout this and the next few chapters. Of course, a trade-off with decoupling logical and physical networks is in ambiguity about the underlying network. When a physical network can contain a variety of logical networks (which may themselves be dynamic), it will require more information and more sophisticated techniques of monitoring and management, as we will see later.

When choosing appropriate technologies for the network, it is important to understand the nature of broadcast for each technology and what role(s) broadcast will play in your design. There are trade-offs between NBMA and broadcast technologies that will be of interest to us, including scalability and simplicity.

One of the fundamental principles of network design is that hierarchies form in the network as groups become larger. Groups can be of users, computers, applications, or higher-level abstractions of these, such as areas or autonomous systems (ASs). (An AS is one way to define an administrative domain—a set of networks that are administered by the same organization—where an AS number identifies the administrative organization.) A group may also be thought of as a collection of computers that have direct access to each other (e.g, an IP subnet or broadcast domain). As groups get larger, the broadcast traffic becomes more and more of a burden on the network, until it (or secondary effects) degrade or disrupt performance. Thus, we want to keep group sizes manageable. As a result, hierarchics form to separate groups.

Group sizes are intertwined with our technology choices and information from the flowspec. We want to size groups so that the steady-state, background broadcast traffic is a small percentage—a good rule of thumb is less than 2%—of the capacity of the technology. For a 10-Mb/s Ethernet, we would expect the background broadcast traffic to be no more than about 200 Kb/s. In order to turn background broadcast numbers into group sizes, we need to estimate how much broadcast traffic a source is likely to generate.

For a broadcast network, this group size would equate to the number of connections to the physical network (a shared Ethernet, Token Ring, or FDDI ring), or to the number of ports on a switch (as in switched Ethernet, Token Ring, FDDI, or ATM) or hub. We need to keep in mind that there are other sources of background broadcast traffic, such as from routing protocols, and that this needs to be taken into account also.

Connection Support

Another consideration for NBMA and broadcast technologies is their connection support, which is whether or not a connection is established by the technology when information is transferred over the network. A connection is associated with the mapping of addresses across the network. These addresses may have end-to-end significance if, for example, we use IP source and destination addresses, or local significance, such as virtual circuit address mapping at ATM switch ports. Connection support is tied to the ability of the technology or service to get state information about the network. In a sense, a connection-oriented technology or service must be able to get and maintain address configuration and status information about its end-to-end connections. This is one form of state information. We will examine three different types of state: *hard state*, *soft state*, and *stateless* (or *no state*).

Hard state is determining and maintaining connection information along the path of the connection, between source and destination. *Stateless* is not having to determine or maintain connection information between source and destination. *Soft state* is between the two, determining and maintaining state until the connection is established, or for a short period of time after the connection is established. *Stateful*, either hard or soft state, is often used to describe a connection-oriented technology, and *stateless* to describe a connectionless technology. Here we will default to these descriptions, but bear in mind that this does not always have to be the case. For example, state can be determined and maintained by the network or transport protocols, making a "connection" at that layer in the network. A connectionless technology does not itself have connection information and does not need to maintain state information (hard or soft state) within the network in order to transfer data.

Sometimes a technology or combination of technologies and protocols may allow an operation somewhere between connection-oriented and connectionless, treating some traffic as if it is transiting a connectionless path and others a connection-oriented path. Deciding how to handle different flows of traffic may be based on source/destination addresses, on flow information (estimated amount of flow, flow type), or some other session-based information.

A trade-off between using a stateful (hard and soft state) or stateless technology is the amount of overhead required to establish and maintain state versus the control over the end-to-end path offered by that state. A connection-oriented technology can offer support for services to a session, based on factors such as cost, delay/latency, or performance, and may be able to support monitoring and verification of the service for each session. If we are interested in supporting specified flows in the network, a connection-oriented (hard or soft state) approach is likely to be appropriate.

There are various types of overhead in supporting connections, in the major resources of the network (e.g., CPU, memory, bandwidth), and also in the monitoring, management, and security requirements. There is also a cost in the setup and teardown times for connections. When the traffic flows for a session are short-lived (e.g., one or two IP packets or ATM cells), then setup overhead (in terms of time and allocation of resources) can substantially reduce the performance of the application.

In order to balance these trade-offs and optimize the use of multiple technologies, some hybrid connection approaches are emerging. They use some state information to make decisions and apply time-outs to eliminate "old" state information. This is what is considered soft state. In Figure 8-5, state is shown being gathered from each device in the end-to-end path of the traffic flow.

Connection support is important when considering scalability and flexibility in evaluating technologies, as well as how services are offered on the network. Basically, the more control we wish to have over the end-to-end service that a network will offer, the greater the tendency is toward connection-oriented technologies. Of course, there are trade-offs in getting more control over an end-to-end connection, and here we need to consider the overhead with connections, the setup and teardown times, and the need for greater configuration control and management. For many environments, the gain in end-to-end control is worth the cost of these trade-offs.

Consider a technology where connections are made for each application session and traffic flow. There will be a delay while the connection is built, and this delay can be significant—up to seconds—depending on how much recent state information is available locally or, if it is not available, how long it takes to get state information (based on the signalling capability of the technology). Some applications may not be able to wait for this connection time and meet the performance expectations of the users. For example, since NFS is a local disk-access substitute, its total network disk-access latency must approximate local disk I/O.

FIGURE 8-5. Network State

System state is gathered from each device in end-to-end path.

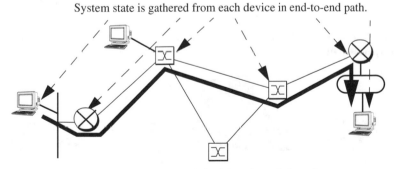

Stateless: Traffic is forwarded without knowledge of system state.
Soft State: System knowledge is short-lived.
Hard State: System knowledge is long-lived or permanent.

FIGURE 8-6. **System State as Part of Network Connections**

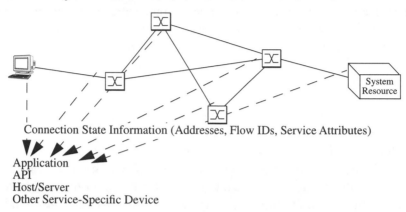

Connection State Information (Addresses, Flow IDs, Service Attributes)

Application
API
Host/Server
Other Service-Specific Device

Additionally, each network node in the path of the connection will keep some state information, local or global, about the connection. This requires memory and CPU that could otherwise be made available to other processes. In Figure 8-6, connection state information—such as host, resource, and network device addresses—are requested by the application/API/host that is establishing the connection, as part of determining if the connection can be set up, configured, and maintained.

The benefits of greater control over the end-to-end service can be substantial in some environments. When specified services are required, a connection-oriented technology with its state information may be the only solution. If a network is being designed for a mission-critical, interactive-burst application (e.g., a visualization application for medical imaging as in Figure 8-7), then it is well worth the overhead cost to design for connections in the network, as long as the connection overhead does not result in delays that are greater than the requirements of the application.

FIGURE 8-7. **Example of a Connection Establishment for a High-Performance Application**

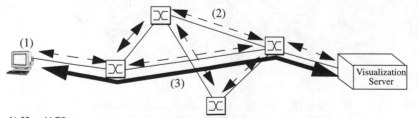

1) Host/API requests access to server resource.
2) State information is used to establish connection, including determining services offered to the host/API.
3) Connection is established.

A compromise can be made between these trade-offs, and the resulting orientation (either both connection and connectionless, depending on traffic type, destination address, and so on, or somewhere between connection and connectionless, where some state information is known) may be optimized for the types of flows in the network. There are other trade-offs here, including ambiguity in the routing of flows in the network, as well as a greater knowledge of the flow types in the network.

8.3.2 Functions and Features of the Technology

Another important design consideration is the set of functions and features that the technology will offer to the system—the sets of users, hosts, and their applications.

Some technologies can be used to help the network adapt to a specific user or application environment. Examples include adapting to a lack of communications infrastructure, such as in underdeveloped countries, in remote areas where terrestrial access is not easily available, or in environments where traditional access is not possible or is prohibitively expensive; adapting to the mobility of users or their resources; or adapting to users/applications that have strict performance requirements or well-understood behavior patterns.

While some of the adaptability will be provided by the various protocols operating in the network, the technology can also support or enhance this adaptability. Where a communications infrastructure or terrestrial access is not readily available, the use of wireless network technologies—by themselves or in addition to other technologies—should be considered. In most cases it will be obvious that a communications infrastructure is not feasible and that a nonstandard means of network access is required. Some extreme environments where nonstandard means of network access have been deployed are research vessels for real-time telemetry, command/control while on the open water; at disaster areas, such as forest fires, earthquakes, and floods; and at remote, inhospitable places, such as on Antarctica, near active volcanoes, even on the surfaces of distant planets (in the case of NASA's Sojourner rover).

These examples indicate that network access is possible for a wide variety of environments, given the right combination of network technologies, services, and protocols—and of course enough funding to deploy and maintain such access.

Similarly, support for the mobility of users may be provided by wireless networks, possibly in addition to having multiple network access points available to the user. For example, to support users who want access to the network from multiple locations both at home and work, and also want access from any location within the workplace via portable computers, then a wireless network would likely be a part of the overall network design. Such mobility also impacts how the user establishes a connection to the network, as in the dynamic allocation of network addresses or authenticating users.

When applications and their flows have performance requirements that are specified or well understood, we may be able to map their requirements to service levels offered by the technology. We would use the service plan of a flowspec such as those developed in Chapters 5, 6, and 7 to identify any specified requirements, then use these requirements to evaluate candidate technologies. In this case, the technology must be capable of supporting specified requirements, which, as we shall see, is much more complicated than most people recognize. Such support may range from Frame Relay committed information rates (CIRs), SMDS access classes, or their equivalents, to ATM quality of service (QOS) or IP type of service (TOS) levels, to combinations of these with resource reservation or allocation mechanisms.

On rare occasions, some of the behavior patterns of the users and/or applications may be well understood or predictable. When this occurs, the design may be able to take advantage of this by mapping network performance levels to flow characteristics, directions, or patterns. Many flow patterns are asymmetric, with much more information flowing to the user than from the user. This was seen in the client-server and cooperative-computing environments discussed in Chapter 5. When it is expected that a flow will be asymmetric, as in Figure 8-8, we can design the network to optimize the directionality of the flow.

Many good examples of this are seen in the usage patterns on the Internet. Web access, for example, is predominately asymmetric, with flows toward users. Services are being developed to support such flows from the Internet, utilizing the asymmetric, broadcast capabilities in cable, radio, and television networks. Hybrid fiber-cable systems and xDSL also allow users, especially residential clients/customers, to take advantage of asymmetry in network flows.

FIGURE 8-8. Asymmetric Flows in a Network

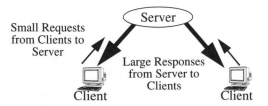

When considering the functions and features of various technologies, we need to understand the requirements of the design environment and how a technology's functions or features will support that environment, as well as those technologies that will provide a value-added service to the customer. When considering the customer environment, we want to consider distance limitations, locations without infrastructure, locations that are mobile, or any way that the environment complicates or constrains the design.

Distance limitations may force constraints on the delay or reliability characteristics. For example, it will be impossible to guarantee a 40-ms round-trip delay for a flow if the distance is transpacific. This will impact the design in how the communications are provided (e.g., satellite versus cable), or how the flow is modeled (e.g., changing from a transpacific cooperative-computing environment to a local client-server environment with data migration). We want to look for design environments that have long-distance, high-delay communications paths, as these will create high *bandwidth*delay* products (which describes how much information can be in transit across a network at any given time). Since a high bandwidth*delay product means that there will be a lot of data in transit, this requires either large amounts of buffering on the sending side, highly reliable connections, good error and flow control, or all of these in the network.

Many designs face infrastructure constraints. If the design includes access to isolated or restricted areas, or if mobility is required, then use of a wireless technology should be considered.

Value-added service may be one or more support services, such as accounting, security, or network management, or value-added for a specific design environment. Some of the ATM features such as LAN emulation (LANE) or multiprotocol over ATM (MPOA) could be considered value-added, as well as the security features in the access lists of SMDS.

Capacity Upgrade Paths

Part of the function and feature set of a technology is its ability to be upgraded, particularly from a capacity perspective. Most, if not all, technologies have evolutionary paths that upgrade capacity with time. Part of the design process is to consider these upgrade paths and how they may be a part of planning where to put each technology, and when they should be upgraded or replaced.

If a technology (such as shared Ethernet) traditionally supports 10-Mb/s capacity, and is currently capable of supporting 100 Mb/s to 1 Gb/s, this information can be used in capacity planning to upgrade areas of the network as individual, composite, and backbone flows increase in capacity, or as specified flows are added to the network.

Technologies that can use the synchronous optical network (SONET) hierarchy (such as HiPPI or ATM) can have a capacity growth path based on selected SONET levels. Each SONET optical carrier (OC) level is a multiple of the base rate, OC-1 (51.84 Mb/s). This comes from the size of a SONET frame (9 rows by 90 columns) and the clock rate (125 microseconds), resulting in 8000 frames per second:

$$\text{(9 rows)*(90 columns)*(1 byte/row-column)(8000 frames/second)*(8 bits/byte)} = 51.84 \text{ Mb/s}$$

Commonly used (or expected) SONET OC levels are as follows, where the lowercase "c" in OC-Nc refers to a concatenated service, and where N SONET payloads are combined over a common path and the redundant overhead is removed, resulting in more efficient transmission.

SONET Level	Rate
OC-3c	155.52 Mb/s
OC-12c	622 Mb/s
OC-48c	2.488 Gb/s
OC-192c	9.953 Gb/s

There are many factors to consider in deciding on an upgrade path for your network. Some of these factors are how dynamic your NIC cards are (i.e., whether they can support multiple rates), the types of cable and distances of cable runs available in your infrastructure, and the types of optics in your network elements. In addition, some upgrade paths can be accomplished by configuration changes in the network elements or by software upgrades.

Common upgrade paths include Ethernet from 10 Mb/s to 1 Gb/s; FDDI from 100 Mb/s to 1 Gb/s; high-performance parallel interface (HiPPI) from 800 Mb/s to 1.6 Gb/s to SuperHiPPI at 6.4 Gb/s; ATM from 1.5 Mb/s to 622 Mb/s (currently); and Frame Relay from 56 Kb/s to 45 Mb/s. Some of these are shown in Figure 8-9.

There are also expansions into both higher and lower capacities for some technologies. Looking at ATM, Frame Relay, and SMDS in Figure 8-10, we can see how each service has overlapped into other service capacities.

Network designs should take into account the capacity upgrade paths of candidate technologies, and the upgrade paths can be one of the criteria for choosing a technology for each part of the network, especially for areas in the design environment that will interconnect other areas and are likely to be dynamic, like backbone areas.

FIGURE 8-9. **Expected Capacity Ranges for Selected Technologies**

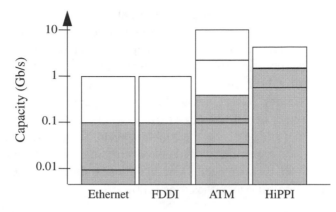

FIGURE 8-10. **Overlap in ATM/SMDS/Frame Relay Capacity Ranges**

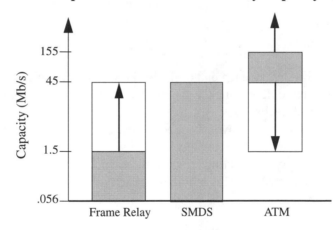

In using capacity upgrade paths as a criterion, as with the other criteria, we want to consider the scalability of our network design based on growth in the numbers of users, computers, applications, and networks; but we should also consider the differences between composite, and backbone flows and how they affect scalability.

From Figures 8-9 and 8-10, we can see that each technology has a range of rates and that many of the ranges overlap. For many of these technologies, a capacity upgrade requires a change in hardware, in network interfaces for the computers and/or at the network elements. As part of evaluating candidates for capacity upgrades, we want to consider the potential cost of changing hardware.

Backbone Flows

Capacity upgrades are particularly important to consider for backbone flows. Backbone flows are the focal points in consolidating flows, or where hierarchies are established. As such, they are more susceptible to growth in capacity, and they usually need to be more scalable than any other part of the network.

In predicting the growth of backbone flows, we can use the method presented in the previous section for scaling all flows, but depending on the hierarchy of the network this may not be sufficient. Generally, when the hierarchy is less than four (the consolidation of traffic across the backbone is a factor of less than four), then the scaling method used earlier will likely be sufficient. When the hierarchy is four or greater, however, then we need to modify the scalability for the backbone. A general scaling guideline for backbones is as follows:

Hierarchy	Scaling Factor
< 4:1	1
4:1 to 6:1	1.5
7:1 to 9:1	2

The hierarchy for each end of the backbone is considered, as well as the largest hierarchy used to determine the scaling factor. This is then mapped to the capacity ranges for each technology.

In Figure 8-11, we have a backbone flow of capacity 3.15 Mb/s and hierarchies of 2:1 and 5:1. We use the greatest hierarchy, 5:1, to determine the scaling factor, 1.5, then multiply this scaling factor to the capacity to get a modified backbone capacity of 4.725 Mb/s. This modified capacity is used to evaluate technologies for the backbone.

FIGURE 8-11. Modifying Backbone Capacities by Degree of Hierarchy

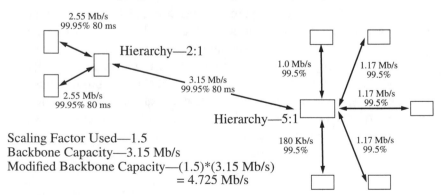

8.3.3 Flow Considerations

Our last evaluation criterion is based on the requirements from the existing or expected flows in the network. The flowspec will be used as the starting point in evaluating candidate technologies based upon the requirements of each individual, composite, and backbone flow for capacity characteristics (capacity planning) and specified services (service planning).

- *Capacity planning* will be used to determine the required capacities of candidate technologies. In the next section we will discuss how to estimate usage and modify flow capacities to reflect this usage. The result will be baseline capacities that we can compare against the available capacities of technologies.

- *Service planning* is also used to evaluate candidate technologies. Each candidate technology will be evaluated on its ability to provide the degree of specified service support required by the flowspec.

Table 8-1 presents evaluation criteria, as applied to some selected technologies.

TABLE 8-1. **Evaluation Criteria for Selected Technologies**

Technology	Broadcast Capability	Connection Support	Functions and Features	Capacity Upgrades
Ethernet	Broadcast	Connectionless	Potential support with CIF	10 Mb/s nominal, 100 Mb/s to 1 Gb/s available; shared and switched versions available
Token Ring	Broadcast	Connectionless	Deterministic for high traffic loads	4 Mb/s and 16 Mb/s available; shared and switched versions available
FDDI	Broadcast	Connectionless	Deterministic for high traffic loads	100 Mb/s, 1 Gb/s expected; shared and switched versions available
ATM	NBMA	Connection-oriented	Specified support through QOS	Available on T1, T3, and SONET OC-3c, OC-12c, with OC-48c and OC-192c planned

TABLE 8-1. Evaluation Criteria for Selected Technologies *(Continued)*

Technology	Broadcast Capability	Connection Support	Functions and Features	Capacity Upgrades
HiPPI	NBMA	Connection-oriented	Specialized as high-performance LAN technology	Available at 800 Mb/s to 1.6 Gb/s, with SuperHiPPI at up to 6.4 Gb/s planned
Frame Relay	NBMA	Connection-oriented	Support through CIRs	Available from 56 Kb/s through T3
SMDS	NBMA	Connection-less from user perspective	Support through access classes	Available at 4, 10, 16, 25, and 34 Mb/s, but also offered at 56 Kb/s

8.3.4 Guidelines and Constraints on Technology Evaluations

We will be using the information from our flowspec to evaluate technologies based on the combined capacity requirements for best-effort services, or on the reliability, capacity, and/or delay requirements for specified services.

In the capacity and service plans of the flowspec, we combined the capacity requirements of all best-effort and deterministic services for each flow, while we chose the highest-performance reliability and delay characteristics for the specified flows. These capacity, reliability, and delay characteristics are used to determine the ability of candidate technologies to support specified services, and the combined capacity characteristics are used to evaluate the capacity characteristics of each candidate technology. Following are two rules of thumb for evaluating technologies based on capacity and service plans:

Rule 1: If specified requirements are specified in the flowspec (the service plan), then either the technology or a combination of technology and supporting protocols or mechanisms must support specified services. This guideline restricts the selection of candidate technologies to those that can support specified services.

We can divide this rule into two portions: support for deterministic services and support for guaranteed services. Let's examine deterministic services first. Recall that a deterministic service provides predictable or bounded operation. The objective of having a deterministic service is to reduce the variabilities in reliability, capacity, and delay in components of the network, in order to offer a more predictable service to end users. While determinism in the service results in a better-understood and more predictable service to end users and applications, it does not mean that the service is guaranteed to provide a particular level of performance.

What will distinguishing between best-effort and deterministic services mean to an operational network that incorporates these design rules? Why not just treat all services, including deterministic services, as best-effort? This is basically saying that all traffic flows are the same, which they most definitely are not. From traffic flows that have no timing requirements (e.g., email), to real-time and mission-critical flows (e.g., telemetry, image processing, and on-line transaction processing), to bursty interactive traffic flows (e.g., Web applications), each flow type has individual performance characteristics that require services from the network. Therefore, we need to be able to recognize services and distinguish between service types.

There are a couple of reasons for distinguishing between services. First, by separating out those flows that have strict capacity, delay, and/or reliability requirements, we are taking the first steps toward offering multiple, various services to end users. As mechanisms for offering services become better understood and widely available, we will be prepared to take advantage of these services in the network design. This is not to say that mechanisms do not exist today, but that they are relatively primitive.

Second, flows that require deterministic services need to be handled differently by the network. Given the nature of deterministic requirements in flows, they are not as tolerant as best-effort flows to variances in network performance. Thus, we need to ensure that deterministic flows receive more predictable performance characteristics from the network. This is the basis for our selection of candidate technologies for deterministic flows.

Example 8.1—Multipart Flowspec

Flows	Reliability	Capacity	Delay
f1		225 Kb/s	
f2	98.0%	900 Kb/s	100 ms
f3		240 Kb/s	80 ms
f4 (g)	99.9%	3.2 Mb/s (g)	45 ms (g)
f5		640 Kb/s	60 ms
Composite Flows			
CF1	99.9%	240 Kb/s	80 ms
Guaranteed Service		3.2 Mb/s	45 ms
CF3	98.0%	240 Kb/s	80 ms
Guaranteed Service		3.2 Mb/s	45 ms
CF6	98.0%	1.14 Mb/s	80 ms
CF7	98.0%	1.14 Mb/s	80 ms
CF8	98.0%	1.14 Mb/s	80 ms

Backbone Flows

BB1		240 Kb/s	80 ms
BB2		240 Kb/s	80 ms
BB3		240 Kb/s	80 ms
BB4		240 Kb/s	80 ms
BB5	98.0%	1.14 Mb/s	80 ms

In this flowspec, we have best-effort service for individual flow f1; deterministic service for individual flows f2, f3, f4, f5, composite flows CF1, CF3, CF6, CF7, CF8, and backbone flows BB1, BB2, BB3, BB4, BB5; and guaranteed service for individual flow f4 and composite flows CF1, CF3. The deterministic service requirements are for reliability, capacity, and delay, while the guaranteed service requirements are for capacity and delay.

For all of the flows that have deterministic requirements, individual flows f2, f3, f4, f5, composite flows CF1, CF3, CF6, CF7, CF8, and backbone flows BB1, BB2, BB3, BB4, BB5, we want to choose candidate technologies that can support these requirements. Since deterministic service is a predictable, or bounded, service, we want technologies that can provide service predictability, or bounds. Some mechanisms to consider:

- QOS levels in ATM
- CIR levels in Frame Relay
- Access classes in SMDS
- NBMA or broadcast technologies, using the resource reservation protocol (RSVP)

These options provide more predictability than traditional best-effort services, yet do not guarantee service to the end user.

For example, we have the options of using ATM with a constant bit rate (CBR) or variable bit rate (VBR) service level; ATM, Frame Relay, SMDS, HiPPI, dedicated circuits, Ethernet, Token Ring, FDDI, or a combination of these, with RSVP.

Support for guaranteed service is much more stringent than for deterministic services. In the flowspec above, we have guaranteed service for individual flow f4 and composite flows CF1, CF3. For these flows, we want to choose technologies that can meet guaranteed capacity and delay requirements. In order to offer a service guarantee to a flow, a technology must be capable of

- Determining the state of the end-to-end path of the flow
- Controlling the resources of each network element in the end-to-end path of the flow

- Providing a mechanism to arbitrate who gets or keeps the service when it is contended for

Note that a guaranteed service is meaningful only when it services an end-to-end flow. This means that all components of the system must understand and support the guaranteed service, including the network elements, host interfaces, host operating system, and applications. Thus, a guaranteed service is the most difficult to provision and operate, and will be the most expensive service to offer to end users.

For a service to be guaranteed to a flow, the state of all network elements, as well as the host components, must be determined for that flow. There must be some mechanism to keep and provide state information in all of these elements, and a mechanism to get this information in order to make a service decision.

If a guaranteed service is to be offered to the flow, then the appropriate resources will then be configured in each of the network elements in the flow path, and possibly within the end hosts. Resources that may be configured in the network elements include

- Buffer allocations, including the establishment of multiple queues and prioritizing services across them
- CPU
- Input or output capacity, probably linked to buffer allocations

In addition, the service needs to determine how to handle periods when there are more service requests than available resources (periods of contention). One method is to offer services on a first-come, first-served basis. Using this method, when the resources are fully utilized, no more service guarantees are given until resources become available. This method is not likely to be used on a large scale, as it promotes holding onto a service as long as possible, even if it is not needed. Another method is to use priorities to determine which flows get service during periods of contention. In this method, a flow may get "downgraded" from guaranteed service to deterministic or best-effort service if a higher-priority flow needs the service.

At this time, for guaranteed service requirements we should consider ATM with its service levels, particularly CBR service for guaranteed capacity. It is expected that guaranteed delay and reliability will become available in the near future, and that other technologies will support guaranteed service.

Thus, for the flowspec example, we could select the following candidate technologies for guaranteed service: For individual flow f4 and composite flows CF1, CF3, the guaranteed service is 3.2-Mb/s capacity and 45-ms delay. The candidate technology is ATM, with a CBR service of 3.2 Mb/s for each flow. The 45-ms delay could be provided by designing a dedicated end-to-end path for the flow, keeping the distance below physical (speed-of-light) limits.

$\Diamond \Diamond \Diamond$

Rule 2: If best-effort and/or specified capacities are specified in the flowspec, then the selection of technology may also be based upon capacity planning for each flow. Capacity planning is using the summary capacities from the flowspec to select candidate technologies, and determining scalability of the technologies based on capacities and growth expectations.

In the flowspec we developed capacity estimates for each individual, composite, and backbone flow. Each of these estimates was based on a single session of an application, and did not consider the impact of multiple concurrent sessions. But usually we do not know the application usage patterns of our users. There are, however, some general patterns that we can use. If we can estimate the number of concurrent sessions within a flow, then we will multiply the capacity of that flow by the number of concurrent sessions. If we cannot estimate the number of concurrent sessions within a flow, then we will use the capacity estimate from the flowspec.

When comparing the capacity estimates from the flowspec to the capacities provided by candidate technologies, we want to develop a threshold capacity that will indicate that a technology capacity is insufficient for the flow. In capacity planning, we want to design toward this threshold capacity and make sure that the technology has capacity to spare. If the flow contains only best-effort capacities, then a rule of thumb is for the summary capacity of that flow to be 60% of the threshold capacity for that flow. If the flow contains deterministic capacities, then the rule of thumb is for the deterministic capacity of that flow to be 80% of the threshold capacity, or 60% of the summary capacities of the best-effort component of the flow, whichever is greater.

These rules of thumb are based on experience and should be used as a first attempt to evaluate technologies based on capacity. As you use these rules, you should be able to modify them to better approximate your design environments. For example, if you know the degree of burstiness in the application, you can use it to modify the threshold capacity. Some bursty environments are designed to the threshold capacity divided by the burstiness. Thus, if the burstiness (MDR/SDR) on a deterministic application is 5, then the design is based on 80% of the threshold capacity divided by 5, resulting in 16% of the threshold capacity. Doing this enables the network to accommodate a much higher capacity during times of bursts from the application. To be able to use these guidelines, you need to know if the flowspec used MDRs or SDRs, and what the maximum throughput is for each candidate technology.

Following are some estimates for maximum throughput with TCP/IP. These estimates are from experience, and you should note that these numbers may vary depending on the type of OS you are using.

Technology		Maximum Capacity	Maximum Throughput
Ethernet		10 Mb/s	3–7 Mb/s
		100 Mb/s	80–95 Mb/s
Token Ring		4 Mb/s	4 Mb/s
		16 Mb/s	16 Mb/s
FDDI		100 Mb/s	80–100 Mb/s
ATM:	T3	45 Mb/s	34 Mb/s
	OC-3c	155.52 Mb/s	120 Mb/s
	OC-12c	622 Mb/s	Not yet available
HiPPI		800 Mb/s	350–500 Mb/s
		1.6 Gb/s	Not yet available
Frame Relay		45 Mb/s	45 Mb/s
SMDS		4 Mb/s	4 Mb/s
		16 Mb/s	16 Mb/s
		25 Mb/s	25 Mb/s
		34 Mb/s	34 Mb/s

Example 8.2—Unitary Flowspec

Composite Flow	Area	Capacity (SDR)
F1	WAN	170 Kb/s
F2	WAN	70 Kb/s
F3	WAN	500 Kb/s
F4	LAN	29.5 Mb/s
F5	LAN	6 Mb/s

Backbone Flow	Area	Capacity (SDR)
BB1	WAN	2.07 Mb/s
BB2	LAN	8.7 Mb/s

Since these capacities are SDRs, we will use the guideline that capacity must be less than 60% of the maximum capacity for a candidate technology. To find the maximum capacity needed to support each flow at 60%, we divide each capacity by 0.60, which gives

Composite Flow	Area	Capacity (SDR)	Maximum Capacity Needed
F1	WAN	170 Kb/s	283 Kb/s
F2	WAN	70 Kb/s	117 Kb/s
F3	WAN	500 Kb/s	833 Kb/s
F4	LAN	29.5 Mb/s	49.2 Mb/s
F5	LAN	6 Mb/s	10 Mb/s

Backbone Flow	Area	Capacity (SDR)	Maximum Capacity Needed
BB1	WAN	2.07 Mb/s	3.45 Mb/s
BB2	LAN	8.7 Mb/s	14.5 Mb/s

For WAN flows F1, F2, and F3, candidate technologies include Frame Relay, SMDS, ATM, or dedicated circuits (such as fractional T1). For the backbone WAN flow BB1, we will need capacity beyond T1. We could apply a 4-Mb/s SMDS service, a Frame Relay service with a CIR at or above 4 Mb/s, or an ATM service with a CBR or VBR service at or above 4 Mb/s.

For LAN flow F4, candidate technologies include ATM OC-3c, FDDI, Ethernet (100 Mb/s), and HiPPI. LAN flow F5 candidates are Ethernet (10 Mb/s or 100 Mb/s), Token Ring (16 Mb/s), FDDI, and ATM (at 25 Mb/s, T3, or OC-3c). Backbone LAN flow BB2, at 14.5 Mb/s, could be handled with Token Ring (16 Mb/s), Ethernet (100 Mb/s), FDDI, or ATM (25 Mb/s, T3, or OC-3c).

◊ ◊ ◊

If growth expectations are available, we can use them in combination with the flowspec to estimate scalability for the network design. We may base growth estimates on the number of users in the network, as in the following example.

Example 8.3—Estimating Scalability

Composite Flow	Capacity	Maximum Capacity	Users
F1 (LAN)	12.7 Mb/s (SDR)	21.2 Mb/s	900
F2 (WAN)	1.35 Mb/s (SDR)	2.25 Mb/s	1200
F3 (LAN)	31.5 Mb/s (MDR)	39.4 Mb/s	1600
F4 (LAN)	1.05 Mb/s (SDR)	1.75 Mb/s	250

Backbone Flow	Capacity	Maximum Capacity	Users
BB1 (LAN)	44.0 Mb/s (MDR)	55 Mb/s	1250
BB2 (WAN)	1.8 Mb/s (SDR)	3.0 Mb/s	1950

Where total number of users = 2100
User growth estimates are 20% for year 1, 25% for year 2, and 10% for years 3 to 5

Note that maximum capacity was calculated with a factor of 60% (0.60) for capacities based on SDR, and a factor of 80% (0.80) for capacities based on MDR. Now we apply the growth estimates for each year of the 5-year series:

	Maximum Capacity (in Mb/s)					
Flow	Year 0	Year 1	Year 2	Year 3	Year 4	Year 5
F1	21.2	25.4	31.8	35.0	38.5	42.3
F2	2.25	2.7	3.4	3.7	4.1	4.5
F3	39.4	47.3	59.1	65.0	71.5	78.7
F4	1.75	2.1	2.6	2.9	3.2	3.5
BB1	55.0	66.0	82.5	90.8	99.8	109.8
BB2	3.0	3.6	4.5	5.0	5.4	6.0

This chart provides us with an estimate of expected maximum capacity for the next 6 years. When looking at a chart such as this, a reasonable question is: How much of this is useful? Experience has shown that network technologies cycle about every 3 years, so a reasonable approach is to base technology choices on 3-year growth. This 3-year cycle is actually part of a more sophisticated approach, using the 3-year cycle as a sliding window, where the first 6 months (or 1 year) is well-known (and well-budgeted), and the outlying 2.5 or 2 years is budgeted based on best guesses regarding expected technologies.

Another reasonable approach is based on the customer's typical cycle time. If the customer changes out other equipment every 5 years, for example, then it is probable that budgeting for networks will occur along the same cycle. We would then use a 5-year estimate.

In this example, we will base our estimate on a 3-year cycle. In scaling our design for the third year, we have:

Flow	Maximum C (Year 0)	Maximum C (Year 3)	Users (Year 3)
F1 (LAN)	21.2 Mb/s	35.0 Mb/s	1485

F2 (WAN)	2.25 Mb/s	3.7 Mb/s	1980
F3 (LAN)	39.4 Mb/s	65.0 Mb/s	2640
F4 (LAN)	1.75 Mb/s	2.9 Mb/s	412
BB1 (LAN)	55.0 Mb/s	90.8 Mb/s	2062
BB2 (WAN)	3.0 Mb/s	5.0 Mb/s	3218

The third-year estimate helps us to determine if a technology choice will support planned growth, and if not, if the choice should be changed or a design modification planned by year 3. LAN flows F1 and F3 are in the range of 100 Mb/s Ethernet, FDDI, or ATM OC-3c. If T3 ATM was chosen for any of these flows, it would have to be reevaluated by year 3. Backbone LAN flow BB1 is at the border of performance for 100 Mb/s Ethernet or FDDI by year 3, yet is well within limits for ATM OC-3c. HiPPI may also be a consideration for the LAN flows. At year 3, LAN flow F4 is still well within limits for 10 Mb/s Ethernet or 4 Mb/s Token Ring. For WAN flows F2 and BB2, services will have to be above T1 rate. At this point, Frame Relay, SMDS, and ATM are all candidates.

Another method to achieve scaling is through the proper choice of an interconnection mechanism, which is discussed in Chapter 9.

Constraints on Candidate Technologies

There are two potentially major constraints on the selection of candidate technologies: the cost of each candidate and preexisting networks.

When a list of candidates has been developed, we can prioritize the list, much the same way we prioritized the flows in Chapter 6. If we already have a cost-prioritized list of flows, we can apply that cost information to the area that the flow is in, and the candidates for that area. For example, let us consider the following list of cost-prioritized flows (where costs are nonrecurring network hardware and installation for technologies, and may include first-year service costs for services):

Composite Flow	Cost (Budget)	Candidate Technologies
BB1 (LAN)	$425K	100 Mb/s Ethernet or FDDI ATM OC-3c
F2 (WAN)	$350K	ATM T3 Frame Relay T3
F3 (LAN)	$200K	10 Mb/s Ethernet 16 Mb/s Token Ring
F4 (LAN)	$125K	10 Mb/s Ethernet 4 Mb/s Token Ring

For each area (in this case, each LAN/WAN and Flow ID), we would compare the equipment and installation costs for each technology to the budget allocated for that area. This would either eliminate some candidates or result in a cost-prioritized list of candidates.

When there are existing networks, we will need to consider their characteristics—both the constraints they impose on the design and the features that they offer to it. From the flow considerations, the composite and backbone flows can be impacted when they connect to an existing network. If we have a requirement in the flowspec for a capacity of 40 Mb/s, but the flow directly connects to a 10 Mb/s Ethernet, then either the requirements and/or flow analyses were not done correctly, the existing technology needs to be upgraded, or the flow cannot be supported by the design. During this evaluation and selection process, analyzing flows that connect to existing networks should identify when an existing network needs to be upgraded or replaced.

Existing networks may support the new design. For example, it may be possible to use existing LAN cabling for switched or faster LAN technologies. Likewise, some WAN technologies, like ATM, Frame Relay, or SMDS, may already provide connectivity with existing hardware, and may only require a reconfiguration or software upgrade to support a higher-capacity backbone or composite flow.

The result of evaluating technologies based on the criteria presented in this section is to select a list of candidates for us to apply to the design. While a process has been presented here, you will likely want to modify it by adding or eliminating sections. You may also find that one or more of the sections—connection orientation, multicast support, offered capabilities and services, or performance upgrades—are not appropriate for your design. The section on flow considerations, however, should be applicable to all designs.

8.4 Making Technology Choices for the Design

Now that we have developed some evaluation criteria for candidate technologies, we can begin the process of evaluating candidates for our design. In this section, we develop some general guidelines for evaluating technologies, with the goal of producing a reasonable number of candidates for each area of the design. Two candidates per area is reasonable; if one candidate is obviously above the rest, then the evaluation process was successful; when there are several candidates (more than two), either the evaluation process needs improvement, the requirements and flows have not been sufficiently described, or the candidate technologies are very similar based on the evaluation criteria. In the latter case, you should reexamine the requirements and flow that you used.

In evaluating candidate technologies, we will use the evaluation criteria from the previous section. In addition, we will consider constraints imposed upon the selection of technologies, based on cost or the precondition of existing networks. In making technology choices, we will first segment the network into workable sizes, then apply a method that is termed *black box* to isolate each area, and then apply the evaluation criteria and design guidelines to each area. The result will be one or more technology candidates for each area of the design.

8.4.1 Sizing the Network

One of the problems we face in designing networks is that they are usually so large that it is hard to absorb detailed information about the whole design. This is one of the most common complaints about designing a network—where to begin. What is needed is a way to segment the design into workable parts, here termed *areas*. The area concept that is developed here will be similar to the flow boundaries we used in the last chapter, as well as routing, addressing, and administrative areas that are used later in this book. Sizing the network is a first step toward making the design workable.

There are a few different ways to size and segment the network. We could segment the network based on geography, concentrations of users, or flow hierarchy. At times, all of these methods will produce similar results, so you should choose the method that makes the most sense and works best for you. Sizing the network by geography is done by segmenting the network into areas whose sizes are based on geographic sections. These sections may range from countries, states, or cities to areas within a city, campuses, buildings, or parts of a building. If a network is being designed to interconnect offices in various cities, one way to size the network is to divide it into individual city networks (LANs or MANs), and a WAN to interconnect them, as in Figure 8-12.

FIGURE 8-12. Sizing the Network Design at the LAN/WAN Level

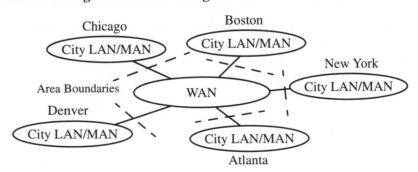

FIGURE 8-13. Sizing the Network at the Campus Level

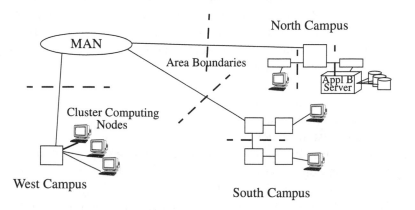

At a campus level, we segment the network by buildings or parts of buildings, such as in the example in Figure 8-13 of a campus network design.

Similarly, we can divide the network design based on the numbers of users or on their relative concentrations. This may or may not equate to divisions based on geography. Instead of showing geographic information, we describe the numbers of users, perhaps including groups that they belong to within the organization. In Figure 8-14, boundaries are placed between groups of users, regardless of their locations.

FIGURE 8-14. Sizing Based on User Concentrations

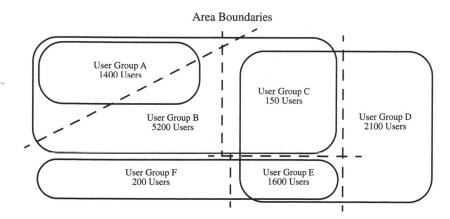

This method is particularly useful when virtual groups of users are to be supported. Virtual user groups are either groups that are not tied to a particular location, or groups that are dynamic in their locations, affiliations, or applications. Since at this point in the design process, we have some flexibility in describing user groups and their user concentrations, and in evaluating several methods for supporting virtual user groups, now is the time to design for these groups. In doing so, we can optimize the design for them.

Arguably the most useful way to size the network is by flow hierarchy. This method uses the flow analysis of the previous chapter to show where potential hierarchies may exist in the network. In addition, this method has the benefit of showing end-to-end service needs (via flows), which will be important when evaluating and applying technologies to the design. Consider the flow hierarchies of a flow diagram such as those shown in Figure 8-15.

Here we can use the locations where individual, composite, and backbone flows meet as borders to divide the network. These are usually where the flow boundaries were placed during the flow analysis. In the example above, we placed borders at five locations, resulting in six different network areas.

In a sense, sizing by flow hierarchy incorporates the geographic and user-group methods. Since flows are end-to-end between users, applications, and hosts, and their requirements have location information built into them, the geography and user-group information make up part of the flows.

FIGURE 8-15. **Sizing Based on Flow Hierarchies**

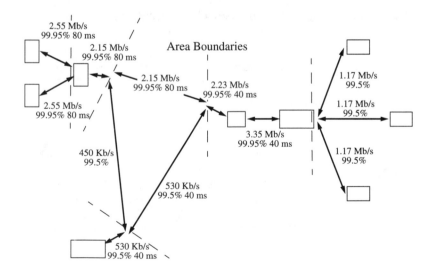

The goal of sizing the network is to segment the design into areas that are of workable sizes. This means that the numbers of users, hosts, networks (existing as well as planned), flows, and potential connections outside of this area are small enough so that it is possible for a single technology or service to reasonably support that area. This requires an understanding of how the various technologies size and scale. As you work through this chapter, you will find that sizing the network overlaps with evaluating and applying the technologies, so that as you analyze the network, sizing and technical evaluation of the network will overlap.

Some related parameters for sizing your network include the sizes of broadcast domains, the types of services requested by users, and the performance characteristics of flows in the network. A *broadcast domain* is a group of addresses that are all reachable by a single address, the *broadcast address*. As a broadcast domain increases in size, or as the number of broadcast protocols operating in a domain increases, the amount of broadcast traffic increases, impacting the overall performance of the network. It is desirable to keep the size of a broadcast domain reasonably small, especially if growth in the size of the network is expected.

An Alternate Method for Sizing Designs

One sizing method that is used often in the field is to size the network based on functions and features. For example, a WAN can have some distinguishing characteristics that separate it from LANs (besides distance). A WAN may incorporate service providers—local and interexchange carriers—that will affect its design. Likewise, there are locations in designs where many flows come together. These locations can have characteristics similar to Internet network access points (NAPs).

This method of sizing leads to five types of areas in the design (see Figure 8-16): WANs, which often use service providers and are focal points for network consolidation; NAPs, which interconnect and integrate (or separate) the other areas; specialized areas, which have requirements and flows that dictate particular technologies; backbones, where several flows are consolidated; and general areas, which focus on more traditional requirements, where capacity planning, scalability, and cost-effectiveness are primary considerations. This method is offered as a simple, workable hybrid of the other methods. You should consider this method and the others as a start toward developing your own sizing method.

FIGURE 8-16. Sizing Based on WANs, NAPs, Backbones, and Specialized and General Areas

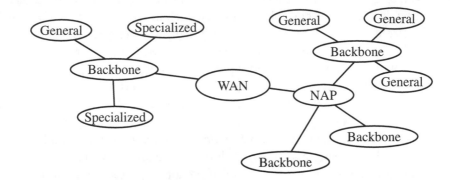

8.4.2 Isolating Areas—The Black Box Method

With the areas separated, we are ready to make the technology selections for each individual area in preparation for putting the areas back together. The black box method is a way to isolate each area, which makes the selection process easier. One of the challenges in doing network design is being able to focus on a particular area of the design. Some environments—and the network designs for those environments—are so large that it is easy to get lost within the design. The black box method helps to overcome the enormity of the design.

The black box method hides areas of the design that we are not currently focusing on, as in Figure 8-17. In this sense it is very similar to the traditional notion of a black box in engineering.

FIGURE 8-17. A Black Box as Applied to a Network Design

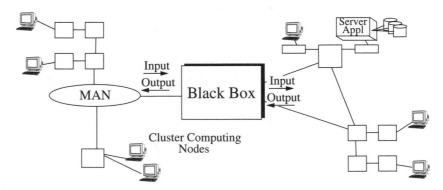

In Figure 8-17, the inputs to and outputs from the black box equate to the flows and flow information for each area of the design environment. We can use the black box method at any level of the design we choose, to hide entire networks (such as existing networks), areas or parts of areas, geographic or topological features (regions of a country, a campus, a building), or network elements (routers, switches, CSUs, circuits). At the extreme, a black box can hide everything except a single network element, or be used only at the edges of the design, leaving everything within the design exposed. The black box method is applied to each area of the design until the technology selections have been made to all areas.

8.4.3 Applying Evaluation Criteria and Guidelines

As each area of the design is isolated with the black box method, we apply all of the information we have developed so far—requirements, flowspec, design goals, evaluation criteria, and guidelines—to make technology selections for the area. How you apply all of this information depends primarily on what you have selected as your design goals, as well as how these design goals translated into evaluation criteria. The clearer your evaluation criteria, the easier it will be to apply them to the design.

As you proceed through this process, you should reevaluate your selections as the areas come close to completion. This is done to ensure that, for the overall design, the technology selections are coherent. This provides balance to the design, so that we do not ignore the entire network by focusing on its individual areas.

Example 8.4—Minimizing Cost in the Design

You may have chosen a design goal of minimizing cost for a network to interconnect three campuses in a metropolitan area, and translated that goal into an evaluation criteria of setting cost limits for each area, based on an overall cost estimate and the flowspec. For this example, the overall budget for networking is $400K, with $50K of that allocated for recurring service costs. This flowspec is based on the two-part flowspec, modified here to include estimates of users for each flow.

In modifying the flowspec, we first estimate the user populations for each area of the network. This can be done during the requirements analysis process, through getting the numbers of planned network users at each location. For this example, we have shown the numbers of users for each area, giving us Figure 8-18. The totals for each campus are as follows: Area A, 450 users; Area B, 1500 users; Area C, 150 users. The total planned for the network is 2100 users.

FIGURE 8-18. **User Estimates for Example 8.4**

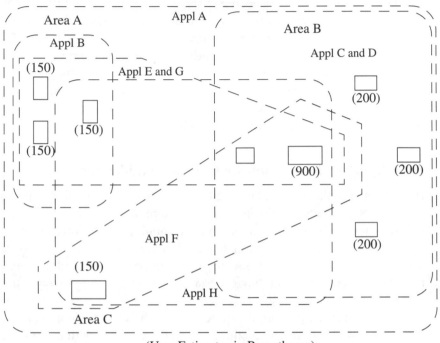

(User Estimates in Parentheses)

These user estimates are applied to each flow of the flowspec, including composite and backbone flows. In applying the users to the flows, we take the sum of the users from each location where the flow applies. For any application that impacts all flows (such as Application A/flow f1), it is not considered in the composite or backbone user estimates. If flow f1 was included in these estimates, the result would be that all backbone and composite flow would have user estimates of 2100, making them useless in the cost comparisons later.

Users are estimated by summing user counts for each application area. Application E, whose flow (f5) covers all of Area A as well as the headquarters (HQ) building of Area B, has an estimate of (150 + 150 + 150 + 900 =) 1350 users. Application H, whose flow (f8) covers Area C, part of Area B, and part of Area A, has an estimate of (150 + 900 + 150 =) 1200 users.

When estimating users for the composite and backbone flows, we can choose to either take the sum of users for each flow, which will count some users multiple times, or to count a user only once. We choose to count a user only one time. This means that, for a flow like CF1, which includes flows f5, f7, and f8, we would count the Area A users (450 users) and Area B users (900 users) once, resulting in an estimate of (450 + 900 + 150 =) 1500 users. If we had just taken a sum of all the flows, the user estimate would have been (1350 + 1350 + 1200 =) 3900 users. The listing of user estimates for all flows is presented below.

Two-Part Flowspec for Example 8.4

Flows	Reliability	Capacity	Delay	Users
f1		50 Kb/s		2100
f2		800 Kb/s		450
f3		120 Kb/s		1500
f4	99.5%	1.0 Mb/s		1500
f5	99.0%	500 Kb/s	80 ms	1350
f6		80 Kb/s	40 ms	1050
f7	99.95%	1.2 Mb/s	100 ms	1350
f8	99.5%	400 Kb/s		1200
Composite Flows				
CF1	99.95%	2.15 Mb/s	80 ms	1500
CF2	99.5%	530 Kb/s	40 ms	1200
CF3	99.95%	2.23 Mb/s	40 ms	1500
CF4	99.95%	2.55 Mb/s	80 ms	1350
CF5	99.95%	2.55 Mb/s	80 ms	1350
CF6	99.5%	1.17 Mb/s		1500
CF7	99.5%	1.17 Mb/s		1500
CF8	99.5%	1.17 Mb/s		1500
Backbone Flows				
BB1	99.95%	2.15 Mb/s	80 ms	1500
BB2	99.5%	450 Kb/s		1200
BB3	99.5%	530 Kb/s	40 ms	1200
BB4	99.95%	3.35 Mb/s	40 ms	1800

The flows and their performance characteristics are presented in Figure 8-19.

FIGURE 8-19. **Flowspec Diagram for Example 8.4**

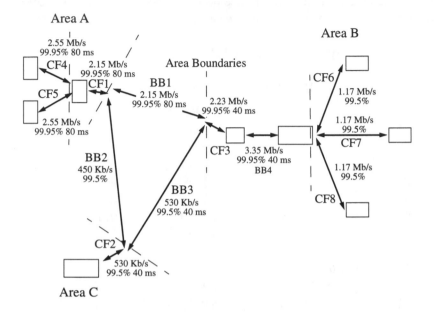

While setting cost limits is a primary evaluation criterion, you may have chosen a secondary criterion to be sharing network capacity between multiple applications, using the capacity plan from the flowspec. This would fall in line with the primary criterion, being one way to minimize costs in the network. Let's say that other criteria that are important are performance and ease of use (see Figure 8-20).

FIGURE 8-20. **Evaluation Criteria for Example 8.4**

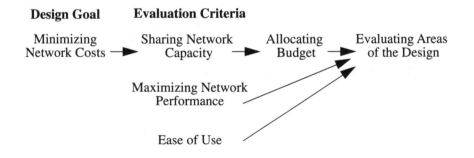

The next step in the process is to apply budget information to the flows. One way to apply the budget is to distribute it across the flows based on the ratio of users for each flow. In this method, the budget allocation for each flow would be a fraction of the total budget, determined from the ratio of the users for that flow divided by the total number of users for all flows.

Another method to apply the budget is to distribute it to each administrative area of the design. In this example, this would likely be each area (A, B, and C). In order to be able to apply this method, we would need to estimate how much of the budget can be allocated to each campus. This information may have been determined during the requirements analysis process.

A third method would be to use some outside constraint on applying budget information. These constraints are often in the form of directives from management.

We will use the first method for this example. Taking the ratio of (users for a flow)/(total users for all flows) for each composite and backbone flow, and multiplying by $400K (the other $50K is handled differently, as we will see in a moment), we get flows with budget allocations:

Flows	Users	Percent Allocation	Budget
CF1	1500	8.8%	$35.2K
CF2	1200	7.0%	$28.0K
CF3	1500	8.8%	$35.2K
CF4	1350	7.9%	$31.6K
CF5	1350	7.9%	$31.6K
CF6	1500	8.8%	$35.2K
CF7	1500	8.8%	$35.2K
CF8	1500	8.8%	$35.2K
BB1	1500	8.8%	$35.2K
BB2	1200	7.0%	$28.0K
BB3	1200	7.0%	$28.0K
BB4	1800	10.4%	$41.6K
Total		100.0%	$400.0K

We can pick any area of the design to begin applying the black box method. One way to determine where to start is to prioritize the budget allocations and take the highest allocation as the starting point. Our secondary criterion for this example is sharing network capacity. This criterion points to the backbone flows (as they are where multiple flows are carried between flow boundaries), so we begin there.

FIGURE 8-21. **Black Boxes Applied to Isolate Backbone Area**

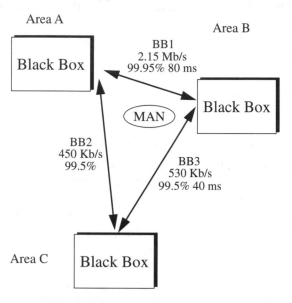

The design is sized into areas based on the flow boundaries shown in Figure 8-19, starting with the area that contains backbone flows BB1, BB2, and BB3. In order to isolate this area, the other areas of the design are covered with black boxes, as shown in Figure 8-21.

Having isolated these backbone flows, we can now apply the evaluation criteria to technology choices. For these three flows, we have:

Flows	Reliability	Capacity	Delay	Users	Budget
BB1	99.95%	2.15 Mb/s	80 ms	1500	$35.2K
BB2	99.5%	450 Kb/s		1200	$28.0K
BB3	99.5%	530 Kb/s	40 ms	1200	$28.0K

These flows are in the MAN environment and can be supported by either dedicated circuits, an extension of a LAN technology (depending on distance), or a service provider. We would consider technologies and services that can be implemented given the budget allocations, and that would meet or exceed the performance requirements listed above. Technology candidates include Frame Relay, ATM, SMDS, Ethernet, and dedicated circuits. Since we do not discuss vendor- or provider-dependent choices, an evaluation of technology costs are not presented here. What we would do here is choose a candidate that meets the implementation costs for these flows ($91.2K), plus the budget given for the recurring costs for service ($40K), and has performance characteristics that are closest to the requirements of the flows.

For example, we might have chosen a local provider's Frame Relay service for this area of the design. If this met the budget allocations, it can also meet the capacity requirements (except the 2.15 Mb/s capacity of BB1, if the service is T1). Given that the design is for campuses that are in close proximity to each other (within approximately 60 miles), the delay characteristics are likely to be met. The only other performance consideration is for reliability. If we were to take the deterministic performance requirements of this example more seriously, then the design goals may be driven more by performance than by cost. In that case, a different technology may be chosen. Having made a choice for this backbone area, we can move on to another area of the design. We would choose the remaining backbone area, BB4, along with composite flow CF3.

Figure 8-22 shows these flows isolated from the rest of the design. We could also have used this method twice, once to isolate BB4 and another time to isolate CF3. For these flows we have:

Flows	Reliability	Capacity	Delay	Users	Budget
CF3	99.95%	2.23 Mb/s	40 ms	1500	$35.2K
BB4	99.95%	3.35 Mb/s	40 ms	1800	$41.6K

This area is a campus environment. CF3 describes the requirements for taking flows from the MAN environment into Area B. BB4 describes the same requirements as CF3, and adds the requirements of flows within Area B. The total budget for these flows is $76.8K. This portion of the network will be implemented and supported by the Area B staff and will use a LAN technology, such as Ethernet, Token Ring, or FDDI. The choice of technology will be driven by cost, but any of the candidates above can support the capacity requirements of these flows, and the delays are well within distance limits. If Ethernet turns out to be the least expensive technology, it would be the primary candidate for this area.

We would apply this process to each of the remaining areas, making technology choices based on the flow information for that area. The result would look like Figure 8-23.

FIGURE 8-22. Black Boxes Are Moved to Isolate Another Area of the Design

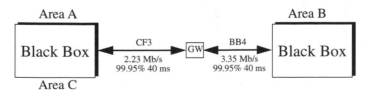

FIGURE 8-23. **Technology/Service Choices for Example 8.4**

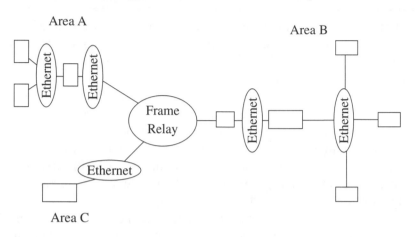

Note: Choices are used to illustrate process.

The next step for this example would be to consider interconnection strategies for the design.

◊ ◊ ◊

8.5 Case Study

Step 1   Establishing Design Goals. Our manufacturing design environment can be considered high-performance, and in talking with the customer, we learn that they want us to place performance as the highest priority, given the budget that they have allocated to this project and that this customer considers high-performance to primarily mean high reliability. Our design goal will be to maximize performance for the network, particularly for those flows that contain the mission-critical and real-time applications.

For our mission-critical application, we will focus on optimizing reliability in the network. This will occur primarily when we look at interconnection mechanisms in the next chapter, as well as when we look at the physical design and routing protocols, as these mechanisms, the physical plant, and routing protocols can provide higher reliability to the design.

For our real-time application, we will focus on optimizing delay in the network. Since it is likely that the delay characteristics of our MAN will be well within the minimum application delay requirement (40 ms), delay should not be a problem. We do need to be careful not to add large sources of delay into the design. This will be important when we look at network management, administration, and security, as these are some potential sources of delay.

Step 2   Developing Criteria for Technology Evaluation. Along with our reliability and delay considerations, we will be using the capacities from the flowspec as part of our evaluation criteria. We will also be using the criteria that are presented in this chapter.

Step 3   Sizing the Network. We will segment the design into areas so that we can apply the black box method. The areas that are shown in Figure 8-24 are based on the flow boundaries that we used earlier in the flow analysis. This will split the design into three campuses (SF, Oakland, and SJ), and the SF and Oakland campuses are each split into two areas (see Figure 8-24).

Step 4   Making Technology Choices. We will now apply the black box method to each area in the design. Let's start with the area between the campuses—the MAN environment. Applying black boxes to each campus, we isolate the backbone flows (see Figure 8-25).

FIGURE 8-24. **Design Segmented into Campus and Building Areas**

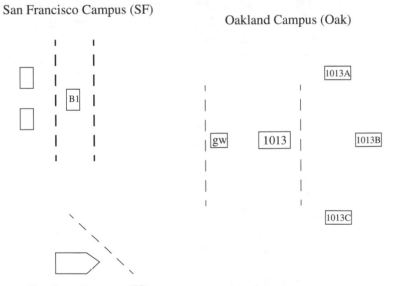

FIGURE 8-25. Black Boxes Used to Isolate BB1 and CF6

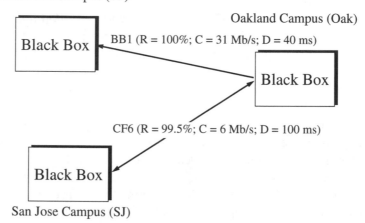

San Francisco Campus (SF)

Oakland Campus (Oak)

BB1 (R = 100%; C = 31 Mb/s; D = 40 ms)

CF6 (R = 99.5%; C = 6 Mb/s; D = 100 ms)

San Jose Campus (SJ)

For both of these backbone and composite flows, the distances involved in the design do not raise any red flags. If the design spanned a distance whose delay was close to any of the delay requirements of our applications, or was greater than the HRT, then these would raise a red flag. The reliability characteristics for these flows, particularly the mission-critical flow with a 100% reliability, will be considered here, as well as when we look at interconnectivity mechanisms, the physical plant, and routing protocols later in this book. From a capacity perspective, both the backbone flow BB1 (at 31 Mb/s) and the composite flow CF6 (at 6 Mb/s), have a number of technology options available.

Since this is a MAN environment, it is likely that we will use a service provider for flows BB1 and CF6. We consider Frame Relay, SMDS, ATM, ISDN, and ADSL as possible options. For BB1, based on the capacity from the flowspec (31 Mb/s), the choices lie somewhere between a DS3 and an OC-3c. For the flexibility of upgrading to an OC-3c and getting a service offering (and rate) from a provider, we would recommend ATM at DS3 as a candidate for BB1.

Looking more closely at CF6, we see that the flows that make up CF6 are somewhat asymmetric, as shown in Figure 8-26.

FIGURE 8-26. A Closer Look at Flow CF6

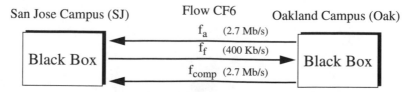

San Jose Campus (SJ)   Flow CF6   Oakland Campus (Oak)

f_a (2.7 Mb/s)

f_f (400 Kb/s)

f_{comp} (2.7 Mb/s)

FIGURE 8-27. **Black Box Used to Isolate BB2, CF3, CF4, and CF5**

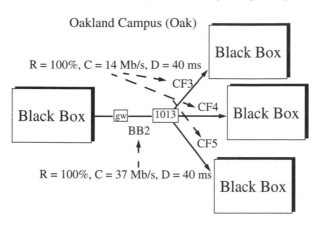

We can take advantage of this asymmetry by choosing a technology that optimizes for asymmetric flows, such as ADSL or ATM. Given the capacity of this flow, and that we have chosen ATM for BB1, it would be easier to support both flows as ATM from the same provider. When we factor in the expected growth rate of 50%, ATM will allow for expansion in CF6's capacity. BB1, which is at the limit for ATM/DS3, will need to be upgraded if its capacity requirement increases much beyond 31 Mb/s.

If the service provider offers alternatives to these technologies, we would want to consider them as well. Some locations may have carriers that offer metropolitan FDDI or Ethernet, which could be used for CF6 and BB1. For the building environment at the SJ campus, we will use a 10 Mb/s Ethernet switch.

We can now remove the black box from the Oakland campus, and place a black box on the MAN and on the SF and SJ campuses, giving us Figure 8-27.

BB2 has the most strict requirements of any of the flows in this area. Since Applications A, D/G, F, and C/E all have flows between SF and/or SJ and Building 1013, BB2 is the most critical flow in this design. We would expect this flow to be the first to grow, and it will likely grow by the greatest amount of any of the flows, since most flows are reflected in BB2. So we will plan for the greatest capacity increase and reliability for this flow. At 37 Mb/s, we are already at the bound for ATM at DS3, but OC-3c is a candidate, as well as FDDI, 100 Mb/s Ethernet, HiPPI, and Fibre Channel. While HiPPI and Fibre Channel offer high levels of capacity, connecting them to ATM in the MAN and whatever technologies we choose for CF3, CF4, and CF5 would unnecessarily complicate the design for this area.

With the performance characteristics and the importance of the flows between Building 1013 and the SF campus, we should be prepared to consider supporting end-to-end services between these sites. ATM QOS levels is a likely candidate to support these services, and using ATM at OC-3c rate for BB2 will allow us to run ATM from the MAN environment to the Oakland campus. In addition, with OC-3c for BB2, we will have a good bit of growth capability. An ATM OC-3c link will provide a seamless interface with the ATM DS3 service in the MAN, and will be compatible with the upgrade to OC-3c in the MAN. ATM/OC-3c is our technology candidate for this flow.

Flows CF3, CF4, and CF5 have the same characteristics, and we will be able to take advantage of this by focusing on one of the flows. CF3, like CF4 and CF5, has a capacity characteristic of 14 Mb/s. Its flows are between Buildings 1013A and 1013, which are within the Oakland campus. In discussions with the customer, we have determined that this campus environment should not be a problem for our network. There is a well-protected conduit system connecting the four buildings in this campus. This gives us some interesting options for this environment. One option is to extend the ATM network between 1013 and 1013A, 1013B, and 1013C. This has the appeal of providing ATM QOS between these buildings, but given the environment and the applications' performance requirements, this may be a bit of overkill. The applications used in this environment are important to the company, just as in the MAN environment, but here we have more control over the environment. Another option is to choose an Ethernet or FDDI environment, probably a switched environment. A 100 Mb/s switched Ethernet would be relatively easy to install, configure, use, and maintain, and will provide adequate performance for the applications. This is our technology candidate for flows CF3, CF4, and CF5.

The final area that we will consider is the SF campus, shown in Figure 8-28.

FIGURE 8-28. Black Box Used to Isolate CF1 and CF2

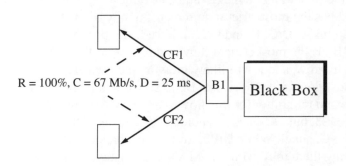

FIGURE 8-29. **Technology Candidates**

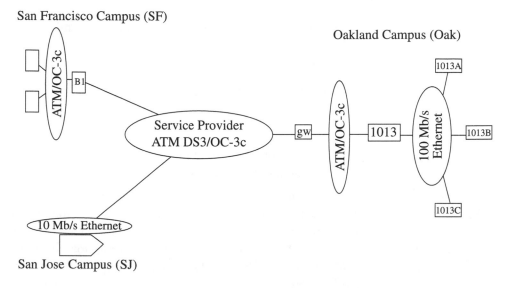

As with the Oakland campus, the flows in the SF campus are equivalent. Given a 50% growth factor, we expect that the capacity of each flow will approach 100 Mb/s. Most of this capacity is local to the campus, from flow f_b(53 Mb/s). From both a capacity perspective and in providing a seamless service from Building 1013 to the SF campus, ATM at OC-3c is a candidate for this area.

The black boxes are now removed from the design environment, and the resulting technology candidates are shown in Figure 8-29.

8.6 Concluding Remarks

In choosing the network technologies that will be used in the design, we have used requirements, traffic flows, and design criteria to help us make the most informed choices. In the next chapter we will learn about the mechanisms to connect these technology choices, thus bringing the design together.

Exercises

1. For the following primary design goals, list at least two secondary or derivative design goals. Explain your answers.

   a) Minimizing WAN costs

   b) Simplifying network troubleshooting

   c) Scaling the network:

        –From LAN to WAN

        –To double its backbone throughput

        –To increase the number of users by 50%

2. For a LAN design environment for 150 users, you have been given the design goals of making the network easy to use and administer, and maximizing the performance of the network by choosing the highest-performance technologies available. Explain the trade-offs between these two design goals, and develop a simple chart that shows these trade-offs for the following technologies:

        –Ethernet (10bT)

        –Fast Ethernet

        –Gigabit Ethernet

        –ATM (OC-12c backbone/OC-3c access)

        –HiPPI

   Consider the needs for network management for each of these technologies, including help-desk or network operations center (NOC) support.

3. Some common technology evaluation criteria are presented in Section 8.3. List other criteria that you would use in evaluating network technologies, or provide some examples of the criteria in 8.3.

4. In the design of Figure 8-30, two backbones (BB1 and BB2) connect three regions of the network. What scaling factors should you use on these backbone capacities? What are the new capacities for the backbone flows?

5. In Figure 8-31, you want to prepare to make technology choices for the Chicago Campus MAN; the WAN connection from Chicago to Toronto, Boston, and Philadelphia; and the Internet connection in Chicago. Determine the placement of black boxes in each area in order to isolate the flows for each of these connections.

FIGURE 8-30. Figure for Exercise 4

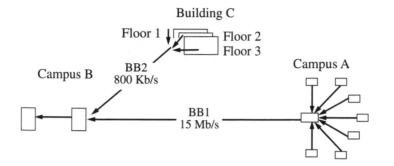

FIGURE 8-31. Design for Exercise 5

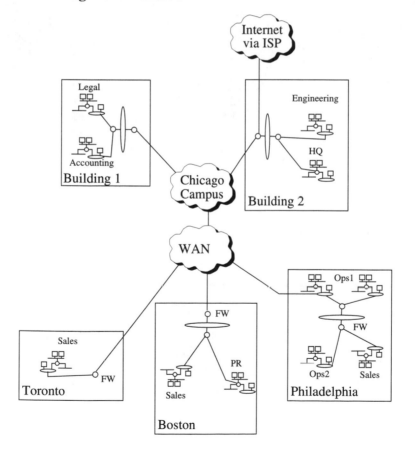

CHAPTER 9

Logical Design: Interconnection Mechanisms

9.1 Background for Logical Design

Having made technology selections for each area of the network design, we can now focus on mechanisms that connect these choices together, as well as on optimizing the overall design for our design goals. These mechanisms, termed here *interconnection mechanisms*, bring the logical design together.

Interconnection mechanisms include using a shared medium, where all hosts are on the same network and there is no interconnection; using bridging, switching (such as Ethernet/FDDI/Token Ring switching), ATM switching, frame switching, and SMDS; and using network-layer routing.

Other interconnection mechanisms are hybrids of switching and routing that attempt to combine both mechanisms in order to optimize both network-layer and link-layer (or subnetwork-layer) solutions, to adapt to existing technologies, or to allow for the creation of virtual networks by the end users. These hybrid mechanisms include LAN emulation (LANE), multiprotocol over ATM (MPOA), the next-hop resolution protocol (NHRP), and switching based on flow or end-to-end information. Despite what some vendors like to tell their customers, there is no all-encompassing, "right" mechanism. Each of the mechanisms listed above have their advantages and disadvantages, and each can be successfully applied to network designs.

Understanding interconnection mechanisms can be somewhat tricky, as more and different mechanisms are being developed, while routing and switching are being integrated into mechanisms that optimize performance (at the trade-offs of complexity and cost) for some environments. Basically, the trend in interconnection mechanisms is toward convergence at the link and network layers. We are losing the separation of functions at each layer, resulting in a lot of options, and making solutions harder to understand by everyone. Instead of having lots of network devices that performed a specific function (like routing), we now have devices that integrate several functions into one box.

The integration of link- and network-layer functions is not necessarily good or bad, just different from what we are used to. As long as we have some clue about what each mechanism does and what the trade-offs are between mechanisms, we can make them useful in our network designs.

As you go through this section, you will see that there are many reasons for planning routing, switching, and hybrid mechanisms in a network design. There are also designs where a shared medium with no interconnections is warranted. In general, we look at several factors in evaluating interconnection mechanisms, including scalability of the network, optimizing certain flow models, providing external connectivity to the network, and applying support services to the design. We start with the simplest interconnection mechanism, consisting of no interconnections at all—a shared-medium mechanism.

9.2 Shared Medium (No Interconnection)

With a *shared-medium mechanism*, areas are collapsed and their technologies combined to form a larger version of an area network. Figure 9-1 shows a shared-medium network.

This is done either through directly combining networks, through physical media or hubs, by adding repeaters between areas. The result is that the collapsed areas all share a common IP addressing structure, and all hosts on the network are directly accessible by each other.

FIGURE 9-1. **A Shared-Medium Network**

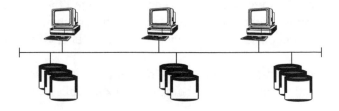

While this is the simplest solution, it has major trade-offs, primarily the lack of scalability. As we discussed earlier, as the number of users/applications/hosts sharing a common address group grows, the overhead associated with multicast, address resolution and network-layer functions also grows until network performance is degraded or the network becomes unusable. As a result, a hierarchy forms to isolate or hide parts of the network from each other. When does this hierarchy occur, and when should we plan to provide hierarchy in the network? This is where scalability, flow-model optimization, external connectivity, and support services need to be considered.

In the previous chapter we looked at scaling the network, based on the growth in users, applications, hosts, or networks. Scaling was achieved by selecting candidate technologies that could either handle the expected growth in capacity, based on MDR or SDR, or had planned upgrades in the technology to meet the expected increase in capacity by the time it was needed. Another way to meet growth expectations is to plan hierarchy in the design.

Planned hierarchy is the introduction of methods to isolate and hide networks and their traffic from one another. This could be done by adding new networks or segmenting existing ones, as in Figure 9-2.

When this is done, the shared media is separated and interconnected by bridges, routers, switches, or hybrids of these. The rules of thumb for capacity planning developed earlier for scaling networks can be applied here—with slight modifications—to show when hierarchy needs to be introduced into the shared-medium network:

1. When the maximum data rates (MDRs) for the expected traffic flows on a shared-medium network approach 80% of the capacity for the technology used in that network

2. When the sustained data rates (SDRs) for the traffic on a shared-medium network approach 60% of the capacity for the technology used in that network

FIGURE 9-2. **Planning Hierarchy in the Design**

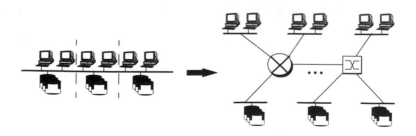

The performance modifiers examined during the flow analysis can be used here to modify these rules, as necessary.

In these rules, traffic is the statistical sum of all application/user/host information flows over that network. This is determined by either sampling the flows over the network (if there are existing networks where this can be done), using existing information from traffic studies, or estimating the traffic based on each application's MDRs/SDRs, percentage utilization of that application on the network, and number of simultaneous sessions of that application.

Given that many of today's applications and computers can easily reach the maximum throughput of most technologies, including 10/100 Mb/s Ethernet, FDDI, Token Ring, Frame Relay, ATM (OC-3c and below), and SMDS, planning an interconnection mechanism in the design, even when the MDR/SDRs are presently low enough for a shared-medium network, is a forward-thinking approach.

Redundancy is also an indication of the need for an interconnection mechanism. The higher the degree of redundancy, the greater the need for an interconnection mechanism—and protocols—that can reroute traffic quickly. When we apply interconnection mechanisms to the design, we will use degrees of redundancy to determine when to apply them.

A shared-medium mechanism does not optimize for most of the flow models described during the flow analysis. In particular, when client-server, collaborative-computing, or distributed-computing flow models are indicated in the design, we should automatically consider an interconnection mechanism for the design. As discussed in Chapter 5, these flow models have characteristics that are optimized by creating separate, logical paths for each.

When external connectivity is expected, an interconnection mechanism must be added to the design. When the connectivity is to the Internet, that mechanism must be IP routing or a protocol gateway.

Interconnection mechanisms are closely tied to support services. When security, administration, and network management are being considered in the design (which is true for almost every design today), then an interconnection mechanism should be considered. As we will see later in this chapter, the mechanism selected for connecting networks will play a role in how security and network management are implemented.

9.3 Switching and Routing: Comparison and Contrast

There is often confusion about the differences between *switching* and *routing*, and the evolution of hybrid mechanisms complicates the issue. Before discussing switching mechanisms, it is important to understand what switching and routing are. Both switching and routing are methods of moving information between networks, based on network- or link-layer addresses.

From a network-layer perspective, switching can be considered more oriented toward connections than routing. Switches create connections (or abstractions of connections) for the duration of the information flow that they are switching. So, while an ATM switch will establish a connection between ATM switches and/or hosts (based on E.164 or NSAP addresses) for the duration of a cell stream (when SVCs are employed), an Ethernet switch will establish a connection across the switch for the duration of transmission and receipt of an Ethernet frame from a host to a switch port, while a flow switch will establish a connection for the duration of a flow. Routers, on the other hand, are oriented toward connectionless transfer, although connections may occur at the transport layer. Routing decisions are local to the router, which does not (usually) know how the information will be routed beyond its neighbors.

Currently, switching is generally at the link layer, while routing is generally at the network (IP) layer. Link-layer Ethernets, Token Rings, FDDIs, or HiPPIs do not use network-layer information in switching decisions. Thus, network-layer addressing treats a group of interconnected switched networks as a single IP network, which has implications for network-layer services. Routing, when done at the network layer, separates interconnected networks via IP. Examples of convergence of switching and routing can be seen in integrated private network-to-network interface (I-PNNI) and in IP switching. I-PNNI uses link- and network-layer information in making forwarding decisions and communicates this information to devices at both layers. IP switching, when not implemented as merely IP routing in hardware, also combines link- and network-layer information to make forwarding decisions.

Switching may or may not have input and output buffers associated with it. When switches do not have buffers, they must switch quickly enough to pass the traffic without storing it in memory. This makes the switch very fast, but also means that the traffic is lost (dropped) and must be retransmitted if it cannot be switched at that time. In effect, it does not act like a store-and-forward device. When the switch does have buffers, it can keep the traffic resident for a short period of time, reducing the likelihood of it being dropped, but also slowing the switching time. Thus, switches with buffers begin to have delay characteristics like routers, albeit with usually much smaller and more consistent delays. Routers are store-and-forward devices, with relatively large buffers to allow the router to process traffic as well as to handle bursts of traffic. Routers are more tolerant of traffic bursts than are switches, but the processing and wait times in buffers result in longer and more variable delays in the network.

Since routers store traffic for short periods of time, they are likely devices to add support services to. Routers will usually have much more network management, security, and user interface capabilities than switches. As we will see later in this book, routers are starting to shed some of these support services (even some of the network-layer services) to devices specialized in these services, such as route servers and security firewalls.

What this all boils down to is that routers make forwarding decisions based on network-layer information, and have large buffers to handle traffic variability, while switches make forwarding decisions based on link-layer information, and have very small (or no) buffers in order to pass traffic rapidly. Both of these capabilities are usually needed in the network, which is part of the reason for the emergence of hybrid mechanisms.

9.4 Switching

Switching can be viewed as a relatively simple (and usually cheap) way to achieve scalability and to optimize some flow models. There is an old statement, "bridge when you can, route when you must," that may be modified to "switch when you can, route when you must." This statement is somewhat misleading, however, as it incorrectly implies that routing should be avoided at all cost.

The basic trade-offs between switching and routing are simplicity and speed versus complexity and function. Switches are great when the design is simple and the speed of switching is a benefit. As the design becomes complicated (e.g., large amount of growth expected, crossing administrative domains, connecting to other networks, the need to accommodate diversity in media or technologies), routers offer network-layer and support services that help with the complexity. From this perspective, switches can be thought of as a first or intermediate step in interconnecting networks, leading to routing as the complexity or distances increase.

For scalability, you can use the capacity-planning guidelines to determine if switching is needed in the design. In optimizing flow models, we want to look at switching for client-server, cooperative-computing, and distributed-computing flow models. How can a switch help to optimize certain flow models? Switches can make multiple connections through the switch at the same time, allowing multiple simultaneous flows at media speeds through the switch. When a flow model suggests

FIGURE 9-3. **Flows in a Distributed-Computing Environment**

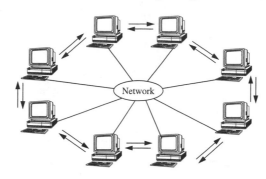

multiple simultaneous flows, the proper placement of switches can optimize the network for that flow model. Consider a distributed-computing environment, as in Figure 9-3.

Here the flows in this environment are between neighbor computing nodes, and have strict performance requirements. Instead of having the flows share the same network, they may be interconnected with one or more switches (see Figure 9-4), isolating the flows and reducing the required capacity over any particular network.

When the environment is local—such as a computer room, building, or campus LAN—a switch provides a simple, easy, and fast solution to handle multiple simultaneous flows. While a router could also be used here, it will likely have greater end-to-end delays in this environment, and be a more complex solution. The switching approach also applies to client-server and cooperative-computing environments.

If the distributed-computing environment was separated by a LAN/WAN flow boundary, then the end-to-end delay characteristics and complexity of the environment (in terms of connecting to a service provider, or to other networks) would make routing a candidate for interconnection, at least for the WAN connectivity.

FIGURE 9-4. **Switching in a Distributed-Computing Environment**

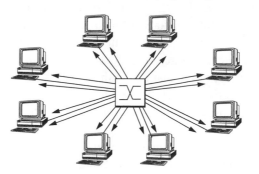

FIGURE 9-5. **Routing in a WAN Distributed-Computing Environment**

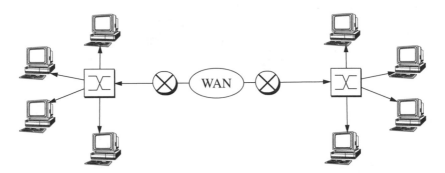

In the design environment of Figure 9-5, the switches will optimize the end-to-end delays of flows in each local computing group, while the routers provide administrative support across the WAN. The end-to-end delays across the WAN are large enough to mask the differences in switch and router delay characteristics.

9.4.1 ATM Switching

There has been a great deal of debate about where ATM is most useful, in the backbone environment or directly to the desktop. When ATM first hit the general networking world (for many people, at the 1992 Interop conference), it appeared the probable successor to existing technologies. It did have a serious impact on SMDS, and appeared to threaten Frame Relay, Ethernet, Token Ring, and FDDI. There has been some backtracking since then, reducing the scope of ATM to network backbones and WANs. This is partly due to the inherent complexity and overhead of ATM, the lack of large operational ATM networks (relative to the numbers of new networks based on existing technologies), and the slow growth in services-based networking. What, then, are the roles of ATM in today's and future networks?

First, it is important to note that this backtracking should be expected. Proponents of ATM have tried to accomplish quite a bit in a short amount of time, for a variety of reasons. But this does not mean that they have been heading in the wrong direction. What many network designers and developers have known is that each technology, service, and interconnection mechanism has its purpose, and no single technology, service, or mechanism is the one "right" answer. Like the home builder who has a wide variety of specialized tools, or the software developer who relies upon many different algorithms, techniques, or specialized code fragments, the network designer uses network technologies and interconnection mechanisms, and it is good design practice to be able to use all available tools and to know where and when to apply them. ATM is no exception.

ATM can be used in backbone environments, in the WAN, and to the desktop, depending on the requirements of the system. This is where the requirements and flow analyses can give some insight into the design, in identifying where each tool (such as ATM) may be applied. But we need to understand what the trade-offs are with ATM, and the implications of using it to the desktop, particularly if it is end-to-end between applications. There are some general trade-offs with ATM. One is the ability to support end-to-end services versus added complexity. Another is perceived high performance (particularly in capacity) versus overhead.

ATM can provide some support to end-to-end services, and this service support is growing. As we saw in Chapter 1, services can be important and are becoming required in some environments, but there is an added complexity in the resulting network. In order to support end-to-end services, state information has to be kept about the connection and the services requested/offered. Services to different applications are likely to be merged somewhere within the network, particularly if the service levels are the same, and this merging has to be managed by the network. And the dynamic nature of networks means that connections will be broken, reestablished, and rerouted, and service state will either move with the connection or be reestablished, both of which will take considerable resources in the network.

While the cost of complexity is high, the potential benefits can be great. End-to-end services may be the only (or the best) way to support emerging applications. As this generation of services-based networking matures, end-to-end services will be a distinguishing feature of successful networks.

ATM can also provide high levels of capacity, and the combination of ATM over SONET gives a known path for performance upgrades. ATM is either developed or in the planning/developing stages for SONET OC-48c and OC-192c. There is a capacity overhead with ATM, as with all technologies and protocols, but it is (apparently) higher with ATM. This is due to the small, fixed cell size of ATM. At 53 bytes, with 5 bytes of header and 48 bytes of data, the initial overhead is 5/53 or 9.4%. When segmentation and reassembly and the ATM adaptation layers (AALs) are considered, the overhead can grow to 5 bytes of header and up to 8 bytes of AAL, or $(5 + 8)/53 = 24.5\%$. And this does not include the overhead from SONET.

ATM options focus on interconnecting ATM with traditional technologies and providing network-layer functions with ATM. LAN emulation (LANE) provides an ATM infrastructure that interconnects technologies such as Ethernet and Token Ring together, and to ATM. LANE emulates Ethernet and Token Ring services across the ATM network. In order to accomplish this, it provides support for the characteristics of these technologies, particularly address resolution, broadcast capabilities, and their connectionless nature. To the network layer, the emulated LANs look like a bridged network, and routers are used to interconnect networks (although interemulated LAN cut-throughs are likely to be available soon).

There are three mechanisms to introduce LANE into a design environment. First, it can be used to introduce ATM into the backbone, yet minimize the impact to the end users by not making changes to the end-host configuration and NIC. This can be very important in an environment where there is a large existing base of Ethernet and/or Token Ring hosts. Second, it can be used as an intermediate step in migrating to other ATM options, such as RFC 1577, native ATM, NHRP, or MPOA. By introducing ATM into the backbone in the first mechanism, we can migrate hosts from the LANE environment to another ATM environment. Third, we can use LANE to tie together groups of Ethernet or Token Ring hosts, as a permanent solution when the hosts do not need more than Ethernet or Token Ring connectivity or performance.

A major reason for using LANE is to keep existing Ethernets and Token Rings in place. This saves money in the Ethernet and Token Ring host interfaces that are in an existing network. ATM can be brought into the network, for example, as a backbone, and LANE used to connect hosts as Ethernet- or Token Ring–attached hosts. In addition, LANE can help minimize the impact of network modifications to the end users, so they don't see any changes to their connectivity.

However, these benefits come at a cost. A trade-off in being able to capitalize on an existing investment in the traditional technologies by using LANE as an interconnection mechanism is in the increased complexity of the network. LANE emulates Ethernet and Token Ring environments, and the mechanisms used to provide this emulation can result in events on the network that are difficult to understand or solve. This is primarily due to added components, such as LAN emulation clients (LECs), LAN emulation configuration servers (LECSs), LAN emulation servers (LESs), broadcast and unknown servers (BUSs), and special multicast servers (SMSs); the virtual circuit connectivity between components; and the reduction in straightforwardness in the underlying infrastructure. Thus, more knowledge about the structure, state, and operations of the network is required, possibly through the use of LANE-specific network-management software and hardware, or skilled, specialized staff.

On the other hand, being able to continue to use existing networks while integrating ATM into the infrastructure can save substantial amounts of time and money, while allowing those who will operate and manage the network to utilize their existing knowledge of traditional technologies. Therefore, if a design has a significant number of existing networks based on Ethernet and Token Ring, LANE should be one of the considerations as an interconnection mechanism, with the caveat that there will be a complexity cost, in terms of required LANE and network-knowledgeable staff.

These trade-offs can be applied to the design goals discussed earlier. If a primary design goal, or evaluation criterion, is minimizing cost for the network, then LANE will be an option if you have a large base of existing Ethernet- and Token

Ring–attached hosts. If the primary goal is maximizing ease of use and manageability, LANE is less clear as an option, as it will provide ease of use to the end users (since their interfaces to the network will look the same), but manageability of the network will likely decrease with the added complexity of LANE. From the network performance design goal, LANE can be seen as an intermediate step in improving the performance for the end users. If the users were previously on a shared Ethernet, then LANE can improve their performance, but LANE will not improve performance beyond switched Ethernet or Token Ring performance. Where LANE does improve performance is in the backbone network, as we can bring in a high-performance backbone (say ATM/OC-3c or OC-12c), and attach hosts with LANE, then migrate hosts as needed from LANE to either a direct ATM connection or to another high-performance technology (e.g., Fast/Gigabit Ethernet, HiPPI, or Fibre Channel) connected to the ATM backbone.

Classical IP over ATM networks, based on the specifications in RFC 1577 (also termed 1577), interconnect networks via ATM and IP in a more straightforward, albeit IP-centric, fashion. RFC 1577 networks treat ATM as another underlying technology for IP, and all interconnections are done with routing. This may also change, as with LANE, by having the option of cut-through paths in the ATM network. A trade-off here is in not taking full advantage of ATM, along with some potentially strange interconnectivity patterns, versus simplicity and a straightforward interconnection at the IP layer.

RFC 1577 does not take full advantage of the switching and service capabilities of ATM, but instead forces ATM to mold itself to an IP structure. If your existing network is a large IP network, then changing the IP addressing and routing may be quite difficult. Starting with 1577 can be an intermediate step in integrating ATM into such networks, with a plan to migrate from 1577 to another mechanism that takes more advantage of ATM. RFC 1577 can be useful in areas where network multiple technologies meet, such as at backbones or corporate-internal NAPs.

In Figure 9-6, three logical IP subnets (LISs) are configured over a common ATM network. For each LIS, all hosts and routers must be able to connect to each other, and traffic between LISs must be sent to a router common to them. The scalability of ATM is reduced in this environment, unless multicast and address resolution mechanisms are added to the network. Basically, ATM provides the link-layer infrastructure for an IP subnet, and interconnections between subnets are routed. This can result in strange traffic flows when multiple LISs are built on a large-scale ATM infrastructure. For example, if LISs cross the WAN environment, flows that would stay in the LAN may cross the WAN in order to be routed (see Figure 9-7). In a situation such as this, it is clear that a direct switched path is preferable to the long-distance routed path.

FIGURE 9-6. **ATM in a Classical IP Environment**

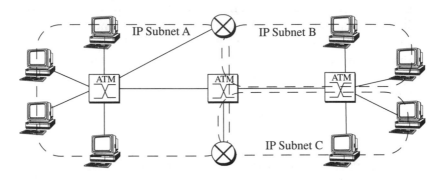

While there may be times when switching is more optimal than routing in this environment, it is not permitted. When cut-through routing is available, however, then 1577 begins to look more like NHRP or MPOA in its behavior.

A key benefit to this strictly IP-interconnected environment is that IP is relatively well understood. Since ATM is treated as yet another link-layer technology, the reliance on ATM is minimized. There is no reason why the link layer cannot be replaced with Frame Relay, Fibre Channel, HiPPI, or SMDS, as necessary.

Switching provides an interconnection mechanism for improving the overall capacity characteristics of the network and, when designed properly, can optimize flows. As the design becomes complicated, however, routing should be considered part of the interconnection mechanism.

FIGURE 9-7. **Example of Suboptimal Flows in Classical IP Over ATM**

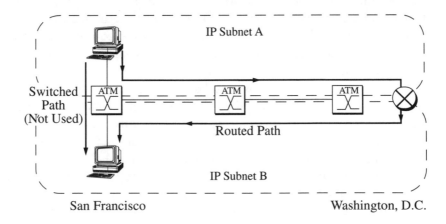

9.5 Routing

Routing can be applied to the design as the sole interconnection mechanism, or as an addition to a switching mechanism. In either case, it provides support for complex and very large network designs—consider the size and complexity of the Internet—and offers features beyond the switching mechanism. From a scalability perspective, the same capacity-planning guidelines can apply to routing. Thus, when the MDR/SDRs of traffic flows are high enough to warrant segmenting a shared-medium network, then routing could be used as the interconnection mechanism, and routers placed between the networks.

Routers are also convenient devices to place support services, such as security, network monitoring and management, user interfaces, and accounting and administration. Routers support these services well, although their performance can suffer when too many services are placed on them. They can be placed at locations in the network where traffic flows are consolidated, and since they route at the network layer, they have access to network-layer information (e.g., source/destination IP addresses, port numbers, protocol information) that happens to be useful to support services. Since routers examine network-layer information, it is logical to use that information for other purposes, such as filtering traffic based on the source IP address, or keeping counters of packet information for access by the simple network management protocol (SNMP).

When routers have support services in place, they make good locations to demarc administrative boundaries. This is enhanced by the routing protocols, which understand administrative boundaries through autonomous system (AS) numbers, and routing areas. One feature of having such administrative boundaries is the ability to apply policies, or higher-level abstractions of routing, to the network. As administrative features evolve, the ability to provide accounting information about the network will become important.

Another key aspect of routing is the inherent support for redundancy. By its nature, routing is closely tied to redundancy. In fact, without redundancy there really is no need for routing. As the degree of redundancy and/or the number of paths increases, routing increases in importance.

All of the features listed above help to make routing a logical choice for external connectivity. When connecting to the Internet, IP routing is required. As trust declines in allowing outside connections to internal corporate or personal resources, the security, monitoring, and administrative abilities associated with routers become essential in operating a network with external access. The combination of routing, external connectivity, and support services have led from placing routers between internal and external networks to the concept of the isolation LAN (iLAN) as a boundary for external access. This concept, enhanced by the proliferation of

FIGURE 9-8. **Evolution from Routers to iLANs to Intranets**

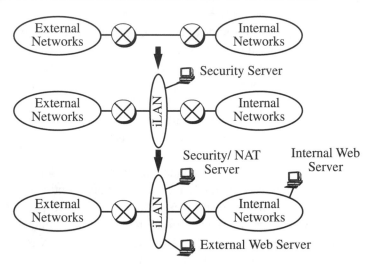

Web-type information access and transfer, has led to a new term for networks, the *intranet*. In the intranet of Figure 9-8, not only is there a separation of administrative responsibilities, but information itself is also separated into internal and external resources.

9.6 Hybrid Switching/Routing Mechanisms

There are benefits with both switching and routing, and some methods have been developed that bring them together in various fashions. Some that we will consider here are ATM options, such as LANE and MPOA, NBMA hybrid mechanisms, service switching, and IP switching. These interconnection mechanisms have similarities that are rooted in the contrasts between switching and routing, as well as the other factors discussed earlier—multicast capability, connection orientation, offered abilities and services, performance upgrades, and flow considerations.

9.6.1 NHRP

The next-hop resolution protocol (NHRP) is one method to take advantage of a (shorter, faster) data-link-layer path in an NBMA IP environment. For example, if we have multiple IP subnetworks using the same NBMA infrastructure, instead of using the standard IP path from source to destination, NHRP can be used to provide a shorter path directly through the NBMA network, as in Figure 9-9.

FIGURE 9-9. **NHRP Flow Optimization in an NBMA Environment**

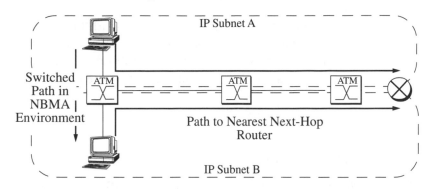

NHRP provides a path through the NBMA network toward the destination. If the destination is directly on the NBMA network, then the path will be to the destination. When the destination is beyond the NBMA network, then the path will be to the exit router from the NBMA network closest to the destination.

NHRP is one method for diverging from the standard IP routing model to optimize paths in the network. A strong case for the success of a method such as NHRP is the open nature of the ongoing work on NHRP, through the Internetworking Over NBMA (ION) Working Group of the IETF, along with its acceptance as part of the MPOA mechanism.

9.6.2 MPOA

MPOA applies NHRP to LANE to incorporate LANE environments into multiprotocol environments, and to allow optimized switching paths across networks (or subnets). MPOA is an attempt to build scalability into ATM systems, through integrating switching and routing functions into a small number of NHRP/MPOA/LANE-capable routers, and reducing the routing functions in the large number of edge devices.

MPOA builds on LANE to reduce some of the trade-offs discussed earlier with LANE. First, by integrating LANE with NHRP, paths between networks (or subnets) can be optimized over the ATM infrastructure. We now also have an integrated mechanism for accessing other network-layer protocols. The complexity trade-off with LANE is still there, however, and is increased with the integration of NHRP and MPOA. There are numerous control, configuration, and information flows in an MPOA environment, between MPOA clients (MPCs), MPOA servers (MPSs), and LECSs. In each of these devices reside network-layer routing/forwarding engines,

MPOA client-server functions, LANE client functions, and possibly NHRP server functions.

It should be noted that, until link-layer and network-layer functions are truly integrated, perhaps through a common, distributed forwarding table (combining what we think of today as switching and routing tables), where and how information flows are configured, established, and maintained by the network will be quite confusing. MPOA may be an answer toward this integration, as well as I-PNNI or NHRP.

9.6.3 Service Switching

Service switching based on flow or end-to-end information is a term that is used to generically describe mechanisms for optimizing paths in a hybrid switching/routing environment, with the major differentiator being the criteria for determining when to route or switch traffic (see Figure 9-10). Multiple vendors are developing their own standards for hybrid mechanisms, and since neither networking vendors nor vendor-specific mechanisms are discussed in this book, the generic term is used instead.

For example, one criterion for determining when to route or switch is the amount of traffic in an application's session, or the size and duration of the flow. The concept behind this is to amortize the cost of setting up and tearing down connections over large amounts of traffic. It really does not make sense to go through the overhead of setting up a connection (say, via ATM) through the network to send one or a few units of information, which is likely for some traffic types (*ping*, NFS, DNS, http, UDP in general), while for traffic types that typically transfer relatively large amounts of information (FTP, TCP in general) this overhead is a small percentage of the transferred information.

FIGURE 9-10. **Using Flow or End-to-End Information to Make Forwarding Decisions**

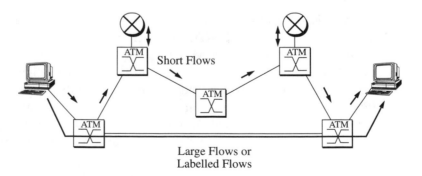

We can use some general rules, such as counting the number of cells/packets that have the same destination address and session type, or using the port number, to determine when to switch or route. For example, we may choose to route all UDP traffic and switch all TCP traffic, or switch traffic with particular port numbers. While this method provides some optimization between switching and routing, it by itself does not address end-to-end services. It appears that this method is particularly useful when switching a large number of connections of different types of information, which is likely to occur over backbones or at traffic aggregation points in the network.

Another mechanism is to take a more generic approach to distinguish traffic types. By allowing devices (i.e., routers) to create labels to identify a particular characteristic of traffic (protocol, transport mechanism, port ID, even user- or application-specific information), these labels can be exchanged between devices to allow them to handle labelled traffic in special ways, such as providing priority queues, cut-through routing, or other service-related support for the traffic. This type of mechanism has the advantage of being configurable for a particular environment, especially if it can support user- or application-specific requirements.

Now let's take a look at the interconnection mechanisms presented in this chapter, along with evaluation criteria. Table 9-1 presents a summary of this information. When an interconnection mechanism is evaluated against a criterion, it may be optimized for that criterion (+), it may have a negative impact on that criterion (–), it may have no effect on that criterion (0), or it may not be applicable to the criterion (N/A). Each interconnection mechanism is evaluated against design goals and criteria developed in this chapter. You can use this information as a start toward developing your own evaluation criteria. There will likely be customer- and environment-specific criteria that can be added to what is presented here, or you may develop a set of criteria that is entirely different, based on your experience, perspectives, customers, and environments.

TABLE 9-1. **Summary of Evaluation Criteria for Interconnection Mechanisms**

	Shared Medium	Switching	Routing	LANE	MPOA	1577	NHRP	Service Switching
Scalability	–	0	+	0	+	–	+	0 to +
Optimizing Flow Models	–	+	0	0	+	0	+	+
External Connectivity	–	–	+	–	0	+	0	0

TABLE 9-1. **Summary of Evaluation Criteria for Interconnection Mechanisms** *(Continued)*

	Shared Medium	Switching	Routing	LANE	MPOA	1577	NHRP	Service Switching
Support for Services	0	0 to +	0	0	+	–	+	+
Cost	+	+	–	+	+	0	+	+
Performance	–	+	+	0	0	0	+	+
Ease of use	+	+	0	–	–	0	–	–
Adaptability	–	0	+	+	+	0	+	+

9.7 Applying Interconnection Mechanisms to the Design

Interconnections are important from at least two perspectives: the degree of concentration of networks or flows at the interconnection (*hierarchy*), and the number of alternate paths provided by the interconnection (*redundancy*).

9.7.1 Hierarchy

Throughout the first part of this book, we looked for locations where information came together in the network, whether it was applications, users, flows, or broadcast domains, and examined where boundaries between areas occur. Such locations point to a consolidation of information, which leads to the formation of hierarchies in the network. Hierarchies play an important role in interconnection mechanisms, for as they indicate consolidation points in the network, they are likely to show where multiple technologies interconnect.

Some metrics for measuring hierarchy in the network are the concentration of flows, technology connections at or within an area, and the number of networks or areas that are interconnected. We can describe the degree of hierarchy as low, medium, or high, based on the following criteria:

Degree of Hierarchy	Concentration of Flows/Connections
None	1:1
Low	2:1
Medium	3:1 to 5:1
High	6:1 or greater

9.7.2 Redundancy

Redundancy, or the number of alternate paths in the network, is an important part of providing reliability in the network. Another commonly used term associated with redundancy is *diversity*. Looking at the number of alternate paths is a fairly simple view of redundancy and is not end-to-end, but in order to evaluate end-to-end redundancy, we must consider all components in the end-to-end path, a far more complex task. This simplistic view of redundancy is sufficient for determining criteria for interconnection.

During the requirements and flow analyses, we have discussed and shown service metrics for reliability, but until this section we have not yet been able to do much in the network design to support it. Where mission-critical applications and specified reliability in flows occur, redundancy is likely to be indicated. There are two components of redundancy to consider, the number of paths at convergence points and the degree of redundancy provided by alternate paths. In providing alternate paths in the network, there will be locations where these multiple paths converge. It is these convergence points where redundancy affects the interconnection mechanism.

Alternate paths can provide a variety of degrees of redundancy in the network. Consider the following examples.

Low-Redundancy Path

First, an alternate path may not be immediately available when the primary path is disabled. There may be some configuration (possibly even human intervention) required to make the alternate path operational, which means that there will be a significant delay—on the order of minutes—while the alternate path is brought up. Furthermore, the performance characteristics of this alternate path may be (quite a bit) less than the primary path.

Figure 9-11 shows a path with a low degree of redundancy. This means that the end user/application will encounter a disruption in service (either in terms of delay or loss of application session) and a degradation in perceived performance.

Medium-Redundancy Path

A higher degree of redundancy is when the alternate path is readily available, but this path has a lower degree of performance than the primary path. Readily available means that the alternate path may be immediately available, or there may be a short wait—milliseconds to seconds—while flows are rerouted across the alternate path, but no human intervention is required. Such a path could be termed being in *hot-standby*.

FIGURE 9-11. **Low-Redundancy Path**

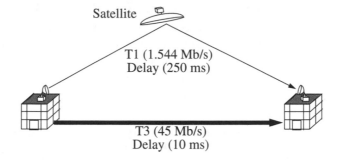

In Figure 9-12, the redundant path (the T1) is ready to work and can be cut over quickly by the routing protocol. It has a lower capacity, however, and would likely result in degraded performance for its users. This is a medium degree of redundancy, and means that the user/application will (usually) not notice a disruption in service, although there will be a degradation in perceived performance when the alternate path is established.

High-Redundancy Path

The highest degree of redundancy is where one or more alternate paths are readily available, and the performance of each alternate path is the same as the primary path. In Figure 9-13, the redundant path is equal in performance—both capacity and delay—to the primary path.

This is a high degree of redundancy, and means that the user/application will not usually notice a disruption in service but will enjoy the same level of performance with the alternate path. Ideally, this degree of redundancy means that users never notice when the primary path fails. If equal performance paths are used, as in Figure 9-13, and the traffic load is shared between the T3s during normal operations, then this would not be considered high-redundancy but would be medium-redundancy. If the normal traffic load is shared between the equal paths, then the loss of the primary path would result in degraded performance and service to the users.

FIGURE 9-12. **Medium-Redundancy Path**

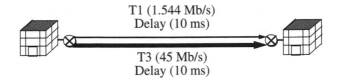

FIGURE 9-13. **High-Redundancy Path**

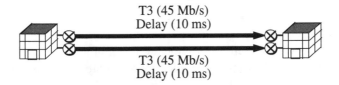

An obvious trade-off between the degrees of redundancy is in cost. Providing a low degree of redundancy is relatively cheap, while a high degree of redundancy is almost, if not equal to, building a second, backup network.

We can describe the degrees of redundancy as low, medium, or high, based on the following guidelines:

Degree of Redundancy	Number of Paths	Description of Redundancy
None	No alternates	Service failure
Low	1 alternate, unequal	Service disruption and performance degradation
Medium	1 or 2 alternates, unequal	No service disruption, but performance is degraded
High	2 or more alternates, equal	No service disruption or performance degradation

The guidelines for hierarchy and redundancy in the network are useful not only in developing interconnection mechanisms, but also in developing network management, security, and addressing and routing strategies for our design.

9.8 Case Study

Step 1   Determining the Degrees of Hierarchy in the Design. This design environment has varying degrees of hierarchy. As we can see in Figure 9-14, the flow hierarchy ranges from 1:1 at the SJ campus, to 2:1 at the SF campus, to 3:1 at the
Oakland campus. Using the metrics in Section 9.7, this results in flow hierarchies
that range from none to medium.

Step 2   Determining the Degrees of Redundancy in the Design. Given that one
of our applications is considered mission-critical for our design, and that the reliability requirement is 100% for some of our flows, redundancy will be a critical part
of our interconnectivity strategy. Figure 9-15 shows the flows that have the highest
reliability requirements.

For these flows, we want to provide additional measures of reliability. Two of
the options that we will want to consider are alternate, redundant paths between and
within campuses and redundant network hardware at each campus.

FIGURE 9-14. Flows and Flow Hierarchies in Design Environment

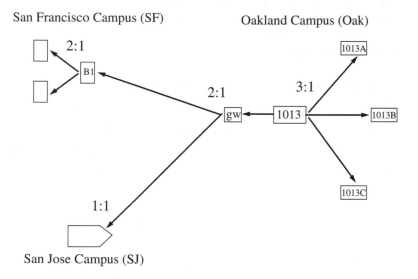

FIGURE 9-15. **Flows with 100% Reliability Requirement**

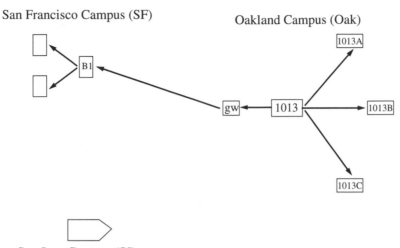

From Section 9.7, we will label these flows as medium to high redundancy, which means that we will design alternate paths that have performance that is equal or unequal to the primary path. For the connection to the SJ campus, we will label that connection as low to medium redundancy, and will provide an alternate that is unequal to the primary path.

Perhaps the biggest factor in redundancy is the cost of provisioning alternate paths. When considering how to provide redundancy in the network, you should look at all of the components in the redundant path and determine what your limiting factor or weak link is. There can be many components in a path, as shown in Figure 9-16. To provide a fully redundant path is expensive, often more than just twice the cost of the primary path. When getting redundant service in the MAN or WAN environments, consider the demarcation points at each site. Redundancy to multiple provider central offices or even to multiple carriers will improve redundancy to the demarc points.

From the previous chapter, recall that our candidates for network technologies were ATM at DS3 and/or OC-3c in the MAN, SF, and Oakland campuses, and 100 Mb/s Ethernet in the Oakland campus. For redundancy, we will look at the ATM environment between SF and Oakland, and also within the Oakland campus environment.

FIGURE 9-16. **Locating the Limiting Factor in a Redundant Path**

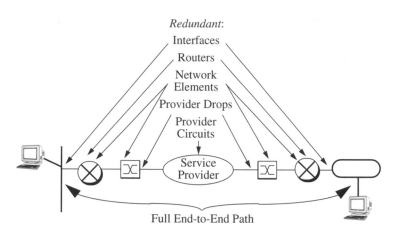

In discussions with the customer, we offered a number of alternatives for applying redundancy to the design, based on the levels of redundancy shown in Figure 9-16. Their original choice was to provide full, end-to-end redundancy between Building B1 in SF and Building 1013 in Oakland, but the original cost estimate for the redundant path (about 85% additional cost) resulted in a scaling down of the plan. As an optional plan, a recommendation was made to provision redundant ATM virtual circuits between all campuses, including the SJ campus, and to bring those circuits into ATM interfaces at routers at each site. The routers would be at the campus/MAN interface of each campus and would connect to ATM or 10 Mb/s and 100 Mb/s Ethernet switches. Figure 9-17 shows the design with routers and switches added.

At this point, we have ATM switching within the SF campus, 10 Mb/s Ethernet switching within the SJ campus, and both ATM and 100 Mb/s Ethernet switching within the Oakland campus. All of these switching environments are separated by IP routers, which also terminate the MAN ATM service from the service provider. RFC 1577 was chosen for ATM in this design, to provide simplicity at the network layer.

FIGURE 9-17. **Routers and Switches Added to Design**

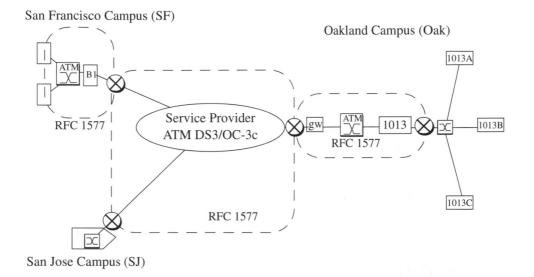

9.9 Concluding Remarks

While we have covered a number of interconnection mechanisms in this chapter, there are many more that you should explore in detail. The variants of Ethernet, including switched Ethernet and 100/1000 Ethernet, as well as FDDI switching, are important, relatively straightforward interconnection mechanisms that are comparable to ATM switching for many environments.

We have also alluded to variants of ATM switching and IP routing in the section on hybrid mechanisms. This is a rapidly changing area and one that shows promise. Material to help you understand hybrid mechanisms—as well as all of the mechanisms discussed in this chapter—is listed below.

Suggested Further Reading

1. Cole, R., Shur, D., and Villamizar, C. IP over ATM: A framework document. *RFC 1932*. April 1996.

2. Heinanen, J. Multiprotocol encapsulation over ATM adaptation layer 5. *RFC 1483*. July 1993.

3. Heinanen, J., and Govindan, R. NBMA address resolution protocol (NARP). *RFC 1735*. December 1994.

4. LAN emulation over ATM, Version 1.0. ATM Forum. January 1995.

5. Laubach, M. Classical IP and ARP over ATM. *RFC 1577*. January 1994.

6. Perez, M., Mankin, F.A., Hoffman, E., Grossman, G., and Malis, A. ATM signaling support for IP over ATM. *RFC 1755*. February 1995.

7. Perlman, R. *Interconnections: Bridges and Routers*. Addison-Wesley, Reading, MA, 1992.

8. Private network-network interface specification, Version 1.0 (PNNI 1.0). ATM Forum. March 1996.

Also examine the Internet-drafts from the Internetworking Over NBMA (ION) Working Group of the IETF.

Exercises

1. Using the rules of thumb for capacity planning given in Section 9.2, recommend whether or not hierarchy needs to be introduced in the following shared-media environments:

   a) A 10-Mb/s Ethernet network that is bursting at a 9-Mb/s MDR

   b) A 100-Mb/s FDDI network that supports an SDR of 40 to 45 Mb/s

   c) A 10-Mb/s Ethernet network that has the composite flow CF1, whose SDR consists of

   $-f_a$, a client-server flow with a capacity of 400 Kb/s

   $-f_b$, a distributed-computing flow with a capacity of 1.2 Mb/s

   $-f_{eng}$, a real-time video stream with a capacity of 2.7 Mb/s

2. Consider a design environment where we have an existing base of PCs and workstations with Ethernet interfaces. Their current capacity needs are beyond 10 Mb/s, and they want to keep their investment in Ethernet NICs. We are migrating from a shared network, and are looking at IP routers, Ethernet 10- and 100-Mb/s switches, and LAN emulation as possible options. Compare and contrast these options, disregarding capacity for the moment.

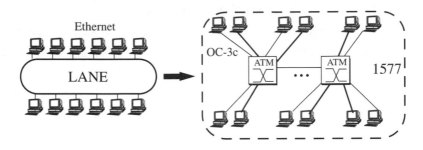

FIGURE 9-18. LANE and 1577 Environments for Exercise 9.3

What distinguishing characteristics of the design environment indicate each of these options? What requirements of the design environment would we need to be better able to make a choice?

3. We are going to use LANE as a step to migrate our Ethernet hosts to a 1577 environment. Our hosts will start with Ethernet NICs and end up with ATM OC-3c NICs in the 1577 environment (see Figure 9-18).

   Design the LANE environment, showing all LANE servers (LECS, LES, BUS, SMS) and the connectivity between them and with the clients (use 12 clients). Show how clients will be migrated from the LANE environment to the 1577 environment (the ATM switches shown in the 1577 environment in Figure 9-18 are also in the LANE environment) as their NICs are upgraded from Ethernet to ATM OC-3c. What changes need to be made in the host configurations as they are migrated to the 1577 environment?

4. For each of the following environments, would you recommend routing or switching? Why? Explain your choices.

   a) A work group of 100 workstations within a building who use client-server applications and share a common IP subnet address

   b) Connecting your LAN to the Internet via a dedicated T1 from an ISP

   c) A backbone between several different organizations within a corporation. Each organization wants to be secure from the others and requires that you monitor traffic between organizational boundaries

5. In many of the hybrid mechanisms, a flow can have either a routed path or a switched path, depending on the flow's characteristics. Given the characteristics of switching and routing discussed in this book and in Exercise 9.3, when would you recommend that a flow be switched, and when should it be routed? Present recommendations based on

a) Duration of the flow in terms of the number of cells, frames, and packets

b) Type of flow, by protocol or application

c) Service requirements of the flow (i.e., performance requirements)

d) Destination (and possibly source) of the flow, as link-layer or network-layer addresses

Are there other flow characteristics that you should consider? If so, give examples.

CHAPTER 10

Logical Design: Network Management and Security

10.1 Integrating Network Management and Security into the Design

At this point in the design process, we are ready to integrate management and security into our network design. Most of this chapter is targeted toward the design considerations of network management and security, with a brief discussion about the different types of management and security. There are some excellent books available on the subject, several of which are presented as suggested reading at the end of the chapter.

Network management and security have previously been afterthoughts in most designs. They were intended for a relatively small user base, but, given the proliferation of the Internet and Web applications, the number of network users has increased dramatically. In addition, most network designs counted on users not being malicious, which was generally true up until a few years ago. Today and in the future, networks are a resource whose integrity should be measurable and verifiable.

We will begin by defining and characterizing management for a network design, and how to plan for monitoring, configuring, and troubleshooting the network. We will then examine network management protocols and instrumentation requirements. This will lead to some of the architectural aspects of applying a network management to the design.

10.2 Defining Network Management

Network management consists of a variety of tasks—monitoring, configuring, troubleshooting, and planning—that are performed by users, administrators, and network personnel. One of the first challenges in developing network management in the design is to define what network management actually means to the organizations that will be performing the tasks and receiving the end service—the customers.

Network management tasks fall into one or more of four categories:

- Monitoring for event notification
- Monitoring for metrics and planning
- Configuration of network parameters
- Troubleshooting the network

10.2.1 Network Elements and Characteristics

A network element is a component of the network that can be managed. This includes hosts, routers, switches, DSUs, hubs, NICs, even cable segments. Networks and network elements have characteristics that can be measured. These characteristics are grouped into end-to-end characteristics, and link and element characteristics.

- *End-to-end characteristics* are those that can be measured across multiple network elements and may be extended across the entire network or between hosts. Examples of end-to-end characteristics for network elements and network traffic are availability, capacity, delay, delay variation (jitter), throughput, various error rates, network utilization, and burstiness of the traffic on the network. These characteristics may be modified depending on the types of traffic on the network.

- *Link and element characteristics* are specific to the type of element being managed. These characteristics are in addition to those that define end-to-end connections. For example, some element characteristics for an IP router would include the IP forwarding rates (in packets/second), the buffer utilization of the router, and any logs of authentication failures.

10.2.2 Monitoring and Metering

Monitoring is obtaining values for the end-to-end, link, and element characteristics. The monitoring process involves collecting data about the desired characteristics, processing some or all of this data, displaying the (processed) data, and archiving some or all of the data.

FIGURE 10-1. **The Monitoring Process**

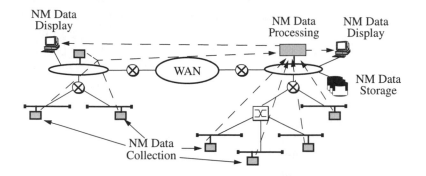

Data are collected usually through a polling or monitoring process involving a network management protocol (e.g., SNMP) or proxy service. As we will see later in this chapter, several techniques may be used to get this data, as well as to ensure that the data are current. When the data are gathered, they may or may not reflect the characteristics that we wish to monitor. The values for some characteristics may be derived from the gathered data, while other values may be modified (e.g., added, time-averaged, turned into delta values). This is processing of the data.

The raw (unprocessed) and postprocessed data are ready to be displayed. There are many potential techniques to display data, including standard monitor displays, field-of-view or wide-screen displays, special-purpose displays, even virtual reality displays. How the data are displayed depends on what the data are being used for, and there may be many different types of displays for one set of characteristics, networks, or management systems.

At some time during this process, some or all of the data are saved to a (semi) permanent media or system. This part of the process may itself have many parts, including *primary storage*, which could be at the network management server; *secondary storage* at a storage server for the network; and *tertiary storage*, which is usually the most permanent—and slowest—storage within the system. Secondary and tertiary storage are often termed *archives*. Figure 10-1 shows each part of this process occurring on a separate device, but they may all be combined on one device.

10.2.3 Monitoring for Event Notification

An event can be described as a problem or failure in a network element, or when a characteristic crosses a threshold value. Events are similar to transients, which are short-lived changes in the behavior of the network. Thresholds may be set on end-to-end or element characteristics for short-term or immediate notification of events. This is termed here *real-time analysis*.

Real-time analysis usually involves short *polling intervals* (requests for data for monitored characteristics), so there is a trade-off between the number of characteristics and network elements polled for real-time analysis versus the amount of resources (capacity, CPU, memory, storage) needed to support real-time analysis. In some cases, the amount of network traffic generated by the periodic polling of multiple characteristics at many network elements can impact the overall performance of the network. For example, if a network has 100 network elements, each element is monitored for 8 characteristics, each characteristic generates an average of 4 bytes of data, and we plan to poll for these characteristics every 5 seconds. If we generate a poll for each individual characteristic, then we would have 800 polls and 800 responses every 5 seconds. If the average size of all polls and responses is 64 bytes, then the amount of traffic is

(800 polls + 800 responses)*(64 bytes/poll or response)*(8 bits/byte)

or 819 Kb each 5 seconds. At best case, this is averaged over the 5 seconds for 164 Kb/s, or it all occurs at roughly the same second for an 819-Kb/s peak every 5 seconds. This would be a problem if the polls/responses were crossing a T1 or slower speed network, or if we grow from 100 to 1000 to 10,000 polled devices.

When this occurs, some modifications need to be made in how management is designed into the network.

10.2.4 Monitoring for Metrics and Planning

The same end-to-end and element characteristics that are used for event monitoring can also be used for trend analysis and to plan for future network growth. When data are collected for the purpose of long-term analysis, the process is termed *metering*, and the measured values are *metrics*. Metrics are used for trend analysis in various ways. In doing continuous, uninterrupted data collection, usually at a long polling interval, we can establish long-term baselines, and use these baselines to note trends where measured values deviate from them.

10.2.5 Generating the Characteristics Set

As part of the design process, we want to generate a working set of end-to-end and element characteristics, and plan for the design to have the facilities to monitor these characteristics at short- and long-term polling intervals. Later in this chapter, we will develop some guidelines on where monitoring facilities should be placed in the design.

Most network elements require some level of configuration by the network personnel. For each network element, we want to generate a table of configuration parameters, to establish the methods for adjusting these parameters, and to know and understand the effects of adjusting the parameters. In order to manage a network properly, it is important to understand how the configuration parameters affect each network element, as well as the end-to-end characteristics.

We also need to understand the effects of problems with the network elements and how to correct such problems. Troubleshooting, which consists of problem notification, isolation, identification, and resolution, can be aided by knowing likely failure modes in the network, their effects, and the possible steps to correct them.

It should be noted that in generating a set of working characteristics, including these configuration parameters and failure modes, what we are really doing is going through a detailed review of how the network operates or will operate. This can be quite complex and time-consuming, but the result is that you will better understand what is happening in the network, thus making you better prepared to operate and manage it.

10.3 Designing with Manageable Resources

We will now take a look at some of the popular network management protocols, the requirements for management protocols and instrumentation, and the impact of management instrumentation on the network design. *Instrumentation* is the set of facilities provided by the network elements for accessing element characteristics and configuration parameters. Network management protocols are used to couple this instrumentation with monitoring, display, processing, and storage to form a complete management system. There are currently two major network management protocols: the simple network management protocol (SNMP and SNMPv2) and the common management information protocol (CMIP)/CMIP over TCP/IP (CMOT).

SNMP has seen widespread use and forms the basis for many popular commercial network management systems. It provides facilities for collecting and configuring parameters from network elements. These are done through the SNMP commands *get* (to collect a parameter), *get-next* (to collect the next parameter in the list), and *set* (to configure a parameter). There are also provisions for the unsolicited notification of events, through the use of traps. A *trap* is a user-configurable threshold for a parameter. When the threshold is crossed, the values for one or more parameters are sent to a specified location. The benefit of trap generation is that polling for certain parameters can be stopped or the polling interval lengthened, and instead an automatic notice is sent to the management system when an event occurs.

Parameters that are accessible via SNMP are grouped into management information bases, or MIBs. Parameters can be part of the standard MIB (currently MIB-II) or a proprietary MIB. There are other MIBs that are also standard, with each

MIB having parameters specific to a type of network element. For example, there are MIBs for routers, switches, and circuits (e.g., T3). There is also a remote moni-toring MIB (RMON MIB), which provides information about a LAN segment. There are also enterprise-specific MIBs, with parameters that are either proprietary or specific to a particular vendor's product.

SNMP version 2 (SNMPv2) builds on SNMP, providing more secure authenti-cation (SNMP authentication consists of plain-text community strings), the ability to retrieve blocks of parameters, and trap generation for most parameters.

CMIP/CMOT provides for parameter collection and setting, as with SNMP/SNMPv2, but also allows for more types of operations. Many CMIP/CMOT fea-tures, such as globally unique object naming, object classification, alarm reporting, audit trails, and test management, can also be provided by SNMPv2 by creating new MIBs to support these abstractions.

In general, SNMP/SNMPv2 is simpler to configure and use than CMIP/CMOT, helping to make it widely accepted. It is usually easier to instrument a router or any other network element with SNMP/SNMPv2 than with CMIP/CMOT. SNMP/SNMPv2's simplicity has also caused some problems, particularly in modern switching and routing network elements. With hot-swapping and autoconfiguration of interfaces, the correlation of physical slots with logical interfaces can be dynamic. SNMP/SNMPv2 has not been able to handle this dynamic nature. As technologies/services evolve to decouple the physical and logical networks, man-agement protocols will need to support this dynamic nature.

10.3.1 Instrumentation Methods

Methods to access network management parameters include SNMPv2, end-to-end monitoring tools, and direct-access methods. SNMPv2 provides access to MIB-II, other standard MIBs (e.g., DS1 MIB), enterprise-specific MIBs, and remote moni-toring MIBs (RMON MIB, SMON MIB, AToM MIB). End-to-end monitoring tools include utilities such as *ping*, *traceroute*, and *tcpdump*, while direct-access methods include telnet, FTP, TFTP, and connections via a console port.

An example of a base set of parameters to monitor can be developed from the standard MIB-II. The following parameters can be collected on a per-interface basis:

Parameter	Description
ifInOctets	Number of bytes received
ifOutOctets	Number of bytes sent
ifInUcastPkts	Number of unicast packets received

ifOutUcastPkts	Number of unicast packets sent
ifInNUcastPkts	Number of multicast/broadcast packets received
ifOutNUcastPkts	Number of multicast/broadcast packets sent
ifInErrors	Number of errored packets received
ifOutErrors	Number of packets that could not be sent

These parameters can be used for both short-term event monitoring and long-term metering of throughput and error rates. In addition, the following parameter may be collected to determine availability:

| ifOperStatus | State of an interface (up, down, testing) |

This parameter could be used in conjunction with end-to-end monitoring (e.g., *ping*) to verify availability, as well as to (roughly) measure delay.

In developing a network management plan, the instrumentation requirements for each network element should be collected. These requirements would be for each network element and could be grouped into similar categories, such as forwarding elements (routers, switches, switching hubs), pass-through elements (DSUs, simple concentrators, simple bridges), hosts, and passive devices such as those that use RMON.

Some ways to improve the network management design are to ensure that the element instrumentation is accurate, dependable, and simple. There are a couple of ways to ensure accuracy in the instrumentation: testing and taking alternate measurements. If a lab environment is available, some limited network conditions can be replicated and tested. For example, the packet forwarding rates in routers can be tested by generating known quantities of traffic by hosts and/or traffic generators, and comparing the results in the routers to those from the hosts/traffic generators.

Parameters can also be verified from the operational network. This is done by taking alternate measurements of the same parameter at different points in the network. We may be able to get link-layer information from DSUs, routers, and switches in the path of a flow, and, by comparing that information, determine where there are discrepancies in parameter measurements.

For a network management system to work properly, the instrumentation needs to be dependable. A network management system that is the first thing to crash when network transients occur is useless. This may seem obvious, but few current management systems are truly robust and dependable. Ways that dependability can be enhanced in the design is to physically separate and replicate the management components. By having multiple systems collecting, processing, displaying, and storing data for different parts of the network, and by building hierarchy in the management information flows, the loss of any single component of the management system will have less impact on the network's manageability.

10.4 Network Management Architecture

A network design should consider the data flows for management information, as we did earlier for user network traffic. When an end-to-end network connection fails, one or more methods for network monitoring, configuration, and troubleshooting should remain in place. Some architectural issues we will consider in this section are

- In-band versus out-of-band monitoring
- Centralized versus distributed monitoring
- Capacity and delay requirements
- Flows of management data
- Configuration of network management

In designing a management architecture, the components of the management system (displays, storage servers, processors) are superimposed on the network design, giving us the placement of monitoring nodes, potential checks and balances in monitoring, and insight on what monitoring data is needed in each area of the network, or what is common to the entire network.

Monitoring nodes are network elements or hosts that collect information about portions of the network. It is common for there to be a single monitoring node responsible for collecting all required information for the network, but there are some benefits to having multiple monitoring nodes distributed throughout the network. Communications between the monitoring nodes and network elements, or between monitoring nodes themselves, may be in-band or out-of-band with the user network traffic.

10.4.1 In-Band/Out-of-Band Monitoring

In-band monitoring is having the network management data flow over the same network that the user network traffic uses. This makes the network management architecture relatively simple, but means that when problems occur on the network, management data flows are impacted as well, and it may prove difficult to monitor or troubleshoot the network. A primary objective of the network management system is to be able to do event monitoring when the network is under duress, for example, when congested with traffic, suffering from network hardware/software/configuration problems, or under a security attack.

Out-of-band monitoring is providing different paths for network management data flows and user network traffic (see Figure 10-2). This type of monitoring has the distinct advantage of allowing the management system to continue to monitor the network during network events, effectively allowing you to see into portions of the network that are unreachable through the network. Out-of-band monitoring may be provided by ISDN (i.e., the D-channel), by a separate Frame Relay connection or ATM virtual circuit, or via a POTS connection.

The trade-off is that out-of-band monitoring makes the network design more complex and expensive. One way to compromise between in-band and out-of-band monitoring is to provide out-of-band monitoring at a redundancy degree of 1. Recall from previous chapters that a redundancy degree of 1 means that the redundant connection (in this case the out-of-band connection) is at a much lower level of performance, and that it may take time to establish and use this redundant connection. For example, out-of-band monitoring may be through phone lines, as in Figure 10-2.

Some useful considerations for out-of-band monitoring are to provide separate physical network interfaces for monitoring and separate logical connections on switched networks. Full-time or part-time dial-up modems are another useful way to provide out-of-band monitoring, as well as having an alternate method to reach remote network devices.

FIGURE 10-2. Out-of-Band Monitoring

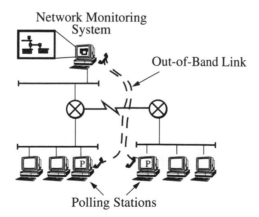

10.4.2 Centralized/Distributed Monitoring

In a centralized monitoring plan, such as that in Figure 10-3, all monitoring data (i.e., *pings*, SNMP polls/responses, and possibly *traceroutes*) radiate from one monitoring node, using in-band or out-of-band paths. This monitoring node is typically a host running a set of network management tools.

In a distributed monitoring plan, such as that in Figure 10-4, monitoring data are collected at localized monitoring nodes and either passed on to display and storage nodes or processed by the monitoring node. When the data are passed on to display and storage nodes without processing, the monitoring nodes act to localize the data collection, reducing the amounts of management data that transit the network and possibly providing backup monitoring capabilities in the event of a loss of any monitoring node.

When the management data are processed before being sent to display and storage nodes, then the monitoring nodes act as local filters, sending only the relevant data (such as deltas on counter values or updates on events). This may substantially reduce the amount of management data on the network, which is especially important if the monitoring is in-band.

Thus, we can have monitoring nodes at strategic locations throughout the network, polling local hosts and network elements, collecting and processing the management data, and forwarding some or all of this data to display and storage devices. The number and locations of monitoring nodes will depend on the size of the

FIGURE 10-3. Centralized Monitoring

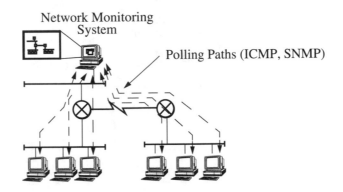

FIGURE 10-4. **Distributed Monitoring**

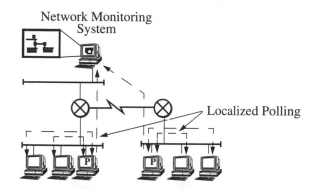

network being designed, the amount of management information expected to be collected, and where the displays and storage devices are located in the management architecture.

10.4.3 Capacity and Delay Requirements

Some rules of thumb for determining the number and locations of monitoring nodes are as follows.

Rule 1. For a LAN environment, start with one monitoring node per subnet. For each subnet, determine the

- Number of hosts and network elements to be polled for parameters
- Number of parameters to be collected
- Frequency of polling (polling interval)

This will give you an estimate of the average and peak data rates for management traffic per subnet. If the rate is greater than 10% of the capacity of the LAN, consider reducing the amount of management traffic generated by reducing one or more of the variables above. If the rate is less than 1% of the capacity of the LAN, this indicates that it may be possible to consolidate the monitoring nodes for some of the subnets.

For most of the standard LAN technologies (Ethernet, FDDI, Token Ring), the management traffic rate should be 2% to 5% of the LAN capacity. As LAN capacities increase, this estimate should be reduced accordingly—for example, a HiPPI

LAN with a capacity of 800 Mb/s should not have an expected management traffic rate of 2% to 5% of 800 Mb/s (16 to 40 Mb/s). An order of magnitude less (0.2% to 0.5%, or 1.6 to 4.0 Mb/s) is more reasonable.

Rule 2. For a WAN/MAN environment, start with one monitoring node per tail site, or at each WAN/MAN–LAN interface. The reasons for monitoring node placement in the WAN/MAN environment are different (for now) from those for the LAN environment. Placing a monitoring node at each tail site or at the WAN/MAN–LAN interface allows us not only to monitor the network at those sites, but also to measure, verify, and possibly guarantee services and service characteristics from the WAN/MAN to each site.

10.4.4 Checks and Balances in Monitoring

While it is appropriate to reduce duplication of effort in network monitoring, it is also advisable to have more than one method for collecting management parameters, in order to validate their correctness. Vendor SNMP agent and MIB implementations are not guaranteed to provide correct information. Therefore, whenever possible, verify their accuracy through a secondary method. Some verification methods include using data from RMON agents, the end host, or traffic analyzers to compare against SNMP-collected data from network elements. Once the SNMP-collected data is proven satisfactory, it may then be used to check the accuracy of other methods for collecting data.

Checks and balances should be repeated regularly, as the accuracy of management data may change with new releases of vendor software and/or hardware.

10.4.5 Flows of Management Data

Network management data typically consists of SNMP parameter names and values. These data are generated by network elements, transported via SNMP to monitoring nodes, and possibly forwarded to display and storage devices. It is important to the network design that an understanding of how the data are generated, transported, and archived be developed.

Management data may either be generated in a query/response (stateless) method, as with SNMP and *ping*, or in response to a prearranged set of conditions (stateful), as with SNMP traps or with SNMPv2. Large numbers of SNMP queries should be spread out over time, not only to avoid network congestion, but also to avoid burdening the network elements and monitoring nodes with any calculations required to generate management parameters.

Management data will consist of frequently generated parameters for real-time event notification and less frequently generated (or needed) parameters for metering or planning purposes. It may be that the same parameters are used for both purposes.

Since frequent polling can generate large amounts of data, storage of this data can become a problem. Some rules of thumb for management data generation and storage are as follows.

- *Rule 1.* Determine which management data are necessary to keep stored locally and which data may be archived. Management data are usually kept local, stored where they can easily and quickly be retrieved, for *event analysis*, which is checking the time before and after an event to determine any indications of the event, and short-term *trend analysis*. Management data that are not being used for these purposes should be archived to tertiary storage, such as tape.

- *Rule 2.* When a management parameter is being used for both event notification and trend analysis, consider copying every Nth iteration of that parameter to a separate database location, where N is large enough to keep the size of this data relatively small, yet is small enough so that the data are useful in trend analysis. If there are indications that more immediate analysis needs to be done, then either a short-term analysis can be done on the locally stored data (from Rule 1, above), or the interval N can be temporarily shortened.

- *Rule 3.* When management data are collected for trend analysis, the data can be stored local to the monitoring nodes, then downloaded to the storage devices when management and/or user traffic is expected to be low, such as late at night.

- *Rule 4.* A management data-archival system should indicate what the archived data refer to and the time period that they were collected. This information (sometimes termed *metadata*) may come from the processing at the monitoring nodes, or from the archival system itself. This metadata is necessary in case environmental parameters of the network elements (e.g., location, IP addresses) change with time.

10.4.6 Configuration of Network Management

The configuration plan for network management should not be as complex as the monitoring plan has been, since network elements will generally not be configured repeatedly and en masse. There is usually no need for a distributed configuration system, although out-of-band configuration access is a good idea. In general, it is useful to have more than one path for network element configuration, with one of the paths being out-of-band. For example, we could have the following in-band and out-of-band paths available: in-band via SNMP/SNMPv2 (using the *set* command), telnet, or FTP/TFTP, and out-of-band via dial-up (e.g., ISDN) connections or through FTP/TFTP via dial-on-demand, switched 56 Kb/s connections.

The most common primary configuration methods are to use either a direct console connection, telnet, or SNMP/SNMPv2. Common backup configuration methods are to FTP/TFTP configuration files to the network element or access via a dial-up method.

Configuration via SNMP/SNMPv2 relies on an enterprise-specific MIB provided by the vendor of the network element. In order to use this enterprise-specific MIB, we need to determine if custom SNMP/SNMPv2 client software has been provided, or if a *schema* (management template) has been provided to use with off-the-shelf management software. When SNMP/SNMPv2 has been chosen as a configuration method, the enterprise-specific MIBs used in the network should be checked to see if they support the parameters that need to be monitored.

When SNMP is used for configuration, it should be noted that the trivial security provided by SNMP (community strings) may not be sufficient for your network. Some security improvements are to use a software command that will enable/disable the ability to modify the network element's configuration via SNMP, or to use SNMPv2 with its stronger security capability. When software is used to enable/disable configuration ability, such software should be authenticated via passwords. This method may also be used with SNMPv2. Other security mechanisms, which will be discussed later in this chapter, may also be used in conjunction with SNMP/SNMPv2.

Many network elements, especially switching/routing elements and hosts, allow direct configuration access via a console interface. Direct configuration is one of the more secure methods of configuration. Unfortunately, there is no standard configuration interface.

10.5 Security

Effective security is the combination of understanding what security means to each of the components of the system—users, applications, hosts, and networks—together with the planning and implementation of security policies and mechanisms.

This section covers how security may be determined and brought into network design. Security is an area of rapid expansion and change in the networking community, so we will present some concepts and mechanisms that should be valid across a wide range of security options. Toward developing a security plan for the network, we will examine user requirements for security, define security policies, perform security risk analysis for the design environment, and develop a security plan.

Security in the network needs to protect network resources from being disabled, stolen, modified, or damaged. This includes protecting hosts, servers, users, and system data, as well as less tangible resources such as an organization's image and privacy.

Attacks against the system range from relatively innocuous unauthorized probing and using of resources, to keeping authorized users from accessing resources (denial of service), to modifying, stealing, or destroying resources. Some first steps in reducing the probability of an attack are to determine the system's requirements for security and to develop a security policy.

10.5.1 Security Policies

There are many trade-offs in security, and it can be a two-edged sword. Sometimes security is confused with control over users and their actions. This confusion occurs when rules, regulations, and security guardians are placed above the goals, objectives, and work that the organization is trying to accomplish. The road toward implementing security starts with awareness and understanding of the possible security flaws in the system, then leads to the removal of those flaws. These flaws are often in the areas of system and applications software, the ways that security mechanisms are implemented, and in how users do their work. This last area is where educating the user can be most beneficial.

Security policies are an important part of the security plan in that they help to define and document how the system can be used with minimal security risks. They can also clarify to the user what the security risks are, what can be done to reduce those risks, and the consequences of not helping to reduce them. At a high level, a security policy can incorporate an overall security philosophy. Two common security philosophies are

- Deny specifics/accept all else
- Accept specifics/deny all else

Deny specifics/accept all else requires a thorough understanding of security threats, as these will become the specifics to be denied. It can also be difficult to verify the security implementation, since it is hard to define "all else" in this philosophy.

On the other hand, accept specifics/deny all else requires a thorough understanding of user requirements, as these will become the specifics to be accepted. It is easier to validate the security implementation, since there are only a few finite "accepted" uses.

Examples of security policies are acceptable use statements, security incident–handling procedures, configuration-modification policies, and network access/firewall policies. Each of these policies has its place in the security plan. An acceptable use statement, configuration-modification policy, or network access/firewall policy should describe not only how system resources can be accessed, used, and modified, but also why, to help users understand the policies that they are being asked to accept. Incident-handling procedures are also helpful, in that they make users aware of what to do when a security problem occurs, making them part of the security process and not just victims of it.

10.5.2 Security Risk Analysis

A *risk analysis* is a process used to determine which components of the system need to be protected and the types of security risks they should be protected from. This information can then be used to determine strategic locations in the logical and physical network designs where security can reasonably be implemented.

Risk analyses are subjective. One of the ways to minimize the subjectivity is to involve representatives from various groups of the organization in the analysis process. This will get many different perspectives in the analysis. You can also perform risk analysis periodically. As an organization grows and changes, the security risks may also change. A periodic risk analysis will ensure that new risks are examined and can also show where new security mechanisms may be applied to the system. In addition, security policies should be reviewed periodically. Subsequent reviews may highlight previously missed risks not initially covered in the policies.

FIGURE 10-5. Example of a Risk Analysis Worksheet

Effect\Likelihood	Mainframes	Workstations (PCs or Macs)	Routers/ Bridges/ Switches	Servers	DNS	Email
Denial of Service	D/D	B/B	A/C	D/D	A/B	A/B
Theft of Data	D/D	A/B	D/C	D/D	C/C	A/B
Corruption of Data	D/D	A/B	A/C	D/D	A/C	A/B
Unauthorized Use	D/D	B/B	C/C	D/D	C/C	B/B
Viruses	D/D	B/B	B/C	D/D	A/B	B/C
Trojan Horses	D/D	B/C	B/C	D/D	B/C	B/C
Physical Destruction	D/D	A/C	A/C	D/D	A/C	A/C

	Effect		*Likelihood*
A	Destructive	A	Certain
B	Disabling	B	Likely
C	Disruptive	C	Unlikely
D	No Impact	D	Impossible

In the example in Figure 10-5, a risk analysis is done on a fictitious company. The analysis couples potential security threats with components of the system, including specific applications, hosts, servers, and network elements. The subjective part is evaluating each threat with a system component, determining the likelihood of a security attack occurring and the effect that each attack would have. Our example indicates that

- A strong user authentication mechanism should be applied to the system.
- Some type of added protection, such as an application firewall, should be used with the email and DNS applications.
- Encryption should be considered for email messages to the corporate office.

These and other security mechanisms are discussed next.

10.6 Security Mechanisms

There are several security mechanisms available today and many more on the horizon. However, not all mechanisms are appropriate for every environment. Each security mechanism should be evaluated for the environment that it is being applied to, based on the degree of protection it provides, its impact on the users' ability to do work, the amount of expertise required for installation and configuration, the cost of purchasing, implementing, and operating it, and the amounts of administration and maintenance required. Security mechanisms covered here are physical security, security awareness, user authentication, packet filters, application wrappers and gateways, encryption, and firewalls.

10.6.1 Physical Security

Physical security is the most basic form of security, and the one that is most intuitive to the user. Nevertheless, it is often overlooked when developing a security plan. Used to protect system resources from physical access and damage, physical security should be addressed even if the campus or building already has access restrictions or security guards. Ways to implement physical security include

- Limiting access to servers, by having protected access (e.g., card key restrictions) and locked rooms, and by not allowing unattended logins at certain locations or for particular hosts or servers
- Providing a backup power source and power conditioning, and by providing secondary backup storage

Physical security also applies to other types of physical threats, such as natural disasters (e.g., fires, earthquakes, and storms). Security from natural disasters includes, in addition to the measures above, protection from fire (using alarm systems and fire-abatement equipment), water (with pumping and other water-removal/protection mechanisms), and structural degradation (through security equipment in racks, attaching racks to the floors/walls, etc.). There are no trade-offs to implementing physical security. It should be a part of all security plans and network designs.

10.6.2 Security Awareness

Similar to security-policy development and risk analysis, *security awareness* involves getting the users involved with the day-to-day aspects of their system security and helping them to understand the potential risks of violating security guidelines. Security awareness can be promoted through security-awareness sessions, where users can have a chance to discuss security, voice their opinions and problems with security, and potentially offer security options; by providing users with bulletins or newsletters on system security and what they can do to help; and by providing users with information on security attacks and system intrusions. As with physical security, there are no trade-offs to providing security awareness to the users. It should be a part of your security plan and network design.

10.6.3 User Authentication

This security mechanism is used to verify that users are who they claim to be, providing protection against unauthorized access to and use of system resources, as well as potential theft and destruction of data. *User authentication* is one of the more common security mechanisms. It is relatively easy to implement and does not have a significant impact on system usage or network performance. Types of user authentication include login ID/password combinations, dynamic password generators, and one-time password generators. A trade-off in providing user authentication is that it requires some administration and maintenance, but the security it provides (especially in conjunction with other security mechanisms) is usually well worth the cost. User authentication should be considered in the network design.

10.6.4 Packet Filters

Packet filters are used to deny packets to or from particular IP addresses or ports (services). This protects the system from unauthorized use, theft, or destruction of resources, and from denial-of-service attacks. While this type of security mechanism is straightforward to implement, it has some drawbacks. First, IP addresses are part of the logical network. As such, they are dynamic, which means that it is hard to map them to physical entities like users or hosts, and they are vulnerable to being improperly applied to other users or hosts. This is commonly known as *address spoofing*. Second, packet filtering takes up network resources, CPU, and memory. The more detailed the filtering rules, or the greater the number of filters, the greater the impact on network resources. Thus, packet filters can impact the performance of the network. Some examples of filters are accepting user traffic from only the corporate office, denying all telnet attempts from the Internet, or denying all external connections with your internal IP address as the source address.

Trade-offs in applying packet filters are discussed above: the possibility of address spoofing and the impact on network resources and network performance. Packet filters can also be complicated, and they require a significant amount of administration and maintenance. Due to these trade-offs, this security mechanism should be considered with caution.

10.6.5 Application Security Mechanisms

Security mechanisms for applications, such as *application wrappers* and *gateways*, are ways to control access to an application, providing protection against unauthorized access, use, theft, or destruction of resources, and denial-of-service attacks. Application wrappers are similar to packet filters, except that acceptable connections are defined on the host running the application wrapper, whereas packet filters are implemented on one or more network elements, such as routers.

Application gateways are used as relays between protected and unprotected systems. This mechanism requires specialized software for each application to be relayed. Application gateways may also be used to disguise internal host names.

Like packet filters, application filters can also be complex and require administration and maintenance. Since they are applied to the hosts, their impact on network resources and performance is less than that of packet filters.

10.6.6 Encryption

While the other security mechanisms provide protection against unauthorized access and the implications of such access, *encryption* protects user and other types of data from being read and used. This is done by ciphering, or encrypting, the data before it is placed on the network, or somewhere along the route in the network. As such, encryption enhances other forms of security by protecting data in case other mechanisms fail to keep unauthorized users from the data.

There are two common types of encryption: *public key* and *private key*. Software and hardware implementations of both are commonly available. Examples include data encryption standard (DES) private key encryption; triple DES private key encryption, and Rivest, Shamir, and Adleman (RSA) public key encryption.

A trade-off with encryption is reduction in network performance. Depending on the type of encryption and where it is implemented in the network, network performance can be degraded by 15% up to 85%. Encryption usually also requires administration and maintenance, and some encryption equipment can be expensive. While this mechanism is very compatible with other mechanisms, these trade-offs should be considered when evaluating encryption.

10.6.7 Firewalls

A *firewall* is usually the combination of one or more security mechanisms, implemented in a host that is placed at a strategic location on the network. The term *firewall* has a wide range of meanings, and firewalls can have different configurations, such as a filtering gateway, an application proxy with filtering gateway, or a combination of all the security mechanisms described above.

One trade-off with firewalls is that they can give an organization a false sense of security. For example, if the firewall is thought of as the ultimate security device, and it is implemented between the organization's network and the Internet, with no other thought to security, then a compromise of the firewall will leave that organization's network wide open. Firewalls can also impact the performance of the network, and they require administration and maintenance.

A key point to remember is that each security mechanism can be useful, and by carefully evaluating an organization's particular security requirements and how each mechanism can support those requirements as well as enhance other security mechanisms, you can incorporate those mechanisms into a plan that will optimize security for the organization.

10.6.8 Security and System Components

Security should be considered at each and every system component—applications, users, hosts, and networks. This section examines methods to enhance system security at each component.

Security at the User Component

Methods of enhancing security at the user component typically involve improving user awareness of security, including informing users of security threats, teaching users to employ strong password construction rules, and warning users against leaving application sessions unattended.

Security at the application component consists of identifying and fixing known software security holes in the application.

Security at the Host Component

Hosts are usually vulnerable for exploitation since they often perform many tasks for multiple users, particularly servers. Methods of enhancing security at the host component include identifying and fixing known software security holes in the host operating system and restricting unnecessary services on the host.

Accounts on the host can be made more secure by limiting the root password distribution and limiting or eliminating the use of group passwords, as well as by frequently reviewing the status of user accounts and disabling unused accounts. File systems on hosts can be protected with access controls. Authentication mechanisms can also be effective here. Hosts should be backed up frequently, logging host activity when feasible. If necessary, host-level encryption can also be implemented.

Security at the Network Component

Methods to enhance security at the network component include limiting the distribution of passwords for network elements, implementing strong password construction rules and authentication mechanisms, keeping up-to-date backup configurations of each network element, and frequently examining and testing filters from outside the network environment. SNMP *set* capability can be limited to a few trusted hosts, along with changing passwords and SNMP community strings (if used) frequently. Like host activity, network activity can also be logged, as feasible, and outgoing traffic can be encrypted at the network level, if necessary.

10.7 Security Examples

10.7.1 External Firewall

An *external firewall* is recommended when there is a perceived security threat from external networks; when systems and network administration of internal resources is limited, poor, or nonexistent; when internal users must have access to external networks; and when connectivity to external networks will not be impacted by firewall performance issues. Figure 10-6 shows where external firewalls are implemented in the system.

FIGURE 10-6. **External Firewall**

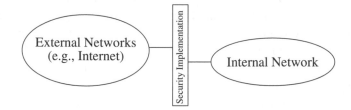

Some of the trade-offs for the enhanced security of an external firewall are as follows:

- May require knowledge of users' service requirements (e.g., telnet, FTP, smtp, http)
- Requires firewall construction and/or configuration expertise
- Network performance degradation up to 30%
- Can make WAN/MAN troubleshooting more complicated
- May require two sets of registered network addresses, or an address translator
- May require additional network elements, such as routers

10.7.2 Internal Firewall

An *internal firewall* is recommended when there is a perceived threat from users either within or external to the network; when systems and network administration of internal resources is not sufficient to meet security requirements; when internal users must have access to other internal or external networks; or when connectivity to internal and external networks will not be impacted by firewall performance issues. Figure 10-7 shows where internal firewalls are implemented in the system.

FIGURE 10-7. **Internal Firewall**

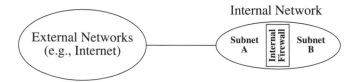

Some of the trade-offs for the enhanced security of an internal firewall are as follows:

- May require knowledge of users' service requirements (e.g., telnet, FTP, smtp, http)
- Requires firewall construction and/or configuration expertise
- Network performance degradation up to 30%
- Can make troubleshooting for all environments—LAN/MAN/WAN—more complicated
- May require two sets of registered network addresses, or an address translator
- May require additional network elements

10.7.3 Distributed Host Security

Distributed host security is recommended when there is a perceived threat from external networks; when internal resources can be adequately protected via systems administration; and when connectivity to internal and external networks would be impacted by firewall performance issues. Figure 10-8 shows where host security is implemented in the system.

Some of the trade-offs for the enhanced security of distributed host security are as follows:

- May require knowledge of users' service requirements (e.g., telnet, FTP, smtp, http)
- Requires consistent and thorough systems and network administration
- Internal network security may be dependent on the security of every host and server within the network
- Security holes in host operating systems or applications will likely affect all internal hosts and servers

FIGURE 10-8. **Distributed Host Security**

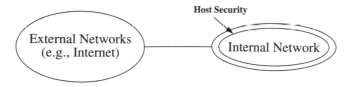

10.8 Network Management and Security Plans

Once the requirements for network management and security have been determined, the steps in developing management and security plans are to

1. Evaluate and select secure, manageable network resources.
2. Evaluate trade-offs in security and network management architectures.

10.8.1 Evaluating and Selecting Resources

There will be a range of network elements that the design could incorporate. Some considerations for evaluating these network elements are methods for accessing and configuring network element parameters; troubleshooting network problems, securing access, configuration, and data; and integrating with the network design.

10.8.2 Evaluating Trade-Offs in Architectures

Given the logical and physical designs for the network, the network management and security architectures can be superimposed on these designs. In doing so, these architectures should balance the needs for security and management with the costs in performance, usability, and resources. This is particularly important when considering the need for real-time management data for event notification, and the concern of generating large amounts of management traffic.

10.8.3 Integration with the Network Design

The network management and security plans affect, and are affected by, the logical and physical network designs. By considering network management and security in the network design, the design is more likely to be effective, robust, and scalable. The logical and physical network designs provide to network management and security plans

- Overall architecture of the network
- Characteristics of the data paths
- Types of network elements that will be required

   The network management and security plans provide the following to the logical and physical designs:

- Requirements for network element instrumentation
- Expectations for in-band/out-of-band data paths, and centralized/distributed management

- Recommendations for the implementation of various security mechanisms

10.8.4 Risk Analysis and Contingency Planning for the Design

At this point in the design process, it is appropriate to analyze the amount of risk in the design, to perform a "sanity check" on the design, and to determine your contingency plans. With all of the flow analysis and design work that has already been accomplished, design risk analysis consists of listing those requirements, flow characteristics, design goals and evaluation criteria, interconnection criteria, and network management and security criteria that may hinder or prevent you from completing the network.

A common risk analysis is in the timely completion of the network. In evaluating technologies, you should know which technologies, functions, and levels of performance will be available at the time the network will be implemented. There is risk in basing a design on technologies that are not yet available, but are expected to be at implementation time. The same is true for technology functions and performance. Your choices of interconnection mechanisms may also incur risks, as these mechanisms are undergoing continual change. Contingency plans for identified risks are ways to back off from the planned design, to implement technologies, interconnection strategies, and network management and security that are less risky and that probably trade off some of your design goals.

For example, you may choose to design your network with ATM switching and with NHRP as your interconnection strategy. In doing a risk assessment, you would look at the state of ATM switch and NHRP deployment, and estimate their availability at the network implementation time. You can develop a contingency plan to implement ATM switches without NHRP, by using MPOA/LANE, or IP routing via 1577. Each contingency plan will impact how you do network management and security, as well as network addressing and routing. By having these contingency plans in place, however, you will be prepared in the event that your desired design cannot be implemented.

Contingency plans may consist of

- Listing alternate technologies and interconnection mechanisms
- Evaluating the functional and performance impact of each possible contingency plan
- Developing a set of logical designs for each plan

The amount of work you should put into risk analysis and contingency planning depends on how certain you are of the components of your design. The closer you are to the leading edge of technologies and interconnection mechanisms, the more important risk analysis and contingency planning become.

10.9 Case Study

We start the process by applying the concepts that were discussed in Sections 10.3 and 10.4 to our design. The primary design decisions are whether we will use in-band or out-of-band monitoring, as well as centralized or distributed monitoring. In addition, we will determine the requirements and flows for our management data.

In deciding between in-band and out-of-band monitoring, we looked at the size of the design environment, the numbers of hosts being monitored, and the expected capacity of the network. Our goal is to keep the amount of management data to a very small percentage of the overall traffic on the network. The numbers of hosts per (planned) subnet are as follows:

Subnet	Hosts
SF	120
SJ	45
MAN	3
Oakland/1013	90
Oakland/1013A, B, C	115

We will also be polling the servers for each of our applications. The frequency of polling was arrived at by discussions with the customer, who felt that the ability to rapidly isolate problems in the network was critical, and that a short polling period was necessary. They requested a polling period of 30 seconds. We recommended that the data be archived to a tape storage system as part of the procedure, and that metrics be developed to chart trends in network traffic.

For the number of parameters, we recommended that they start with the following basic parameters: number of bytes in/out of an interface, number of IP packets in/out of an interface, and number of errors in/out of an interface. If we estimate an average of 64 bytes of SNMP information per variable polled, then the amount of traffic generated on each subnet is

$$(373 \text{ devices})(6 \text{ variables polled/device})(64 \text{ bytes/variable polled}) =$$
$$143 \text{ KB per polling period, or } 1.1 \text{ Mb per polling period}$$

This can be a spike of traffic, which can sometimes occur, but may also be spread out over part or all of the polling period. Thus, it may be a 1.1-Mb/s spike each 30 seconds, or it may be a continuum of management traffic at 38 Kb/s. These are the two extremes, and the actual amount of traffic will be somewhere in between. Since this traffic is generated throughout the network, the total shown above will only occur at the monitoring station (if monitoring is centralized). We are monitoring three campuses, so we can approximate the traffic from each area by the number of devices being polled in the area. For example, since SF has 121 devices (including the MAN device), it should generate approximately (121/373), or 32% of the traffic, which would be 357 Kb per polling period.

Given these estimates of management traffic and the capacity of each subnet, we recommend that in-band monitoring be used and that a centralized monitoring station be placed in Building 1013 at the Oakland campus. From 1013, the monitoring station will SNMP poll each of the routers, switches, and hosts on the network for the variables shown above. At the other campuses, a display will be provided that will allow viewing of the status of the network, but not any configuration changes. We also recommend that dial-up access (either POTS or ISDN) be provided from the monitoring station in 1013 to the MAN/campus routers at the SF and SJ campuses. While there are personnel at each campus that can help troubleshoot the network, the dial-up access will be an additional aid to the network personnel in 1013, especially during off-peak hours.

The traffic information gathered from the MAN/campus routers at each campus will also be used to determine the level of service being received from the MAN service provider. We recommended to the customer that the availability metrics developed earlier be used to measure service, and that the traffic information from the routers be used as part of those metrics. As part of these metrics, the utility *ping* will be used to poll hosts and network elements on a regular basis.

The management design is shown in Figure 10-9.

FIGURE 10-9. Network Monitoring Added to Design

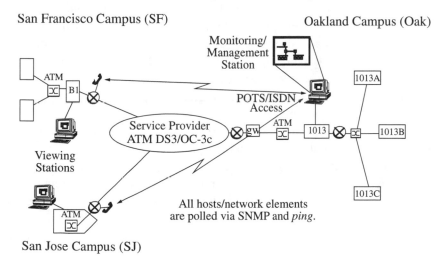

From an access-security perspective, many of the security concerns are minimized by not having Internet access from this network. A security risk analysis was done by the customer, and the biggest concern was the risk of someone accessing one of the routers at the MAN/campus interface and using the router as a base to access other routers or end hosts, or possibly to examine data at that router. We recommended that passwords be used on all router logins, that SNMPv2 security be applied to all network management access, and that user authentication be used (a one-time or dynamic password generator).

From a physical security perspective, there are two major concerns with this design environment: protection against earthquake damage for all sites, and access security at the SJ campus. The SF and Oakland campuses each have communications rooms with rack space where the network elements can be located. Each rack will be bolted to the floor and/or the wall for protection against earthquakes. The SJ building is a shared facility with no computer or communications room. For this campus, we recommended that a room adjacent to the manufacturing floor be cleared for the network equipment. This room will have to be tested to see if it has sufficient cooling and power. In this location, it will not be too close to the manufacturing equipment.

10.10 Concluding Remarks

The logical design of the network is the heart of the analysis and design processes. In the logical design, we use the results of the requirements and flow analyses to prepare the design environment and to make decisions about which technologies we want to use in each area of the design, how to interconnect areas, and how to apply security and network management to the design. In doing all of these functions, the logical design brings many aspects of the design together.

An important first function of the logical design is choosing what we are going to base the design on—the goals for our design. There are some common goals, such as maximizing performance, minimizing cost, and making the network easy to use and operate, secure, and adaptable. There will also be design goals that are specific to your environment. Before we start making decisions about the technologies that we are going to use, it is vital to understand what we are trying to achieve.

To this end, we choose a primary design goal and one or more secondary design goals and examine the trade-offs between these goals. We can use these trade-offs to our advantage. For example, the trade-offs between cost and performance can be used to show the network capabilities that are budgeted for, and how much additional capabilities would cost. When presented properly, trade-offs can be used to argue for greater budgets and higher-performance technologies.

Design goals can be used to evaluate technology choices directly, or can be used to develop other criteria for making such choices. Some evaluation criteria that we considered were

- NBMA and broadcast technologies: broadcast support and connection support
- Functions and features of the technology: capacity upgrade paths and backbone flows
- Flow considerations

There are also guidelines that can be used in technology evaluations:

1. If specified requirements are in the flowspec, then either the technology or a combination of technology and supporting protocols or mechanisms must support specified services.
2. If best-effort and/or specified capacities are in the flowspec, then the selection of technology may also be based upon capacity planning for each flow.

These guidelines are used in the capacity and service plans of the flowspec. We can then make technology choices, by first separating the network into areas, applying the black box method to each area, and using all of our analysis information to make the appropriate selections.

Having made the technology choices, we need to connect them together. There are many interconnection mechanisms, including no interconnection (shared-medium), switching, routing, and hybrid switching/routing. Each interconnection mechanism is appropriate for certain design environments, and we evaluate them based on their scalability, how they work with the flow models of Chapter 5, how they support external connectivity, their support for services, how much they cost, levels of performance, ease of use, and adaptability. In applying each of these mechanisms, we consider the design parameters hierarchy and redundancy.

With our technology choices made and connected together, this is a good time to look at network management and security for our design. As part of the requirements analysis process, we looked at early requirements for network management and security, and we use those requirements here. In bringing network management and security into the design, we need to define what we need from each service and construct a design that includes how network monitoring is done (i.e., out-of-band or in-band, centralized or distributed), how to provide checks and balances in monitoring, and what the management design requires from the network in terms of performance.

For security, we need to establish what policies we want in the system, perform a security risk analysis, and evaluate the available security mechanisms and their trade-offs in the design.

Finally, the logical design is a good place to do a sanity check on the design by performing a risk analysis on the design and considering contingency plans.

Suggested Further Reading

1. American National Standards Institute. *American National Standard for Data Encryption Algorithm (DEA)*. ANSI X3.92. 1981.

2. American National Standards Institute. *American National Standard for Information Systems—Data Link Encryption*. ANSI X3.105. 1983.

3. Atkinson, R. Security architecture for the Internet protocol. *RFC 1825*. August 1995.

4. Chapman, D., and Zwicky, E. *Building Internet Firewalls*. O'Reilly & Associates, Sebastopol, CA, 1995.

5. Cheswick, W.R., and Bellovin, S.M. *Firewalls and Internet Security: Repelling the Wily Hacker*. Addison-Wesley, Reading, MA, 1994.

6. Denning, D.E. *Cryptography and Data Security*. Addison-Wesley, Reading, MA, 1982.

7. Gangemi, G.T., and Russell, D. *Computer Security Basics*. O'Reilly & Associates, Sebastopol, CA, 1991.

8. Kaufman, C., Perlman, R., and Speciner, M. *Network Security: Private Communication in a Public World*. Prentice Hall, Englewood Cliffs, NJ, 1995.

9. Rose, M.T. *The Simple Book: An Introduction to Internet Management*. 2nd ed. Prentice Hall, Englewood Cliffs, NJ, 1994.

See Internet-drafts from the following IETF Working Groups: AToM MIB (ATOMMIB); Benchmarking Methodology (BMWG); Common Authentication Technology (CAT); Distributed Management (DISMAN); Domain Name System Security (DNSSEC); IP Security Protocol (IPSEC); Remote Network Monitoring (RMONMIB); and SNMP Version 3 (SNMPv3). Also check out *The Network Management Server*, available on the Web at *http://netman.cit.buffalo.edu/index.html*.

Exercises

Given the network in Figure 10-10, you will be designing a distributed management scheme and a security scheme. The following exercises refer to the development of this design.

1. This corporate computing environment currently has a network management system at the corporate network operations center (NOC), which monitors only the 13 corporate routers. Design a network management scheme that will allow monitoring the routers as well as all 190 hosts and dial-up routers, keeping the management traffic local to each area (Minneapolis, Los Angeles, and Washington, D.C.).

2. How much management traffic would have been generated in a centralized network management system, assuming data collection of nine SNMP counters on all routers and ICMP *ping* polling on all hosts, with a polling interval of 5 minutes?

3. Add facilities for managing each of the remote sites out-of-band from the corporate NOC.

4. Recommend network security mechanisms for the corporate WAN that maximize network performance for the Los Angeles site and maximize security for the Washington, D.C., site.

FIGURE 10-10. Diagram for Exercises 10.1–10.6

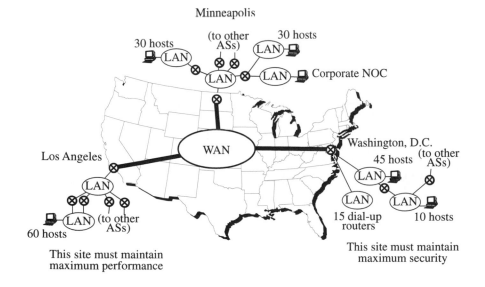

5. How does the addition of out-of-band management from the corporate NOC impact the security of the network?

6. Recommend two ways that the traffic information collected via SNMP counters on each of the routers could be verified.

CHAPTER 11

Network Design: Physical

11.1 Introduction to Physical Design

We now continue the design process with the design of the *physical network*. In the previous three chapters, we developed the design of the logical network, based on making technology choices for each area of the network, determining how the areas could be interconnected, and considering network management and security. While the logical design is the basis for all of the remaining components of the design process—physical design and routing/addressing—the physical design provides the physical information needed to plan and begin network implementation, including diagrams/blueprints of locations, topologies, and architectures.

The physical design is based on commonsense rules about infrastructure, cable plant, equipment placement, and diagramming. For some readers, the concepts, methods, and guidelines presented in this chapter may seem somewhat obvious; however, there is often a loss of continuity between determining the logical connectivity of the network and the translation into its physical layout. Since the physical design is relatively straightforward, we will not spend much time on this part of the process. We will use the physical design to reinforce, complement, and solidify the logical design.

FIGURE 11-1. **Process for Design of the Physical Network**

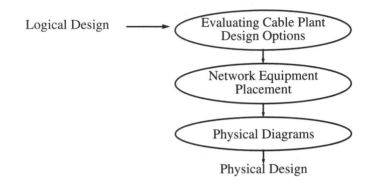

The chapter begins with a discussion about cable plant and physical wiring issues, followed by the placement of equipment in the design. Methods of diagramming the network are then presented, and the chapter finishes with the implementation of coding techniques. The end result of the physical design process will be a set of documents and diagrams that will describe the physical network and may include blueprints and engineering or architectural drawings. This process is shown in Figure 11-1.

11.2 Evaluating Cable Plant Design Options

For the computer network, the physical plant consists primarily of the local wiring—the building and campus cable runs. How the wiring is applied in the design will affect the performance characteristics of the network, particularly the network reliability. In the sections that follow, we will be using fiber optic cable in the discussions and examples, but copper cable could be used as well.

There are two general wiring schemes that we can apply to the design: centralized and distributed. A *centralized wiring scheme* terminates most or all of the cable runs in one area of the design environment, while a *distributed wiring scheme* terminates cable runs throughout the design environment. Both schemes are shown in Figure 11-2.

There are trade-offs to each, and differences between wiring in a campus environment or within a building, as well as differences based on the type of environment you are designing for. Let's first look at the campus environment.

FIGURE 11-2. **Centralized and Distributed Wiring**

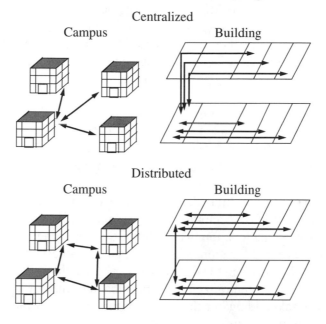

11.2.1 Wiring in a Campus/MAN Environment

In the campus environment—which can be extended into the MAN environment—cable runs are not as protected as they are within a building. In fact, the wiring may at times cross properties outside of the control of the network designer or customer. Therefore, we want the campus wiring to optimize the reliability of the cable runs, which is done through redundancy and quality of the cable plant.

Redundancy can be provided at several levels in the cable runs, and the level of redundancy will differ at each level. Redundancy can vary, from having multiple fibers in a fiber bundle, to multiple cables in a conduit, to providing multiple conduit runs within a path, all the way to providing diverse paths within the campus. Each of these types of redundancy protect against different sorts of damage to the cable plant.

Having multiple fibers in a fiber bundle will provide redundancy if a fiber breaks, but will fail if the fiber bundle breaks. It is rare for this type of damage to occur, however. Multiple cables in a conduit will support a cable break, but not a break across the entire conduit. Multiple conduit runs provide redundancy in a conduit break, but not a failure across the conduit path. The last level of redundancy, multiple paths within a campus, provides redundancy in the event of a path failure.

The reason for showing these different types of redundancy is that there can be a false sense of security in thinking that a wiring design is reliable when it is not. The most likely form of cable damage (outside of the building) in the campus/MAN environment is the physical cutting of cable (the infamous backhoe!), which is usually across the entire path. When this occurs, multiple fibers, cables, or conduits are not much protection. The best protection is multiple, diverse cable paths in this environment.

Another type of protection is the use of high-quality cable, such as "hardened" cable, which is jacketed in metal or composite material. In combination with multiple, diverse paths, hardened cable can reduce the amount of damage when a path is damaged, depending on how the damage occurred (i.e., a backhoe is expensive to protect against).

In order to provide multiple, diverse paths, we would apply a distributed wiring scheme in the campus/MAN environment. It is possible to develop multiple points of entry into the central location in a centralized wiring scheme, which will provide protection at the central location. When the high-risk areas are between buildings, which they usually are, then the distributed wiring scheme is best.

Figure 11-3 shows centralized cable runs that terminate in two different locations in the central building but share parts of their runs in common conduit. This scheme would protect against potential damage at one of the entry points but does not protect against damage at the common runs. Also, damage to any of the cables will result in loss of service to that building. A distributed scheme with diverse cable paths will provide more protection against cable damage and provide alternate paths for service. The diverse paths do not have to be of the same media. For example, we could back up an underground cable run between buildings with a line-of-sight infrared or microwave link, as in Figure 11-4.

FIGURE 11-3. Centralized Wiring Scheme with Multiple Entry Points

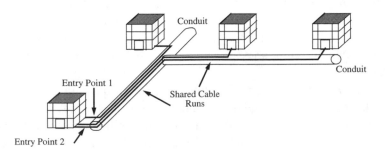

FIGURE 11-4. Diverse Paths of Different Media

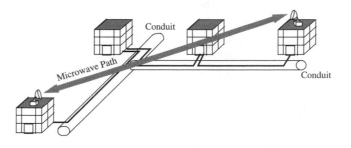

When planning for line-of-sight links or overhead cable runs, it is important to check for any restrictions, rules, or regulations on the installation and use of this cabling and equipment.

It is likely to be hard (and costly) to provide multiple entry points into a central location, and may be more expensive than providing multiple, diverse paths between locations. A trade-off in a distributed wiring scheme is in the difficulty of configuration control and maintenance. A distributed scheme may require changes throughout one or more cable paths when a change in the network design occurs. Figure 11-5 illustrates the differences in configuration changes in centralized and distributed schemes.

FIGURE 11-5. Configuration Change in Centralized and Distributed Schemes

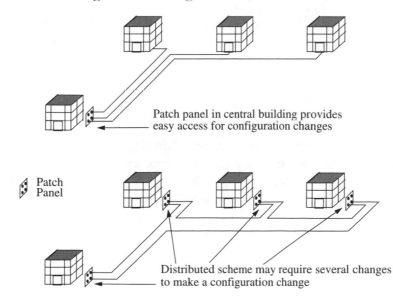

In a centralized campus/MAN wiring scheme, all cable paths terminate in (usually) one area of the design, such as a building. In this scheme, if there is a single point of entry into the building, then path redundancy is traded off for the ease of configuration and maintenance of a centralized scheme. Typically, a centralized wiring scheme has a central location where all of the campus/MAN wiring interconnections are made and all patch panels, fiber monitoring, and testing equipment can be operated. A centralized wiring scheme is also flexible in configuring additions to the cable runs. It simplifies the method of adding new areas (i.e., buildings) to the network by providing a common location to connect to.

11.2.2 Wiring in a Building Environment

Within a building, the need for protection of the cable plant is usually reduced. If the cable is protected by conduit and is placed in walls or ceilings, it is less likely to be damaged than cable runs between buildings. For some building environments, however, this is not the case, and extra protection through diverse paths should be considered. Such environments may have large equipment in close proximity to the cable runs, as can happen in a manufacturing facility or warehouse, or the general environment may be harsh, as in some military or public-safety environments. In general, when the building environment is potentially harsh to the cable runs, then the extra protection of diversity is suggested, as with a campus environment. If the building environment is not harsh, then a centralized wiring scheme should be considered, based on its flexibility, scalability, and ease of configuration.

Figure 11-6 shows a central wiring scheme for a two-story building. The second floor is wired for offices and cubicle pods, and all cable runs are consolidated to one location, Room 212, where a riser allows us to run conduit between floors. The first floor also has office and cubicle spaces, as well as a main computer room, which is where most of the users will access their computing, storage, and application servers.

11.2.3 Choosing a Central Wiring Location

When designing for centralized campus/MAN and/or building wiring schemes, we will need to choose a central location to terminate the cable runs. In addition, this central location should, when possible, also be the place where outside access to the network occurs. This may be access to the Internet, the customer's WAN, or external (outside of the building, campus, or MAN environments) access to the customer's intranet. Even in a distributed wiring scheme, you will need to choose a

FIGURE 11-6. **Centralized Wiring Scheme for Building**

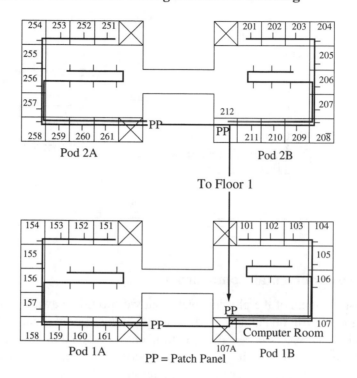

location for external access. Figure 11-7 shows that, for the previous example, the central wiring location would most likely be at Room 107A (or close by), where the wiring from both floors meets. Since this is also close to the computer room, we would have fast and easy access to wiring for the computer room. If possible, this would also be the location where we would terminate external access.

As services, distance-independent computing, and the decoupling of logical and physical networks evolve, they will drive communications between the campus/MAN environment and the building environment to become more equal, in terms of services, access, and amount of information transferred. As this happens, having the central wiring located together with outside access will allow the placement of network and support equipment for all environments in one area, such as in the computer room in Figure 11-7.

FIGURE 11-7. **Central Wiring Location and Outside Access**

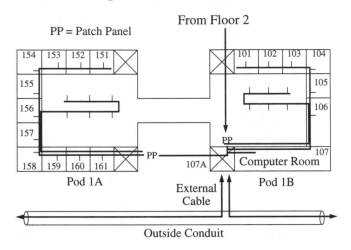

11.2.4 Environmental Components

Other components of the physical plant that we should be aware of for network design are environmental aspects, including heating, ventilation, and, primarily, air conditioning (HVAC), especially in equipment rooms. You should ensure that there is sufficient space for cabling (i.e., conduit access), placement of patch panels and network equipment, and racks to house equipment. The environment will also need sufficient power to run the equipment, and possibly conditioned power and/or backup power. Finally, work areas with equipment should be allocated for technicians and network personnel.

This is particularly important in the central wiring location, as well as in any areas where network equipment is located. When considering the environmental components in the design, you should gather data on each piece of network equipment, such as

- *Heat produced*. These can be summarized for an area to determine the air conditioning requirements.

- *Dimensions*. These can be used to determine the amount of rack space, the relative placement of and overall space for equipment. Patch panels, cable trays, and splice boxes should also be included in the space evaluation. Space for work areas for technicians and network personnel should also be included in this evaluation.

- *Power requirements*. These can be summed for each type of power (i.e., 110V versus 220V 3-phase) to determine the overall power requirements for the area. In addition, we can also evaluate the need for power conditioning or backup power.

All of this information can usually be found in the documentation for each type of network equipment. In developing the layout for your network equipment, don't forget to allow for growth in all of the environmental requirements shown above. A common problem is running out of space for equipment, which you should be able to avoid through careful planning.

11.3 Network Equipment Placement

Issues that affect the placement of network equipment include any existing wiring and wiring plans; various costs for equipment, cable, installation, and overhead; and the impact of equipment, or office moves, on users. In this section we will consider the placement of combinations of hubs, routers, switches, and circuit-level equipment. Some rules of thumb for placing network equipment are as follows:

1. Choose locations that have sufficient environmental support (see previous section). This includes air conditioning, power, and space.
2. Choose physically secure locations.
3. Label all equipment clearly, so that individual components may be easily identified. If possible, set up and follow a coding scheme (discussed later in this chapter).

Distributed and centralized equipment placement schemes typically follow the wiring schemes discussed earlier, though not always. The general trade-offs between distributed and centralized equipment placement schemes are based on redundancy and hierarchy. A distributed scheme can reduce the size of groups (networks, subnetworks, broadcast domains), which creates hierarchies, but it usually places the equipment closer to the users, which makes OAM support more complicated and costly. Distributed schemes can also provide greater redundancy when coupled with a distributed wiring scheme.

In Figure 11-8, equipment is placed in each pod, at patch panel locations, and possibly also within each cubicle area. There will also be equipment in the computer room, and any equipment for external access would be in Room 107A.

FIGURE 11-8. **Distributed Equipment Placement**

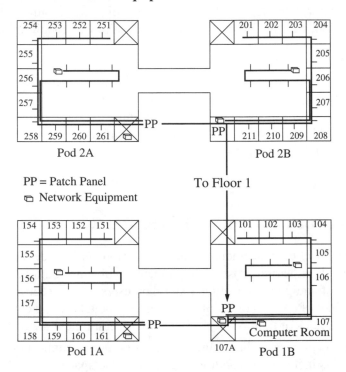

A centralized equipment-placement scheme makes OAM support easier, but makes the distances between user and equipment greater. Centralized placement means that fewer pieces of equipment can be used, but they are larger in numbers of users supported. This can usually reduce the equipment costs, but it may also reduce the degree of redundancy. Note that a centralized equipment-placement scheme may constrain your technology choices, particularly those that are influenced by distance. For example, the lengths of your cable runs may limit deployment of 100/1000-Mb/s Ethernet. Following are some specific guidelines for distributed and centralized placement of hubs, routers, and switches.

Figure 11-9 is a centralized placement of network equipment. The most likely choices for this example are at the central wiring location (Room 107A), the computer room, or both locations. When consolidating equipment in one location, the environmental aspects of the location are critical.

FIGURE 11-9. **Centralized Equipment Placement**

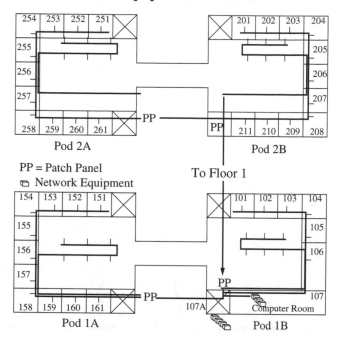

11.3.1 Hub Placement

The number of hubs used in the network can be estimated using the trade-offs described in this section. When users are directly connected to hubs, the maximum distance between user and hub will restrict the placement of the hubs. As hubs are placed closer to users, the number of hubs increases while the number of users per hub decreases. These multiple, smaller hubs can then be connected by a local back-bone. If hubs are placed in a central location, users will need cable connections to the central location, requiring potentially large amounts of cable.

11.3.2 Router Placement

While the number of routers used in the network will be determined by the logical design, the placement of the routers is determined in this section. Generally, if routers are used as administrative demarcs to outside networks (e.g., other customer networks or the Internet), they are placed close to the demarc location of the outside network. If a centralized wiring scheme is used, the demarc is usually also the central location. Routers and hubs can be thought of as two tiers in a network hierarchy to the users, as in Figure 11-10.

FIGURE 11-10. **Routers and Hubs as Tiers in the Physical Hierarchy**

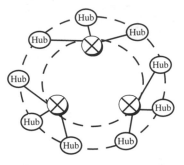

FIGURE 11-11. **Hubs Distributed Across Router Backbone**

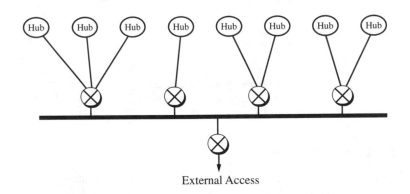

External Access

In this figure, routers interconnect hubs, and hubs interconnect their directly attached users. Figure 11-11 shows that when both routers and hubs are used, routers can act as a backbone for the hubs. This is a distributed scheme for hubs, and possibly also routers. When the hubs are centralized, the routers serving those hubs are also centralized, or collapsed into a single router, as in Figure 11-12.

11.3.3 Switch Placement

Switches are used as an interconnection mechanism, and their placement strategy can be thought of as intermediate between routers and hubs. When switches are used in places where routers would typically have been used, then the switch placement strategy is the same as for routers. In this scenario, switches are used in conjunction with hubs. Switches can also be used to replace or augment hubs. When switches are used in this manner, their placement strategy is the same as for hubs.

FIGURE 11-12. **Collapsed Router Backbone**

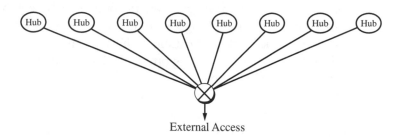

External Access

11.3.4 Circuit-Level Equipment Placement

The locations of circuit-level equipment (e.g., CSU/DSUs, modems, line drivers) are good places to demarc provider services and boundaries outside of the building, campus/MAN environments. It is a good idea to keep demarc locations close together, as it can help in the isolation and identification of problems in the network. Customer-provider demarcs and inside/outside boundaries in the building and campus/MAN environments can be kept close together by the placement of circuit-level equipment close to the circuit/service demarc and the interface to the network equipment, as shown in Figure 11-13.

If a central location has been determined for your design, having the provider demarc all circuits/services at that location, having all outside boundaries terminate at the location, and then locating the circuit-level equipment together with these demarcs and boundaries should keep them close together.

11.4 Diagramming the Physical Design

For each network design, there should be a set of diagrams of the logical design. Accompanying the diagrams for the logical design there will be one or more physical diagrams. Diagrams of the logical design focus on the technology choices for

FIGURE 11-13. **External Circuit and Service Demarcation Points**

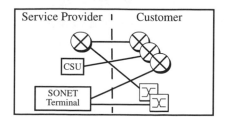

for each area of the network, and on the interconnectivity within and between the areas. Typically, routers and/or switches are the only network equipment explicitly shown on this type of diagram. Diagrams of the logical network are also useful places to trace network-level information, such as port numbers of routers and/or switches, IP addresses, and the routing protocols that you expect to use along with related configuration information.

Port numbers can be developed and assigned to the network equipment and placed on the logical design at this time. (The assignment of IP addresses and routing information will be discussed in the next chapter.) When this information is assigned to the network, it can then be added to the logical diagram. Figure 11-14 is an example of a logical diagram that could have been used to generate a physical diagram like that shown earlier in Figure 11-6.

FIGURE 11-14. Example of a Logical Diagram

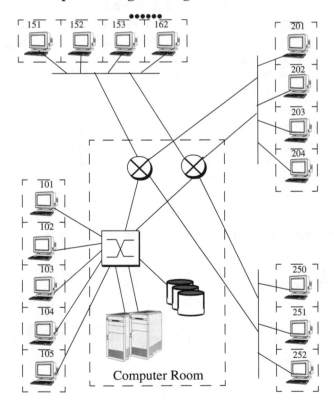

Physical diagrams are complementary to logical diagrams, focusing on physical aspects of the network. The technologies and router/switch placement from the logical diagram is also placed on the physical diagram. On the physical diagram, however, hubs and circuit-level equipment are added. Diagrams of the physical network are also used to trace device locations. This will range from countries, states, and cities to buildings, rooms within a building, even locations within a room (such as positioning within a rack). They can also trace circuit and/or service numbers, cable numbers, and patch panel numbers/ports.

Each of these diagrams serves different purposes. The logical diagram is useful to trace logical connectivity, flows and services, and routing information. The physical diagram is useful to trace physical connectivity, where cable paths lead, distances between computers/users, and how network equipment is interconnected. These differences can be seen in Figure 11-15.

FIGURE 11-15. Comparison of Logical and Physical Diagrams

Logical Diagram

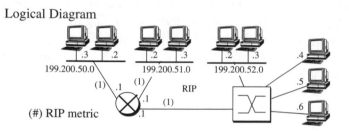

Physical Diagram

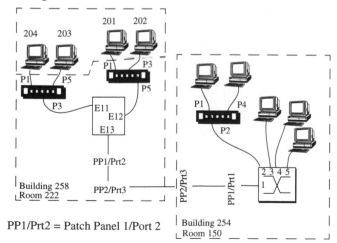

The concepts and guidelines of IP addressing and routing—i.e., *routing information protocol* (RIP) metrics—are discussed in the next chapter, and are shown here only to illustrate what is needed in the physical design.

11.4.1 Maintenance of Diagrams

A major trade-off in diagramming the network is the maintenance and upkeep of the diagrams. The usefulness of these diagrams is related to how accurate and complete their information is. In order to ensure accuracy and completeness, the diagrams should be updated regularly. This type of work sounds like overhead, but is a necessary part of the OAM of a network. There are some good software tools that can be used to help you diagram the network. Some tools provide a database for access to physical and logical design information, to help in accessing and combining this data, such as for inventory control. Diagramming tools (e.g., Visio and Clicknet), along with the analysis and design processes in this book, can be a powerful combination to develop, modify, and maintain your network diagrams.

With time, the design of a network (and the network itself), develops what is termed here *cruft*, which is a form of disarray, missing information, and generally a lack of knowledge and understanding of the design. This *cruftiness* can be minimized by diligence in keeping up with modifications to the design. This is done through developing a process for change in the design, and by keeping track of changes as they occur.

One process for monitoring, evaluating, and documenting change in the design is through a periodic design review. Review cycles that are monthly or quarterly give enough time to process design changes, yet are not so far apart as to deviate significantly from the previous review. In the design review process, potential changes can be introduced and evaluated, and approved changes can then be implemented and documented as part of the "current" design. In this way, changes are made known and discussed, so that there are fewer surprises. In some cases, this review process is also a technical review, where peers may debate among various potential changes and choose the best technical solutions.

11.4.2 Coding Schemes

One method to simplify the description of physical and logical information on the diagrams is to develop a coding scheme to compress the information or make it easily recognizable. One type of coding scheme is based on categorizing areas of the network, such as the end user areas, also known as *leaf sites*, *tail sites*, and *stub areas* (as in open shortest-path first [OSPF] stub areas).

FIGURE 11-16. **Class 1, 2, and 3 Tail Sites**

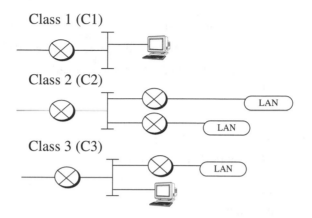

For example, we could categorize tail sites for a WAN by their connectivity to tail site LANs, with categories as shown in Figure 11-16.

- *Class 1 (C1)*. A tail site LAN that has no (router) connections outside of the LAN. Access is limited to directly connected computers.
- *Class 2 (C2)*. A tail site LAN that is connected to other LANs via routers, but has no directly connected computers on its LAN.
- *Class 3 (C3)*. A tail site LAN that has both directly connected computers and router connections to other LANs.

A Class 1 tail site is an example of how an organization with a small number of WAN users might connect to the WAN, or how a secure network might be isolated from the rest of the site's LANs. A Class 2 tail site is similar to the isolation LAN (iLAN) concept discussed earlier in this book, while a Class 3 tail site is the most general and often seen type.

Another type of coding scheme compresses large amounts of site-, network-, or equipment-specific information into a tag. Some common elements of a tag include

- Site name or ID
- Site category (such as the classes shown above)
- Campus/building name and/or number
- Floor number
- Room number
- Rack number
- Equipment type

- IP addresses (local and remote)
- Port numbers
- Type of circuit, technology/service
- Capacity, bandwidth, speed of circuit, technology/service
- Network, data-link, and/or routing protocols used

A tag description:
Site name, ID
Remote IP address/local IP address
Remote port–local port/speed/protocol/class/service

Example of tag:
Acme Corporation, #151-2
199.99.99.1/199.99.99.2
541–542/T1/OSPF/C2/SMDS

This information would then be placed in a database describing all components of the network, and could also be written on actual tags, which would be connected to network equipment, racks, and circuits.

11.5 Diagramming Worksheets

Following are some examples of worksheets that you may use to help in diagramming your network.

Cable Plant

Existing Cable Plant:
(Enter existing cable runs)

Building/Room/Patch Panel<--->Building/Room/Patch Panel

```
    /        /<--->        /         /

    /        /<--->        /         /

    /        /<--->        /         /
```

New Cable Plant:
(Enter new cable runs to be added for new network or network expansion)

Building/Room/Patch Panel<--->Building/Room/Patch Panel

    /   /<--->   /   /

    /   /<--->   /   /

    /   /<--->   /   /

    /   /<--->   /   /

    /   /<--->   /   /

    /   /<--->   /   /

Equipment Layout

Building: _____

Distributed Layout

	Hubs	Routers and Bridges	Switches	Circuit
External Interface, Room: ____				
Wiring Closet, Room: _____				
Wiring Closet, Room: _____				
Wiring Closet, Room: _____				
Wiring Closet, Room: _____				
Wiring Closet, Room: _____				

Centralized Layout

	Hubs	Routers and Bridges	Switches	Circuit
External Interface, Room: _____				
Rack: _____				
Rack: _____				
Rack: _____				
Rack: _____				
Rack: _____				

11.6 Case Study

In our network design, the requirements of each of the campuses are different. At the Oakland campus, we have well-designed conduit and cabling systems, while at the SF and SJ campuses, we have some challenges with the cabling. Let's look first at the Oakland campus. At this campus we have a gateway building (gw) that is the location for demarcing all outside services. We also have a computer room in Building 1013 that we will be able to use for locating network equipment. Each of the other buildings in the campus, 1013A, 1013B, and 1013C, all have equipment rooms that are either ready for network equipment or can easily be made ready. There is already multimode and single-mode fiber between the buildings, along their main conduit run (see Figure 11-17).

All cable runs terminate in the gateway building. We would prefer to have all cable runs terminate in Building 1013, as this is where the computing equipment will be located, or to have a system distributed between all of the buildings, but it would be too expensive for the customer to change the cabling system. At the SF campus, there is a room in Building B1 where network equipment can be located. There is a conduit system that connects each of the buildings, but the cable that is currently in the conduit cannot be used by the customer. Therefore, the customer will have to have cable pulled. We recommended that the customer pull plenty of extra cable at this time, so that they will not have to go back and pull more later, and that they use a distributed cabling scheme between the buildings. Figure 11-18 shows the layout of the SF campus.

FIGURE 11-17. Conduit and Cabling for Oakland Campus

Oakland Campus (Oak)

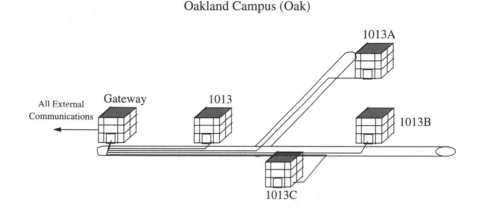

The SJ campus has just one building, and it is where the model fabrication/ manufacturing occurs. This building is basically a warehouse-type structure and does not have typical computer-room or communications-room environments. Our first thought was to put the networking equipment on the manufacturing floor, which would give the customer easy access to it, but the environment is too harsh, and there is a room next to the manufacturing floor where the equipment can be located. The external cabling and conduit are in place, and the service provider is installing their demarc in the equipment room.

FIGURE 11-18. Conduit and Cabling for the SF Campus

Oakland Campus (Oak)

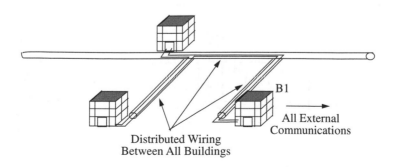

FIGURE 11-19. **Physical Layout of Building 1013**

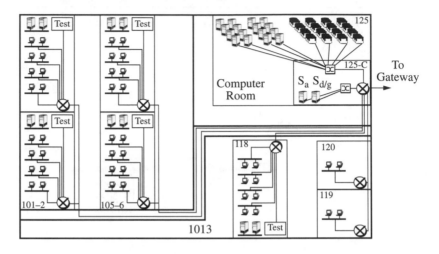

For the physical layout, the customer requested the likely placement of equipment at each building. For the Oakland campus, the main location is Building 1013. In that building, we will connect to the existing LANs, including the computing and storage systems. The physical layout of 1013 is shown in Figure 11-19.

Buildings 1013A, 1013B, and 1013C all have similar layouts, with hubs in each communications room connecting to the gateway building. Figure 11-20 shows the template for each of these buildings.

The gateway building has a simple layout, a series of racks in a caged enclosure. This is where the service providers terminate their circuits and services. All of the other buildings in this campus have multimode fiber runs to this building. Figure 11-21 shows the layout.

FIGURE 11-20. **Physical Layout of Buildings 1013A, 1013B, and 1013C**

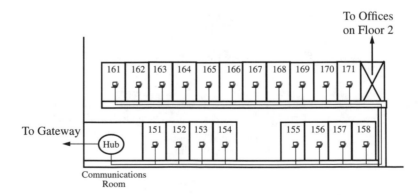

FIGURE 11-21. **Physical Layout of the Gateway Building**

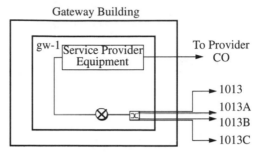

FIGURE 11-22. **Layout of the Buildings in the SF Campus**

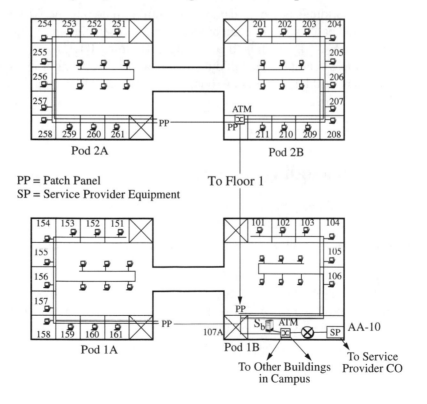

FIGURE 11-23. **Physical Layout of the SJ Campus**

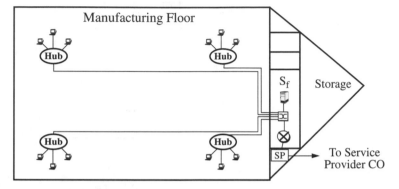

SP = Service Provider Equipment

The buildings at the SF campus are similar in layout and will be connected by a distributed cable system. Each building has a layout, shown in Figure 11-22, except for Room AA-10, which is located only in Building B1.

At the SJ campus, the building houses a manufacturing floor. The network equipment will be located in a room next to the manufacturing floor (see Figure 11-23).

11.7 Concluding Remarks

The physical design of a network complements the logical design. In the physical design, we need to consider the physical plant, including cable placement, redundancy, and environmental factors. The physical design also handles the placement of network equipment and the trade-offs between centralized and distributed placement.

Physical plant decisions are shown by diagramming the physical design. These diagrams describe where network equipment and cable are located, as well as their physical connectivity. Diagrams can also be used to apply codes to the design, to compress location- and equipment-specific information into tags that are associated with the design.

Suggested Further Reading

1. Electronic Industries Association. *Additional Horizontal Cabling Practices for Open Offices*. EIA TSB75. August 1996.

2. Electronic Industries Association. *Additional Transmission Specifications for Unshielded Twisted-Pair Connecting Hardware*. EIA TSB40-A. February 1994.

3. Electronic Industries Association. *Centralized Optical Fiber Cabling Guidelines*. EIA TSB72. October 1995.

4. Electronic Industries Association. *Commercial Building Telecommunications Cabling Standard*. ANSI/TIA/EIA-568-A-95. October 1995.

5. Electronic Industries Association. *Multimode Fiber Optic Link Transmission Design*. EIA/TIA-626. December 1995.

6. Electronic Industries Association. *Standard for Physical Location and Protection of Below-Ground Fiber Optic Cable Plant*. ANSI/EIA/TIA-590-91. July 1991.

Exercises

1. For the campus environment of Figure 11-24, redundancy between Buildings A, C, and D is desired by the company in the campus. There is extra cable in the conduit system from A to C and from D to C, and there is currently no conduit between A and D. Some options that we may have include

   - Using existing cable to provide a redundant cable run from A to D via C; this may be either straight-through from A to D, or with a stop (e.g., at a patch panel or a fiber splice) at C
   - Laying conduit and cable directly between A and D
   - Providing a microwave link directly between A and D

   Given these options, which would you recommend when the area between Buildings A/B/C and D (Area 51) is:

   a) An expressway

   b) An airport runway

   c) A park, owned and operated by the company

   What are your considerations for each scenario? Describe your justifications for each choice.

FIGURE 11-24. Campus Environment for Exercise 11.1

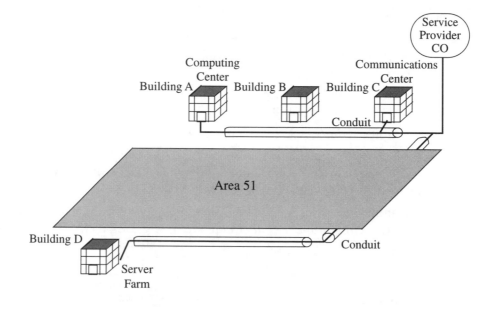

2. For Figure 11-24, the company also desires redundancy to its service provider. They currently connect to one central office (CO) of the service provider. Given that the communications building (C) is the main point of entry for outside communications (such as the service provider), and that the computing building (A) is the termination point of all of the high-performance communications and the focal point of the entire network, how should redundant connectivity be provided using the single CO? Using two COs, at different locations?

CHAPTER 12

Addressing and Routing

12.1 Introduction to Addressing and Routing

To complete the design process, we will examine how to incorporate addressing and routing into the design. Addressing and routing are usually considered at the network layer, such as IP addressing and routing. As we have seen in the logical design, however, these functions can also be incorporated at the link layer. Therefore, as you go through this chapter, remember that these functions can be at the link layer, at the network layer, or at both layers. With the integration of switching and routing in the network, it is likely that addressing and routing will be distributed across both layers.

This chapter begins with discussions on the requirements for routing and addressing in network design, explains how to segment the network into functional areas, and tells how to identify boundaries in the network. A relationship between boundaries and routing flows is then developed, which leads to discussions on the characteristics of routing flows and how these characteristics may be manipulated. It then examines various addressing schemes, including how and where they may be applied. Routing protocols are discussed next, including a comparison of popular interior gateway protocols (IGPs), the routing information protocol (RIP), and open shortest-path first (OSPF). The chapter ends with discussions on choosing and applying routing protocols. The process for integrating addressing and routing into the design is shown in Figure 12-1.

FIGURE 12-1. **Process for Adding Addressing and Routing to the Design**

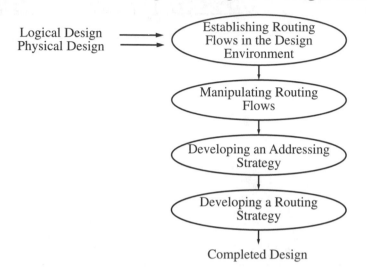

This chapter examines addressing and routing from a network design perspective, but only briefly discusses how addressing and routing are done. There are, however, many good books on the subject, several of which are listed as further reading at the end of the chapter.

12.2 Establishing Routing Flows in the Design Environment

In preparation to develop strategies for addressing and routing, we want to understand how flows will likely be routed through our design environment. As we will see in this chapter, addressing and routing are both closely coupled to the flow of routing information in the network, and the preparation of the design focuses on establishing these flows.

In order to establish these flows, we will need

• The logical layout of the network design

• An understanding of the potential information flows within the network

• The numbers, locations, and purposes of routers in the network (e.g., are they general IP packet forwarding engines, or a filtering and aggregation point?)

The process of establishing routing flows in the network consists of determining the functional areas, identifying boundaries, and establishing the relationship between boundaries and routing flows.

12.2.1 Functional Areas

Earlier in this book, we discussed dividing the logical design into multiple smaller regions, which were termed *areas*. The purpose for doing this is to make the design more workable, by allowing us to focus on one particular segment of the design at a time. These areas are based on geography, user concentrations, or information-flow hierarchies. We will use a similar technique to develop functional areas for our network, to focus on routing flows. It is possible that the areas developed earlier in the design process will become the functional areas for addressing and routing.

Functional areas are based on combining logical groups of users, *work groups*, to simplify the routing architecture. Work groups are users that have common locations, applications, and requirements, or that belong to the same organization. Typically, these work groups are centered around a physical area, such as a building, campus, or city. This may not be the case, though, and groupings may be based on applications or sets of requirements.

Consider Figure 12-2. In this figure there are multiple work groups, in this case based on organizations within a company. Functional areas are created to combine the legal and accounting work groups in Building 1, and the engineering and operations work groups in Building 2. Notice that functional areas were also created for the isolation LANs in each building, as well as for the MAN connecting them. Notice also that the functional areas are bounded by routers.

FIGURE 12-2. Work Groups and Functional Areas

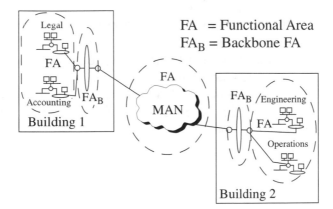

12.2.2 Identifying Boundaries

Boundaries are a physical or logical separation of a network, based on requirements for or administration of that network. Functional areas are one mechanism to identify logical boundaries. Physical boundaries can be identified from

• Isolation LANs

• Physical interfaces on network equipment

• Physical security

   Logical boundaries can be identified from

• Functional areas

• Work groups

• Administrative domains, also known as autonomous systems (ASs)

• Routing management domains

• Security domains

Autonomous systems have AS numbers associated with them. Routing management domains are often the same as ASs, but can be either a subset or superset of one or more ASs. Security domains are places where you put a security device (such as a firewall), and use public addresses outside the security boundary, and private addresses inside.

These boundaries may also be distinguished by the type of routing protocol used to pass routing information across the boundary. There are two general types of routing protocols: exterior gateway protocols (EGPs), which communicate routing information (reachability and metrics) primarily between ASs, and interior gateway protocols (IGPs), which communicate routing information primarily within an AS. The word "primarily" is used here, for EGPs can be used within an AS, and IGPs can be used between ASs. In fact, later in this chapter we will look at ways to combine EGP and IGP use both within and between ASs.

Here we use the term *hard boundary* to describe a boundary where mainly EGPs are used to pass routing information, while a *soft boundary* is a boundary where mainly IGPs are used. Hard boundaries are found between ASs, between an AS and an external network (which may or may not have an AS associated with it), or at well-defined separations between networks within an AS. Figure 12-3 shows some examples of hard boundaries.

FIGURE 12-3. Examples of Hard Boundaries

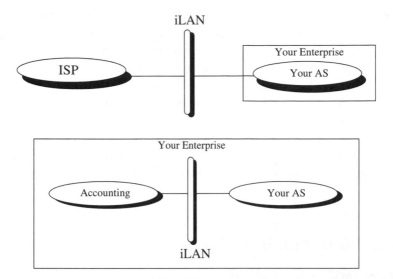

In the first example, an isolation LAN (iLAN) is used to separate an enterprise AS from an Internet service provider (ISP). This is a common hard boundary, and one where an EGP is likely to be used. The second example is less obvious. Here an enterprise wants to restrict communications between certain organizations, in particular the accounting work group. While the entire organization is within an AS, the boundary between the accounting work group and the rest of the AS is similar to an iLAN (it could be considered an internal iLAN), so this is also a hard boundary. An EGP or IGP may be used in this case.

Soft boundaries are usually between functional areas within an AS, as in Figure 12-4. In this figure, all of the interfaces between functional areas are soft boundaries.

FIGURE 12-4. Examples of Soft Boundaries

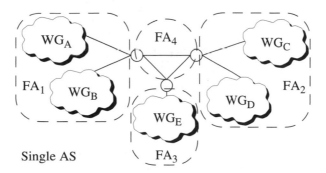

12.2.3 Boundaries and Routing Flows

Why are we interested in determining boundaries for our design environment? Boundaries are important in that they are the focal points for routing flows. Remember from our examples that between functional areas, hard and soft boundaries are located at routers, which aggregate routing traffic. These also happen to be locations where hierarchies are established in the network.

Routing flows are flows of routing information, passed between functional areas. This routing information includes routing initialization, updates, transients, and background traffic such as hellos or keepalives. Boundaries and routing flows are important to the development of a routing strategy, for routing flows can be manipulated, and manipulations occur at boundaries.

12.3 Manipulating Routing Flows

There are several techniques for manipulating routing flows at boundaries. We can supply a default route through our design environment via default route propagation. We can use route filtering to hide routes, and route aggregation to simplify advertisements. We can develop peering relationships between networks or ASs across boundaries. We can also develop routing policies and policy enforcement. To illustrate these route-manipulation techniques, we will discuss each as applied to the example in Figure 12-5.

FIGURE 12-5. Example of Routing Flow Manipulation

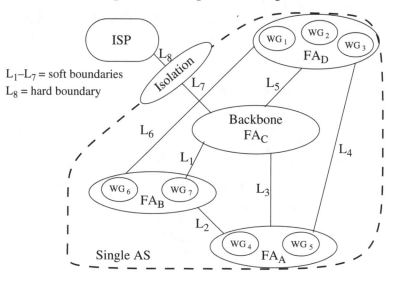

For this example, the following restrictions are requested:

1. Do not advertise Work Group 5 (WG_5).

2. Communications between Work Group 1 (WG_1) and Work Group 6 (WG_6) must occur across Link 6 (L_6).

3. All remaining functional areas (FAs) must use Functional Area C (FA_C) as their primary route.

Now let's see how each of these route-manipulation techniques can be applied to this example to achieve these routing restrictions.

12.3.1 Default Route Propagation

A *default route* is the path through your network you may want some or all FAs to take when there is no better (i.e., more specific) option. Usually, this is the path with the highest available capacity to external networks. *Default route propagation* is the technique used to inform all FAs of the default path; propagation begins at the exit points of the FAs.

For our example, we want the default path to be to the ISP. We would configure default route propagation so that

- FA_C will supply default to all other FAs
- FA_C learns default from the ISP, across the iLAN

This configuration of default route propagation will satisfy Restriction 3 above.

12.3.2 Route Filtering

Route filtering is used to hide networks from the rest of an AS, or to add or modify routes to the routing table. A *route filter* is a statement, configured in one or more routers, that identifies one or more IP parameters (e.g., an IP source or destination address) and an action (e.g., drop or forward) to be taken when traffic matches these parameters. Route filtering is commonly used at hard boundaries. When the IGP OSPF is used, route filtering should not be used to hide networks internal to the OSPF network. This is due to the nature of the route-calculation algorithm in OSPF, which will be discussed later in this chapter. For our example, we would configure route filtering in the following ways:

- FA_A will apply route filtering to keep WG_5 from exiting FA_A. (OSPF is not used in this FA.)

- Route filters are added to prioritize communication between WG_1 and WG_6 over path L_6. This will be different from the default path through FA_C.

   This configuration of route filtering will satisfy Restrictions 1 and 2 in the example above.

12.3.3 Route Aggregation

Route aggregation can be used at both hard and soft boundaries to simplify routing advertisements. Aggregation is accomplished through the use of subnet masks and supernetting (discussed in detail in the next section). For our example, we could use route aggregation to

- Summarize each FA's advertisement to FA_C
- Summarize the whole AS to the ISP at the hard boundary (the iLAN to the ISP), by FA_C

12.3.4 Peering

Peering is the exchange of routing information between ASs, usually between providers with transit networks and large customer networks. This technique is typically used at hard boundaries, and may include policy information. Historically on the Internet, peering was the free and open exchange of routes between large transit networks, but changes in the structure and operations of the Internet have modified peering arrangements, so that now they are somewhat competitive.

   For our example, we could develop a peering agreement with the ISP router and/or other routers on the iLAN. Another example would be a true Internet NAP environment, where there are a number of ISPs located together with a backbone network. In the Internet NAP environment, each ISP develops a peering agreement with one or more ISPs. These peering agreements define whom the ISP will accept routes from, as well as whom they can send routes to.

12.3.5 Policies and Policy Enforcement

A *policy* is a higher-level abstraction of the route filter technique discussed earlier. Just as a route filter takes an action (drop, accept, modify) on traffic that matches one or more parameters (IP addresses), a policy takes a similar action on traffic that matches one or more AS parameters (AS number, list of AS numbers).

FIGURE 12-6. **Policy Enforcement Between ASs**

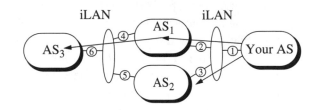

Policies allow an AS to accept or deny traffic, or to modify routing information passed between ASs, based on high-level parameters such as time of day and cost. This allows decisions about routing traffic to be made on a basis other than available routes. Policies are typically applied across hard boundaries and are currently used with the EGP border gateway protocol version 4 (BGP-4), discussed later in this chapter.

Consider a group of interconnected ASs, as in Figure 12-6. Router 1 peers with Routers 2 and 3. Routers 2 and 3 enforce a policy that traffic from our AS must transit AS_1 to get to AS_3 and cannot transit AS_2.

Now we can apply all of the relevant route-manipulation techniques to the example of Figure 12-5. In Figure 12-7, we see that the default route (DR) is supplied to the AS from the ISP, which is then propagated throughout the AS. The default route is to the backbone functional area (FA_C), then to the ISP. To hide

FIGURE 12-7. **Example with Route-Manipulation Techniques Added**

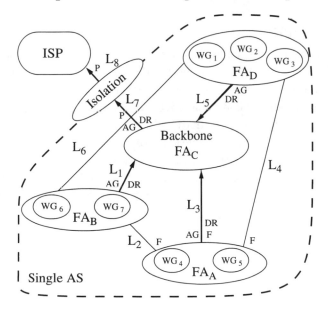

Work Group 5 (WG$_5$) from the rest of the AS, route filters (F) are placed at each exit point in FA$_A$. Route aggregation (AG), accomplished through address masks and supernetting (discussed in the next section), is done at each exit point from the functional areas to the backbone, and from the backbone to the ISP. The ISP may, in turn, aggregate routes further before advertising them to the rest of the Internet. Peering (P) would be done in this example between the ISP and our AS at the iLAN.

These route-manipulation techniques require network addresses and AS numbers. Allocating addresses, address masks, and manipulating addresses are all parts of an addressing strategy for your design, and are covered next.

12.4 Developing an Addressing Strategy

Addressing and routing are closely coupled. Before we continue with routing strategies, it would be useful to discuss some IP addressing strategies, some of which have already been alluded to. The addressing strategies discussed in this section are *subnetting*, *supernetting* and CIDR, and *variable-length subnetting*. Although these strategies are basically themes on a single strategy, we will treat them as separate in order to highlight the differences. It should be noted that the notion of address classes—such as IP address classes A, B, and C—are outdated. We will talk about them briefly here to give some background on the newer techniques, but currently addresses are more often described as the pair (address, address mask length).

12.4.1 Background

IP addressing provides a logical-network counterpart to the (somewhat) physical-network addressing at the link layer. IP addressing is logical in that addresses may be changed (relatively) easily to reflect changes in the logical structure of the network. This flexibility can be an advantage in the design process.

A trade-off with the standard addressing strategy is flexibility in assigning address space versus the complexities of interpreting, understanding, and managing various sizes and types of addresses. IP uses an address mask to show which bits in the address are host and which are network, and this in combination with the class of the address shows if the mask is the natural mask or a subnet mask.

Briefly, the IP addressing structure has been based on multiple classes:

Class	Set Bits (First Octet)	Natural Mask	Number of Addresses
A	0xxxxxxx	255.0.0.0	$2^{24} - 2$
B	01xxxxxx	255.255.0.0	$2^{16} - 2$
C	011xxxxx	255.255.255.0	$2^8 - 2$

Two is subtracted from the number of addresses, as using all 1s is for the broadcast address and cannot be allocated, and using all 0s is usually not done for historical reasons. This structure is relatively simple to allocate, configure, and manage but is not very flexible in its mapping to the number of computers on the network, nor in its efficiency of utilizing address space. Many organizations were allocated Class B addresses, while their address needs—approximated by the number of hosts expected on the network—are often a small fraction of the total space provided by a Class B address. A single Class C address, with ($2^8 - 2 = 254$) addresses, is often too small of an address space, and results in multiple Class C addresses being allocated to a customer.

12.4.2 Subnetting

Making the address mask variable in length gives us more flexibility and better mapping to the number of computers on the network (or planned for in the network design), but is more configuration- and management-intensive. *Subnetting*, or making the address mask larger (into the host portion of the mask), allows us to establish an address hierarchy within our network. This hierarchy is not advertised outside of the network.

For example, consider an addressing strategy for a network with 10,000 computers. This can be supported by a single Class B address, with $2^{16} - 2 = 65,534$ addresses, or by a minimum of 40 Class C addresses, with $40*(2^8 - 2) = 10,160$ addresses. The Class B address should meet the addressing needs for a while but is an inefficient use of space, using only 10,000/65,534 = 15.2%, and is impossible to get (without large amounts of money or influence) anyway. The Class C addresses may be a better use of space, but will require 40 advertisements, both internally and externally, unless some modifications to the strategy are implemented. Let's look at the natural masks for these addresses:

Address (Example)	Natural Mask
Class B (136.178.0.0)	255.255.0.0
Class C (198.9.9.0)	255.255.255.0

Subnetting can be applied to the Class B address to produce a hierarchy of subnets. A subnetting plan can be part of the design, where the variation in the mask length determines the number of subnets and hosts per subnet:

Address	Subnet Mask	Size	Subnets	Hosts/Subnet
136.178.0.0	255.255.255.0	8-bit	254	254
	255.255.240.0	4-bit	14	3556

Figure 12-8 shows a breakdown of a Class B address into various subnet lengths. The numbers of subnets are based on applying the mask size to the address, and subtracting one subnet (the subnet based on all 1s). We allow the subnet based on all 0s to be used, as this has become a de facto practice. Likewise, for the numbers of hosts/subnet we subtract two hosts/subnet, this time both the "all 1s" and the "all 0s." This should be considered in the network design, as address allocations are directly impacted by the subnetting strategy, even if it's not immediately used. Consider the Class B network in our example. If no subnetting plan is in place, computer (host) address allocations may be linear or random, as in Figure 12-9.

FIGURE 12-8. **Subnet Mask Length and Subnet Size**

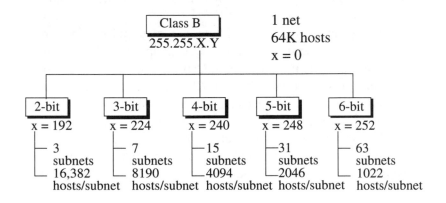

FIGURE 12-9. Class B Host Address Allocations—Linear

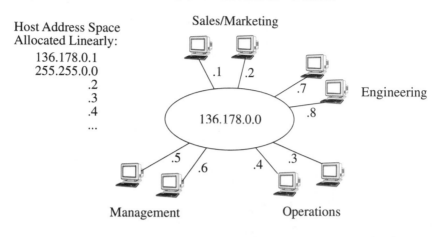

At some point in the future, there may be a need to introduce hierarchy in this network, to isolate work groups, or to reduce traffic loads on backbone networks. If the original address was random, then readdressing is necessary to implement subnetting. On the other hand, a subnetting strategy may be implemented at the beginning, even though the mask is left as the natural mask.

At this point (see Figure 12-10), the network behaves as one large network. With the natural mask in place, no subnets would be recognized. The difference here, however, is that once a hierarchy is needed, subnets can be implemented by changing the natural mask into a subnet mask (see Figure 12-11). No host address changes are needed.

FIGURE 12-10. Class B Host Address Allocations—Hierarchical

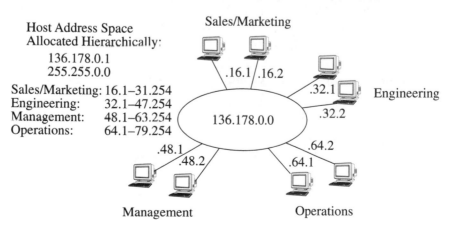

FIGURE 12-11. **Address Hierarchies Implemented with Address Mask Change**

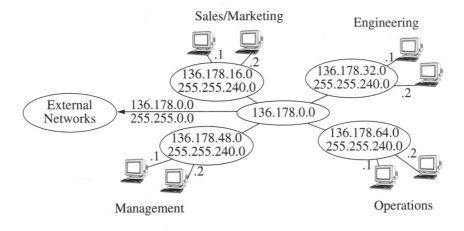

Note that with this strategy, one subnet mask is applied to the network address, producing a number of subnets that are all the same size. There are times when we may want subnets of different sizes, which a variable-length subnetting strategy provides.

12.4.3 Variable-Length Subnetting

We can take the subnetting strategy one step further, and allow for multiple subnet masks within a network. This strategy, termed *variable-length subnetting*, can make more effective use of the address space by creating subnets of different sizes, which can be better mapped to work groups of different sizes.

Variable-length subnetting is recognizing multiple subnet masks for the same network address. Let's take the address we subnetted earlier, 136.178.0.0. During the design process, we found that, for our fictitious company, we needed the following network allocations:

Work Group	Groups	Size/Group (Hosts)
Engineering	3	400
Marketing	1	1950
Administration	1	200
Sales	15	35–90
R&D	1	150
Support	22	10–40

We have determined that each group should receive a subnet. With its natural mask, 255.255.0.0, we have one network capable of addressing $2^{16} - 2$, or 65,534, hosts (actually, interfaces on hosts). From the previous section we saw that, with a 4-bit subnet mask, a Class B network address can have 15 subnets with 4094 hosts/subnet, while with an 8-bit subnet mask, it can have 254 subnets, each with 254 hosts/subnet. None of these masks by themselves will provide what we want.

What we need is a way to combine some large subnets, for engineering and marketing, with some smaller subnets for the administration, sales, R&D, and support organizations. Using variable-length subnetting, we can make the following network address allocations:

Network Address	136.178.0.0
Natural Mask	255.255.0.0
Subnet Mask 1 (4-bit)	255.255.240.0
Subnet Mask 2 (8-bit)	255.255.255.0

Address Allocations	4-Bit Mask	8-Bit Mask
Subnets 1–3 (Engineering)	136.178.16.0	
	136.178.32.0	
	136.178.48.0	
Subnet 4 (Marketing)	136.178.64.0	
Subnet 5 (Administration)		136.178.192.1
Subnets 16–30 (Sales)		136.178.192.2 through
		136.178.192.16
Subnet 31 (R&D)		136.178.192.17
Subnets 32–53 (Support)		136.178.192.18 through
		136.178.192.39

Note that these allocations are not contiguous, that there is a gap between where the addressing with a 4-bit mask ends (136.178.79.0—the end of the 136.178.64.0 subnet) and the addressing with an 8-bit mask begins (136.178.192.1). This was done to leave room for growth in the number of 4-bit subnets, or to create groups of subnets with other masks, such as a 6-bit mask.

12.4.4 Supernetting

Another trade-off with standard addressing and using the natural mask is the explosive growth in route advertisements to the Internet. Looking at the Class C plan for our earlier example, we would need to advertise 40 Class C networks, and more if the efficiency of address space is reduced or if the number of hosts increases.

FIGURE 12-12. **Allocating and Advertising 16 Class C Addresses**

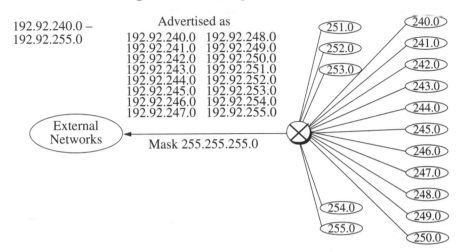

As Class A and B addresses became scarce, Class C addresses were allocated. As we saw above, the number of Class C addresses is much larger than the number of equivalent Class B or A addresses. In the Internet, the number of resulting route advertisements was growing exponentially. A substantial problem with the standard Class C addressing strategy is that the influx of route advertisements could exceed the capabilities of Internet core routers, resulting in a reduction of performance or service breakdown in the Internet. For example, when a group of 16 Class C addresses are configured in a network and the natural mask is used, all 16 addresses are advertised to outside networks. This is shown in Figure 12-12.

This Class C addressing strategy forces a hierarchy on the network design. If the size of the natural address mask can be varied (increased) to create hierarchy through subnetting, why not decrease the size of the natural mask to reduce the hierarchy in the network? This address strategy, called supernetting, reduces the number of routes advertised to the Internet by reducing the size of the network mask, resulting in fewer bits recognized as network. Let's see how this works with our example.

If we look at the third octet of each of the addresses in our group, we find that the first 4 bits of this octet do not change, but the last 4 bits do change. If we mask out only the first 4 bits, and not all 8 bits (as in the natural Class C mask), then we can use one address/mask combination to represent all 16 addresses. Figure 12-13 illustrates this technique.

FIGURE 12-13. **Modifying the Address Mask to Represent Address Groups**

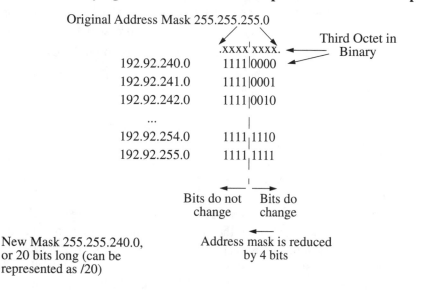

This strategy is also known as classless interdomain routing, or CIDR. Applying CIDR addressing to our 16 Class C addresses yields a single advertisement, as in Figure 12-14.

FIGURE 12-14. **16 Class C Addresses Advertised as a CIDR Block**

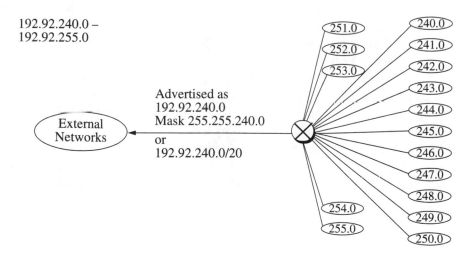

In order for this strategy to work, some rules have to be observed:

1. The number of addresses in a block of Class C addresses (used as a CIDR block) is based on a power of 2 (i.e., 2, 4, 8,... addresses).

2. The ends of the address block must fall on bit boundaries.

3. Avoid having holes in the address space—the CIDR block should be contiguous (although it can be done, as we shall soon see).

Supernetting modifies our view of the network address space: By reducing the size of the network mask, we can determine a network address that can be used as a common address for all of our CIDR block, and ignore the part of the address that is no longer covered by the network mask. This means that these bits can take on any value.

Let's take a moment to look at how the supernetting, or CIDR, strategy works. When we reduce the size of the network mask, we essentially configure the routers to ignore part of the address space. The part of the address space that is ignored can take on any value, and these values make up the addresses of the CIDR block. Consider our example, Class C address 192.92.240.0. Its natural mask is 255.255.255.0, but let's reduce the size of the mask by 4 bits, making it a supernetted mask, as in Figure 12-13.

This figure shows the third octet expanded out into bits. When we reduce the network mask by 4 bits, they are taken from the most significant bits of the last octet—the rightmost 4 bits of the third octet. This results in those last 4 bits being ignored by the network mask. Notice that the rest of the third octet—all of the bits that are now part of the supernetted mask—do not change. These last 2 bits may now take on any value (binary 0000, 0001, 0010, 0011, etc.), equating to the network addresses 192.92.241.0, 192.92.242.0, 192.92.243.0, and 192.92.244.0, and so on, for a CIDR block of 16 addresses.

This CIDR block can be expressed as 192.92.240.0, with a supernet mask of 255.255.240.0. CIDR blocks are often seen with a human-readable mask that shows the number of bits in the mask, which in this case is 20 (remember that the natural mask is 3 octets (24 bits), reduced by 4 bits for the supernet). This can be expressed as a slash between the address and mask size, as 192.92.240.0/20.

The third octet was shown as binary to make it easier to see how the block is formed, and also to show why Rule 2—the ends of the CIDR block must fall on bit boundaries—applies. If, instead of starting with 192.92.240.0 and ending with 192.92.255.0, we decided to have a CIDR block of 16 addresses, starting with 192.92.239.0 and ending with 192.92.254.0, what would happen?

FIGURE 12-15. CIDR Attempted on an Address Block with Offset Boundaries

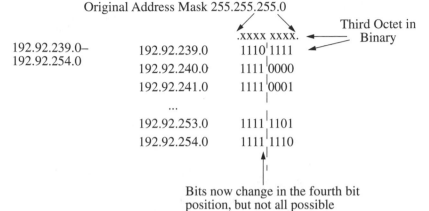

As you can see from the breakout of the third octet in Figure 12-15, these 16 addresses do two things to our mask. First, they change the bits in the third octet that are in the supernetted mask, by changing the fourth bit position, which makes the supernet invalid. Second, they do not take on all values for the ignored part of the address (the part no longer covered by the network mask—the last 5 bits), also making the supernet invalid. The CIDR block 192.92.239.0/20 would not work.

You may now be able to see why Rule 3 applies. If there is a hole in the address block, equating to one or more network addresses not being available for use, then our supernet mask should not allow them to be advertised. But remember that, when the supernet mask is applied, the ignored bits can take on any value. If one of those values corresponds to an address that is not available, we should use that mask. The reason that this rule states that it "should not" be used, instead of "must not" be used, is that indeed it can be used. But this should be done with caution. How can we advertise address space that is not ours, such as holes in CIDR blocks? Consider an organization that advertises a CIDR block (Organization B), and another organization that advertises an address that happens to be in that CIDR block (Organization A). A downstream network receiving both advertisements will use the most specific address match, based on the address mask length (see Figure 12-16).

FIGURE 12-16. Most Specific Address Matches

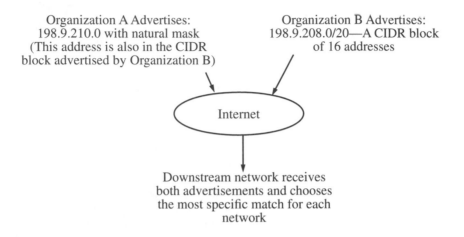

Organization A Advertises:
198.9.210.0 with natural mask
(This address is also in the CIDR
block advertised by Organization B)

Organization B Advertises:
198.9.208.0/20—A CIDR block
of 16 addresses

Internet

Downstream network receives
both advertisements and chooses
the most specific match for each
network

In this figure, the downstream network receives both advertisements
(198.9.208.0/20 from Organization B and 198.9.210.0 (with the natural mask—/24)
from Organization A. For any of the networks within the CIDR block, the downstream network uses the advertisement from Organization B, except for the network
198.9.210.0, for which it has a better advertisement—that from Organization A. It is
a better advertisement because it is more specific: it has a longer mask (/24 instead
of /20) associated with it.

What can we do if we should not use the supernet mask? What usually happens
is that the block of addresses is fragmented into multiple, smaller blocks bound by
the rules listed above. This reduces the effectiveness of the original supernet mask,
by requiring more route advertisements, but it is necessary to ensure that unavailable addresses (likely belonging to someone else) are not being included in our
advertisements.

Now let's examine what we would do if we need 40 Class C addresses in our
network. If, in our analysis of the concentrations of users in the network, we found
that we really needed the equivalent of 40 Class C networks, we would use Rule 1
above to gauge the size of the CIDR block, resulting in a block that is the next highest power of 2 above 40, which is 64 (2^6) addresses.

Next, we want the addresses to fall on a bit boundary. Say, for example, we can
get a CIDR block of 64 addresses that starts with the address 199.99.128.0. For 64
addresses, we need to reduce the natural mask by 6 bits, resulting in a mask that is
18 bits long. The CIDR block 199.99.128.0/18 would give us the address space we
need, with only one advertisement to the Internet.

Routers that receive and pass on such advertisements must understand variable-
length subnetting. If a router is in the path of CIDR advertisements and does not

understand variable-length subnetting, then the advertisement must be expanded into the full list of Class C addresses covered under that advertisement.

12.4.5 Applying Addressing Strategies

When applying any of these addressing strategies, we want to make sure that our network addresses and masks will scale to the sizes of the areas they will be assigned to. We also want to establish the degree of hierarchies in the network. In order to scale the network addressing, we need to know the numbers of

- Functional areas within the system
- Work groups within each functional area
- Networks within each work group
- Hosts within each network

By establishing the scaling and hierarchies for our network, we are applying addressing not only system-wide, but across functional areas, work groups, and networks. The intent here is to look at addressing from many perspectives, so that we do not lose the detail of any particular area, nor fail to see the overall addressing picture. While each of the addressing strategies could be applied to any area of the network, there are areas where each strategy is more appropriate. Figure 12-17 shows where each strategy fits best.

FIGURE 12-17. **Applying Addressing Schemes**

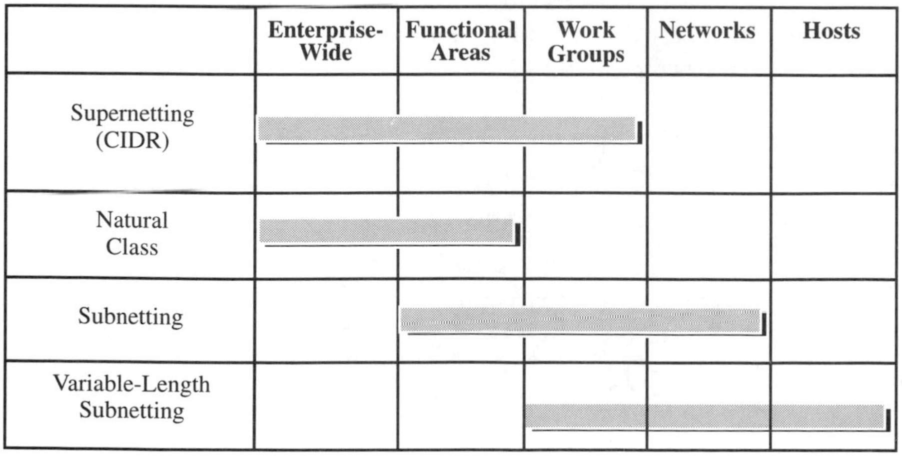

	Enterprise-Wide	Functional Areas	Work Groups	Networks	Hosts
Supernetting (CIDR)	▓▓▓▓▓▓▓▓▓▓▓▓▓				
Natural Class	▓▓▓▓▓▓				
Subnetting		▓▓▓▓▓▓▓▓▓			
Variable-Length Subnetting			▓▓▓▓▓▓▓▓▓		

At the bottom of the hierarchy, where hosts and networks are addressed, variable-length subnetting can provide the flexibility needed to map addresses to a variety of network/host sizes. In the middle of the hierarchy, where there are functional areas and work groups, subnetting is often sufficient. At the top end of the hierarchy, where the systems reside, using the natural mask for the network address or applying supernetting is usually appropriate.

The hierarchies of variable-length subnetting, both internal and external to the network, are shown in the next example, Figure 12-18. Here a hub router connects a number of work-group routers to an ISP. The hub router has the capacity to support up to 10 networks, but is currently connected to 5 networks. Each work-group router should be configured to support 4 networks, each network having 10 to 20 hosts connected to it. We have been assigned the CIDR block 192.92.240.0/20, which we are expected to summarize to the ISP router.

We could break this network into addressing areas, based on the numbers of functional areas, work groups, networks, and hosts. This will help us to choose address mask sizes that are appropriate for the scale of our network.

In our example, there are three distinct areas to address. First, the work groups have four networks with 10 to 20 hosts/network. For this area, we could assign from the CIDR block a Class C per work group, subnetted with a 255.255.255.224 mask, which will support up to 6 networks with 30 hosts/network. The next area is where the work-group routers connect to the hub router. If addresses need to be assigned, we could subnet a single Class C from the CIDR block with a mask of 255.255.255.252, supporting 63 networks with 2 hosts/network (see Figure 12-19). Since these connections are point-to-point between each work-group router and the hub router, we will only need to address two hosts per connection. The third area is the connection between the hub router and the ISP router. Here we will provide the summary advertisement 192.92.240.0/20.

FIGURE 12-18. **Example for Variable-Length Subnetting**

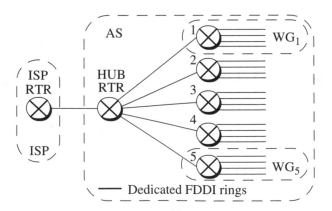

FIGURE 12-19. **Example with Variable-Length Subnetting Applied**

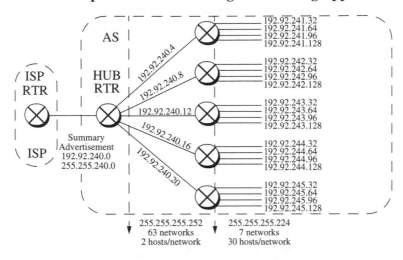

12.5 Developing a Routing Strategy

Now that we have a framework for routing developed and some addressing strategies, let's determine some strategies for applying routing protocols. This section covers the characteristics of some popular routing protocols, the criteria for making selections from these protocols, and where to apply and mix the protocols.

Typically when routing protocols are evaluated, it is on the basis of characteristics that are somewhat distant from the overall design, such as their convergence times, their protocol overheads, which are in terms of capacity (bandwidth overhead), CPU utilization, and memory utilization; and their stability. While these are important characteristics to consider, it is often difficult to relate them directly to the network design. They are, however, indirectly related to the design through two characteristics discussed several times in this book: hierarchy and redundancy.

From the perspective of choosing a routing protocol, hierarchy and redundancy indicate the required complexity and effectiveness of the protocol. Hierarchy describes the degree of connectedness and relative sizes of network areas, while redundancy describes the degree of service consistency, or protection from service interruption. By determining the degrees of hierarchy and redundancy in the network, we relate the characteristics above to the design. For example, convergence time for protocol is directly related to the degree of redundancy in the network. The higher the degree of redundancy, the greater the requirement for uninterrupted service. As this service consistency increases in importance, the routing protocol should be able to converge rapidly when changes in the routed topology occur. This also indicates a requirement for stability in the routed network. Hierarchy tends to place decision making further down the tree. In the case of routing protocols, this usually means that an abstraction of hierarchy, such as the area abstraction in OSPF, is formed.

Recall from the logical design the classifications for hierarchy and redundancy:

Degree of Hierarchy	Concentration of Flows/Connections
Low	2:1 or 1:1
Medium	3:1 to 5:1
High	6:1 or greater

Degree of Redundancy	Number of Paths	Description of Redundancy
Low	1 alternate/highly asymmetric	Service disruption and performance degradation
Medium	1 or 2 alternates/ slightly asymmetric	No service disruption, but performance is degraded
High	> 2 alternates/ symmetric	No service disruption or performance degradation

We can apply these descriptions to our evaluation of routing protocols. In evaluating the routing protocols for our network, we want to make sure that the network is segmented into functional areas.

Other criteria to consider in routing protocols are the relative complexities of the protocols, or their ease of use, and the interoperability of the protocol. These criteria can be more difficult to assess subjectively, for they have implementation dependencies. Some of the many trade-offs in routing protocol choices are simplicity and ease of use versus sophistication and features, and interoperability versus vendor-dependent features.

Some routing protocols are relatively simple to configure and maintain. RIP, for example, is pretty much plug-and-play, as long as you don't try anything fancy. Easy-to-use protocols tend not, however, to provide many features or options, and may not scale well to high degrees of hierarchy or redundancy. As routing protocols increase their feature set, they also become more complex, requiring greater expertise on the part of the network operations staff. At the extreme end of the complexity scale, they may be tunable, allowing the network operators to change parameters within the protocol to optimize the performance or features of the protocol. This can be a great help for networks that have extreme size or performance requirements, but also requires quite a bit of manpower resources in monitoring and maintenance.

Interoperability is the support for operations, performance, and features across multiple vendor platforms. For routing protocols, standards are the start toward interoperability. Standards are necessary, but not sufficient, for protocol interoperability. Do not assume that when an implementation of a routing protocol supports or is based on a standard, that it will interoperate with all other implementations. To be certain of interoperability, you should know which vendor implementations you expect to deploy in the network, then either test interoperability between them in your lab environment, if you have one, or check the results of other testbeds (there are many out there).

At times it may be preferred or necessary to forsake interoperability in order to get features or performance from a particular vendor. For example, we may get a highly desirable feature with a vendor-specific protocol, or a level of support from the vendor that far exceeds that with a standard protocol. While there are times when vendor-specific routing protocols should be considered, it is highly recommended that you always apply caution when considering vendor-specific protocols. If you choose a vendor-specific (nonstandard) protocol, you may become locked into using that protocol, as it may prove expensive to change later to a standard protocol, especially in terms of the knowledge required to run the new protocol.

12.5.1 Protocol Analysis

We will briefly examine and compare the following IGPs and EGP: the routing information protocol (RIP and RIPv2), the open shortest-path first (OSPF) routing protocol, and the border gateway protocol version 4 (BGP-4). In addition, we will also consider the use of static routes. It is expected that you are already familiar with how routing protocols, IGPs and EGPs, work, and that this information will help you in evaluating and choosing the routing protocols for your design. If you need any background information on routing protocols, several excellent references are listed at the end of this chapter.

Static Routes

Although *static routes* are not part of a routing protocol, the concept is included here as a first step in routing. Many people overlook the use of static routes, yet they can be useful in some environments, primarily when a routing protocol is not needed.

The dynamic nature of a routing protocol is needed when alternate routes exist in the network (i.e., there is some level of redundancy). When there is only one route out of an area, a routing protocol cannot adapt to changes in the routing topology (by offering alternate routes). Such an area is often termed a *stub* area (see Figure 12-20).

FIGURE 12-20. **Stub Areas**

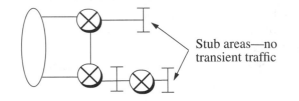

Stub areas—no transient traffic

In this case, a static route can be applied between the stub area and the rest of the network. A trade-off in using static routes is in not having to configure and maintain a routing protocol versus the ability to adapt to modifications in the routing topology. Consider the example above. If an additional connection is provided to that area, then a routing protocol should be configured for the routers and hosts in that area. If there are a large number of hosts and/or routers in that area, they would have to be reconfigured to use the routing protocol. This can be somewhat configuration-intensive. In such a case, or when alternate routes are expected in the future, it may be better to start with a routing protocol to avoid the reconfiguration effort later on.

Static routing is a simple, basic mechanism for default access from a stub area. Whenever it appears that alternate routes may be used in an area, a routing protocol should be configured in that area.

RIP/RIPv2

RIP and RIPv2 are IGPs that are based on a distance-vector routing algorithm. This implies some characteristics of the dynamic behavior of RIP/RIPv2–routed networks. RIP and, to a lesser degree, RIPv2 are relatively straightforward to implement and maintain. RIP has been around for a long time, having been part of the TCP/IP suite shipped with most UNIX systems, and there is a lot of experience with RIP-routed networks. Given the simplicity, longevity, and experience with RIP, interoperability between various versions of RIP should not be a problem.

Due to the nature of the distance-vector routing algorithm used in RIP/RIPv2, they can be slow to converge to a new routing topology when changes occur in the network, where "slow" is on the order of tens of seconds to minutes. They can also form routing instabilities, although there have been several mechanisms developed to minimize the probabilities of their forming (e.g., split horizon, poison reverse, holdown timers). For these reasons, they may not be optimal for areas where high degrees of redundancy or hierarchy are indicated.

RIP/RIPv2 should be considered when there is low to medium redundancy and hierarchy in the network:

Degree of Hierarchy	Concentration of Flows/Connections
Low	2:1 or 1:1
Medium	3:1 to 5:1

Degree of Redundancy	Number of Paths	Description of Redundancy
Low	1 alternate/highly asymmetric	Service disruption and performance degradation
Medium	1 or 2 alternates/ slightly asymmetric	No service disruption, but performance is degraded

OSPF

OSPF is an IGP that is based on a link-state routing algorithm. Like RIP/RIPv2, the choice of routing algorithm affects the characteristics of the protocol. In the case of OSPF, the use of a link-state algorithm results in a faster convergence time when changes in the routing topology occur. Convergence times can be on the order of seconds, or about one or two orders of magnitude faster than RIP/RIPv2. For an area with high redundancy or hierarchy, a fast convergence time may be the single most important feature of a routing protocol and would indicate the use of OSPF.

OSPF also supports an area abstraction, which provides a hierarchy for routing information (see Figure 12-21). The OSPF hierarchy connects these areas via a backbone area, and routing information is internalized within each area. This reduces the size of routing information flows across the OSPF network.

FIGURE 12-21. Example of Hierarchical Relationships Between ASs, Areas, and Networks/Subnets

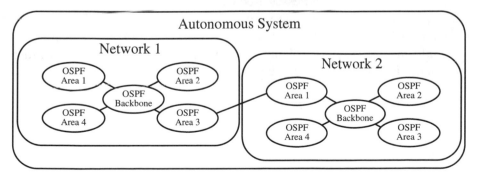

There are trade-offs for the rapid convergence times and area abstraction. One trade-off is in complexity. OSPF may require a lot of configuration during setup, and possibly configuration tuning to reach an optimized steady-state routing topology. OSPF experience is harder to come by than RIP experience, as OSPF has only been available since about 1990. There is more information to understand, monitor, and use with an OSPF network. This information may be helpful in isolating and troubleshooting routing problems, but also requires the skills to use this information. Additionally, interoperability between various OSPF implementations is less certain than with RIP.

OSPF should be considered when there is a high redundancy and hierarchy in the network:

Degree of Hierarchy	Concentration of Flows/Connections	
High	6:1 or greater	

Degree of Redundancy	Number of Paths	Description of Redundancy
High	> 2 alternates or symmetric	No service disruption or performance degradation

Other features of OSPF include

- Equal-cost multipath, allowing multiple paths to be used to the same destination when their OSPF costs are the same
- Route summarization

BGP-4

BGP-4 is a path-vector-based EGP. BGP-4 uses route policies and rules to allow peering between ASs. BGP-4 uses AS numbers, providing an abstraction layer above the network addresses used by OSPF and RIP. Thus, BGP-4 is a natural for applying policies to ASs, as we can develop rules for collections of networks (based on ASs), instead of on a network-by-network basis. There are many good sources of information about BGP-4 and how it works. Some references for further reading about BGP-4 are given at the end of the chapter.

12.5.2 Choosing and Applying Routing Protocols

This section presents some rules of thumb in applying routing protocols to your design. These rules were developed based on the premise of simplifying the applications of routing protocols whenever possible. The three basic rules of thumb are as follows:

1. Minimize the number of routing protocols used in the design. Two routing protocols should generally be the maximum number allowed in a network, and one IGP is best.

2. Start with the simplest routing strategy/routing protocol.

3. As the complexity in the routing design and choice of routing protocol increases, reevaluate the previous decisions.

Minimizing the number of routing protocols is a straightforward rule—don't overcomplicate the routing design by applying too many routing protocols. How many routing protocols is too many is based on the ability of the customer—specifically those responsible for OAM for the network being designed—to support those protocols (but the two-maximum rule is a good idea). Many designs focus on a single IGP within their AS and an EGP for external communications. However, as we will see, there are times when multiple IGPs within an AS and even IGPs and EGPs together within an AS makes sense, as long as the trade-offs in complexity and support are understood.

We also want to start with the simplest routing strategy and work up to more complex strategies as necessary. The simplest strategy is to use static routes, and this would be considered first, for stub areas. If there are no stub areas, or when a routing protocol is indicated, then RIP or RIPv2 should be considered. Recall that RIP/RIPv2 are suggested for low to medium hierarchy and redundancy networks. When the network increases to high hierarchy or redundancy, the OSPF should be considered. The approach is to consider static routes first, for stub areas, then consider RIP/RIPv2 for non-stub areas, or when network complexity is at the level of low to medium hierarchy or redundancy. You will want to consider OSPF when network complexity is at the level of high hierarchy or redundancy, and BGP-4 when an EGP is indicated in the design.

When a more complex routing protocol is being considered, areas where a routing protocol has been selected should be reevaluated. This may or may not result in an upgrade of routing protocol selection for these areas. The intent is to keep the number of routing protocols at a minimum, and to avoid multiple instances of the same protocol in different areas of the network. This rule may be extended to state, generally:

3a When RIP or RIPv2 is indicated, RIP/RIPv2 supersedes the use of static routes.

3b When OSPF is indicated, OSPF supersedes the use of RIP/RIPv2 or static routes.

3c When BGP-4 is indicated, BGP-4 supersedes OSPF or RIP/RIPv2 in backbone networks.

Combining Routing Protocols

While keeping the number of routing protocols (particularly IGPs) in the network to a minimum is suggested, there are times when the benefits of having more than one IGP outweighs the costs of their support and maintenance. When the network is complex enough to have the choice of routing protocol changed from RIP/RIPv2 to OSPF, the areas where RIP/RIPv2 or static routes are already assigned are then reevaluated. There may be areas where the conversion from RIP/RIPv2 to OSPF is beneficial, or where at least there are no additional support or maintenance costs. In other areas, however, such a conversion may not make sense, as it does not offer any additional benefits and may increase the support or maintenance costs. For example, consider the network in Figure 12-22.

In this network we have different degrees of connectivity and hierarchy, and we apply our routing options accordingly. Where there is the greatest degree of hierarchy and redundancy, we apply OSPF. Where the hierarchy is less, we apply RIP. For stub areas we apply static routes.

There may also be times where applying BGP-4 within the network, with either RIP/RIPv2 or OSPF, is appropriate. Applying BGP-4 within the network may be considered when the network is so large that it should be fragmented into multiple ASs, or when the organizations within the network want administrative, management, or security autonomy. In such a case, the boundary between the networks could be treated as a hard boundary. In some cases BGP-4 may just be a simpler, cleaner routing-protocol implementation than OSPF. This is primarily dependent on the structure and operations of the organization that the network is being designed for.

FIGURE 12-22. **Mixing IGPs and Static Routes in the Network**

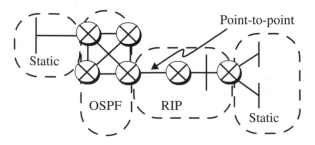

One thing to consider when mixing routing protocols is how information is translated across the boundary between the protocols. Information such as network masks or protocol metrics can easily be lost or misunderstood when crossing routing protocols. There is currently no standard metric translation between dissimilar routing protocols.

Procedure for Applying Routing Protocols

The routing protocols are evaluated for each FA, based on the degrees of redundancy and hierarchy for that FA, and considering any other factors for that FA or features of the routing protocol. When a change is made in the choice of routing protocol, such as from static routes to RIP/RIPv2, or from RIP/RIPv2 to OSPF, or from OSPF to BGP-4, reevaluate FAs where routing protocols have already been chosen. In general, RIP/RIPv2 supersedes static routes, and OSPF supersedes RIP/RIPv2, but remember that you can also consider combining the protocols within the network.

FAs that contain only backbone networks should be considered last, as they are usually the most complex. It is therefore likely that the backbone networks will require the most complex routing protocols. The backbone networks are also where BGP-4 is often considered. In general, for the backbone:

1. If all FAs are using the same routing protocol, that protocol should also be considered first for the backbone.

2. When multiple routing protocols are chosen for the network, consider the more complex protocol for the backbone first.

3. When the hierarchy to the backbone is 6:1 or greater, consider BGP-4 as the routing protocol for the backbone first.

12.6 Case Study

This design is relatively simple from the perspectives of addressing and routing. First, separating the design into functional areas, we get Figure 12-23. Note that in this figure, the connectivity to Building 1013 is shown differently, to account for the cabling of the Oakland campus.

FIGURE 12-23. **Functional Areas for Design**

San Francisco Campus (SF)

Oakland Campus (Oak)

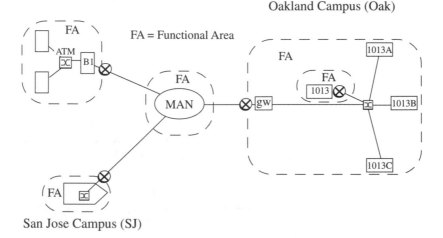

San Jose Campus (SJ)

From discussions with the customer, we find that there are no requirements for separating users, user groups, or areas of the network, and since we have no outside connectivity, we will treat each of these functional areas as having soft boundaries between them. There are no requirements in this design for route filters, aggregation, peering, or policies.

The customer has been allocated a Class C network address, but their network may grow beyond the range of a single Class C address (with 50% growth, they will have about 370 users). We have requested a block of four contiguous Class C addresses for this network, and will use a Class C per functional area. We will subnet a Class C for use between the SJ campus, the MAN, and for the network management links, as these areas will use the smallest numbers of addresses. If the company ever decides to connect to the Internet and does not want to use network address translation or IPv6, then these addresses can be advertised as a CIDR block.

For the choice of routing protocols, we considered RIPv2, OSPF, and BGP-4. With the simplicity of the design and the levels of hierarchy and redundancy in the MAN, we recommended RIPv2 as the candidate routing protocol for this network.

12.7 Concluding Remarks

The addressing and routing strategies described in this chapter complete the design process in this book. An additional area that you may want to consider is how you will apply naming to the design. (There are many good references on this subject listed in the next section.)

You should now have a well-described design, from a set of requirements and flows, to the logical and physical designs, and including the addressing and routing strategies. The analysis and design processes provide you with an abundance of information with which to base the network design.

Where to go from here? There is still a lot to do to bring the design to implementation, and there are many topics that were briefly covered in this book that you can provide more detail for in your designs. Some topics for you to consider:

- Writing an implementation plan for your design

- Developing a request for information (RFI) or request for Proposal (RFP) for network equipment or services

- Evaluating vendors and their products

- Performing acceptance testing on equipment and services

- Determining how to tune your installed network to optimize performance

We hope that you have enjoyed reading and applying this book, and that you have been able to use the guidelines presented effectively. The processes described here are constantly evolving, so if you have comments on how to improve them, please send them to *doowah@fsc.com*.

Suggested Further Reading

1. Albitz, P., and Liu, C. *DNS and BIND*. O'Reilly and Associates, Sebastopol, CA, 1994.

2. Comer, D.E. *Internetworking with TCP/IP* (all volumes). Prentice Hall, Englewood Cliffs, N.J., 1991.

3. Huitema, C. *Routing in the Internet*. Prentice Hall, Englewood Cliffs, N.J., 1995.

4. Moy, J. OSPF Version 2. *RFC 2178*. July 1997.

5. Perlman, R. *Interconnections: Bridges and Routers*. Addison-Wesley, Reading, MA, 1992.

6. Piscitello, D.M., and Chapin, A.L. *Open Systems Networking: TCP/IP and OSI*. Addison-Wesley, Reading, MA, 1993.

7. Rekhter, Y. CIDR and classful routing. *RFC 1817*. August 1995.

8. Rekhter, Y., and Li, T. A border gateway protocol 4 (BGP-4). *RFC 1771*. March 1995.

9. Stevens, W.R. *TCP/IP Illustrated* (all volumes). Addison-Wesley, Reading, MA, 1994.

Internet-drafts from the following IETF working groups: Routing Policy System (RPS); Inter-Domain Routing (IDR); Inter-Domain Multicast Routing (IDMR); and IP Routing for Wireless/Mobile Hosts (MOBILEIP).

And for you hard-core readers, you cannot beat the *DDN Protocol Handbooks*: *Volume 1—DOD Military Standard Protocols*; *Volume 2—DARPA Internet Protocols*; and *Volume 3—Supplement*. They are edited by Feiner, Jacobsen, Stahl, and Ward, and are available from SRI International.

Exercises

Exercises 1 through 4 refer to the design in Figure 12-24:

1. Where are the functional areas for this design?

2. Where are the potential logical and physical boundaries for the design?

3. Given the network address 129.99.0.0, develop a variable-length addressing scheme that best fits the design environment, with the following numbers of users:

AS Number	Building/Site	Department	Users
1	1	Legal	120
		Accounting	370
	2	HQ	1580
		Engineering	200
2	Toronto	Sales	75
	Boston	Sales	110
		PR	45
3	Philadelphia	Ops1	2150
		Ops2	975
		Sales	575

FIGURE 12-24. **Design for Exercises 12.1–12.4**

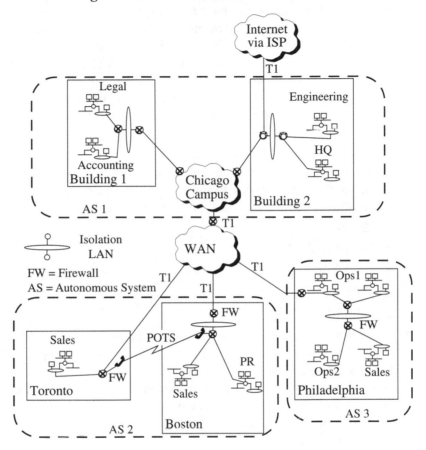

4. You are using BGP-4 in the WAN between AS1, AS2, and AS3. Describe in either plain text or as BGP-4 policy statements how you would

   a) Permit AS3 to communicate with AS1, but not allow AS2 to communicate with AS1

   b) Allow both AS2 and AS3 Internet access through AS1 only between 6 p.m. and 6 a.m. EST each night

   Refer to RFC 1771 for specifics on the BGP-4 specification.

5. Consider the following: You are an ISP and have a group of CIDR blocks to allocate addresses from. You have allocated addresses to a number of clients from a CIDR block of 64 Class C addresses (198.9.128.0 through 198.9.191.0, which can also be stated as 198.9.128.0/18, representing an 18-bit address mask). Now one of your clients wants to stop using your ISP service and move to another ISP,

while keeping the Class C that you had allocated to him (198.9.145.0). You are in a dilemma: you cannot take back the Class C address (his lawyers are better than yours!), yet advertising a CIDR block that contains that Class C address seems to break one of the rules of CIDR addressing. What do you do?
As it turns out, you can allow the (soon to be) ex-client to continue to use the Class C address from your CIDR block, and still advertise the CIDR block. Show how routing based on most-specific route matches allows this to work. Also show what happens to the ex-client's traffic if there is a bug in the Internet and the ex-client's route gets dropped.

6. For each of the following addresses, give its natural mask (in dotted decimal notation—i.e., 255.255.0.0), its subnet/supernet mask (in dotted decimal notation), and the range of networks or subnets permitted by the mask. Also describe any problems and limitations with the address/mask combination, if any.

   a) 129.99.0.0/16

   b) 136.178.0.0/22

   c) 198.9.9.0/28

   d) 192.92.240/20

   e) 192.92.243/20

7. Many design environments are requiring redundant access to the Internet, with the backup connection either in a hot-standby mode or an operational mode (using load balancing between the two connections). Using BGP-4, outline a strategy for providing a backup connection to the Internet, where the connection is in hot-standby mode (i.e., can be made operational by a change to the routing configuration). Figure 12-25 shows what the primary and standby connections would look like.

   What would be required to turn the backup connection from hot-standby mode to a fully operational, load-sharing mode?

FIGURE 12-25. Design for Exercise 12.7

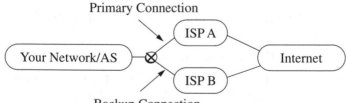

Bibliography

Almesberger, W., LeBoudec, J., and Oechslin, P. Application REQUested IP over ATM (AREQUIPA). *RFC 2170*. July 1997.

Amsden, P., Amweg, J., Calato, P., Bensley, S., and Lyons, G., Light-weight flow admission protocol specification version 1.0. *RFC 2124*. April 1997.

Armitage, G. Support for multicast over UNI 3.0/3.1 based ATM networks. *RFC 2022*. November 1996.

Atkinson, R. Default IP MTU for use over ATM AAL5. *RFC 1626*. May 1994.

ATM Forum. LAN emulation client management specification, version 1.0. af-lane-0038.000. September 1995.

ATM Forum. LAN emulation over ATM version 1.0 addendum. af-lane-0050.000. December 1995.

Baker, D.G. *Fiber Optic Design and Applications*. Reston Publishing Company, Reston, VA, 1985.

Baker, F. Requirements for IP version 4 routers. *RFC 1812*. June 1995.

Baker, F., and Atkinson, R. RIP-2 MD5 Authentication. *RFC 2082*. January 1997.

Baker, F., and Coltun, R. OSPF version 2 management information base. *RFC 1850*. November 1995.

Banerjee, S.K. High speed implementation of DES. *Computers and Security,* Vol. 1, 261–267, 1982.

Baron, S., and Krivocheev, M. *Digital Image and Audio Communications: Toward a Global Information Infrastructure*. Van Nostrand Reinhold, New York, 1996.

Bates, T., and Chandra, R. BGP route reflection: An alternative to full mesh IBGP. *RFC 1966*. June 1996.

Bellcore. *Telecommunications Transmission Engineering, Vol. 1—Principles*. ST-TEC-000051. Bellcore, 1990.

Bellcore. *Telecommunications Transmission Engineering, Vol. 2—Facilities*. ST-TEC-000052. Bellcore, 1990.

Bellcore. *Telecommunications Transmission Engineering, Vol. 3—Networks and Services*. ST-TEC-000053. Bellcore, 1990.

Bertsekas, D., and Gallager, R. *Data Networks,* 2nd ed. Prentice Hall, Englewood Cliffs, NJ, 1991.

Borden, M., Crawley, E., Davie, B., and Batsell, S. Integration of real-time services in an IP-ATM network architecture. *RFC 1821*. August 1995.

Borman, D. TCP and UDP over IPv6 jumbograms. *RFC 2147*. May 1997.

Borman, D., Braden, R., and Jacobson, V. TCP extensions for high performance. *RFC 1323*. May 1992.

Braden, R. Requirements for Internet hosts—application and support. *RFC 1123*. October 1989.

Braden, R. Requirements for Internet hosts—communication layers. *RFC 1122*. October 1989.

Braden, R., and Jacobson, V. TCP extensions for long-delay paths. *RFC 1072*. October 1988.

Braden, R., Postel, J., and Rekhter, Y. Internet architecture extensions for shared media. *RFC 1620*. May 1994.

Bradner, S., and Mankin, A., eds. *IPng: Internet Protocol Next Generation*. Addison-Wesley, Reading, MA, 1995.

Braun, H. Models of policy based routing. *RFC 1104*. June 1989.

Brownlee, N. Traffic flow measurement: Experiences with NeTraMet. *RFC 2123*. March 1997.

Brownlee, N. Traffic flow measurement: Meter MIB. *RFC 2064*. January 1997.

Brownlee, N., Mills, C., and Ruth, G. Traffic flow measurement: Architecture. *RFC 2063*. January 1997.

Buchanan, R.W. *The Art of Testing Network Systems*. John Wiley and Sons, New York, 1996.

Buford, J. *Multimedia Systems*. Addison-Wesley, Reading, MA, 1994.

Callon, R. TCP and UDP with bigger addresses (TUBA), a simple proposal for Internet addressing and routing. *RFC 1347*. June 1992.

Carpenter, B. Architectural principles of the Internet. *RFC 1958*. June 1996.

Carpenter, B., Crowcroft, J., and Rekhter, Y. IPv4 address behaviour today. *RFC 2101*. February 1997.

Case, J., McCloghrie, K., Rose, M., and Waldbusser, S. Introduction to community-based SNMPv2. *RFC 1901*. January 1996.

Castineyra, I., Chiappa, J., and Steenstrup, M. The nimrod routing architecture. *RFC 1992*. August 1996.

Chandra, R., Traina, P., and Li, T. BGP communities attribute. *RFC 1997*. August 1996.

Clark, D. Policy routing in Internet protocols. *RFC 1102*. May 1989.

Clark, D., Jacobson, V., Romkey, J., and Salwen, H. An analysis of TCP processing overhead. *IEEE Communications*. June 1989.

Coltun, R., and Fuller, V. The OSPF NSSA option. *RFC 1587*. March 1994.

Crawford, M. Transmission of IPv6 packets over FDDI. *RFC 2019*. October 1996.

Davie, B.S., and Peterson, L. *Computer Networks: A Systems Approach*. Morgan Kaufmann, San Francisco, 1996.

Deering, S., and Hinden, R. Internet protocol, version 6 (IPv6) specification. *RFC 1883*. January 1996.

Delgrossi, L., and Berger, L. Internet stream protocol version 2 (ST2) protocol specification—version ST2+. *RFC 1819*. August 1995.

DePrycker, M. *Asynchronous Transfer Mode: Solution for Broadband ISDN*. Ellis Horwood, Chichester, England, 1991.

DeSouza, O., and Rodrigues, M. Guidelines for running OSPF over frame relay networks. *RFC 1586*. March 1994.

Dobrowski, G., and Minoli, D. *Principles of Signalling for Cell Relay and Frame Relay*. Artech House, Norwood, MA, 1995.

Droms, R. Dynamic host configuration protocol. *RFC 2131*. April 1997.

Dunlap, K.J, and Mockapetris, P.V. Development of the domain name system. *Proceedings of the ACM SIGCOMM*. August 1988.

Edwards, P.W., Hoffman, R.E., Liaw, F., Lyon, T., and Minshall, G. Ipsilon flow management protocol specification for IPv4 version 1.0. *RFC 1953*. May 1996.

Fuller, V., Li, T., Yu, J., and Varadhan, K. Classless inter-domain routing (CIDR): An address assignment and aggregation strategy. *RFC 1519*. September 1993.

Haskin, D. A BGP/IDRP route server alternative to a full mesh routing. *RFC 1863*. October 1995.

Hawkinson, J., and Bates, T. Guidelines for creation, selection, and registration of an autonomous system (AS). *RFC 1930.* April 1996.

Hinden, R. Applicability statement for the implementation of classless inter-domain routing (CIDR). *RFC 1517.* September 1993.

Jackowski, S. Native ATM support for ST2+. *RFC 1946.* May 1996.

Jacobson, V. Congestion avoidance and control. *Proceedings of the ACM SIG-COMM.* August 1988.

Jain, R. *FDDI Handbook: High-Speed Networking Using Fiber and Other Media.* Addison-Wesley, Reading, MA, 1994.

Jones, P. Resource allocation, control, and accounting for the use of network resources. *RFC 1346.* June 1992.

Kessler, G., and Shepard, S. A primer on Internet and TCP/IP tools and utilities. *RFC 2151.* June 1997.

Kleinrock, L. *Queuing Systems, Vol. 1: Theory.* John Wiley and Sons, New York, 1975.

Lawrence, J., and Piscitello, D. The transmission of IP datagrams over the SMDS service. *RFC 1209.* March 1991.

Mathis, M., Mahdavi, J., Floyd, S., and Romanow, A. TCP selective acknowledgment options. *RFC 2018.* October 1996.

McCloghrie, K. An administrative infrastructure for SNMPv2. *RFC 1909.* February 1996.

McConnell, J. *Internetworking Computer Systems: Interconnecting Networks and Systems.* Prentice Hall, Englewood Cliffs, NJ, 1988.

Metcalf, R. Computer/Network interface design lessons from ARPANET and Ethernet. *IEEE Journal of Selected Areas in Communication.* February 1993.

Minoli, D. *Broadband Network Analysis and Design.* Artech House, Norwood, MA, 1993.

Minoli, D. *Enterprise Networking: Fractional T1 to SONET, Frame Relay to BISDN*. Artech House, Norwood, MA, 1993.

Morse, H.S. *Practical Parallel Computing*. AP Professional, Cambridge, MA, 1994.

Moy, J. Extending OSPF to support demand circuits. *RFC 1793*. April 1995.

Moy, J. MOSPF: Analysis and experience. *RFC 1585*. March 1994.

Moy, J. Multicast extensions to OSPF. *RFC 1584*. March 1994.

Nagle, J. On packet switches with infinite storage. *IEEE Transactions on Communications*. April 1987.

Newman, P., Edwards, W., Hinden, R., Hoffman, E., Liaw, F., and Minshall, T.G. Ipsilon's general switch management protocol specification version 1.1. *RFC 1987*. August 1996.

Newman, P., Edwards, W., Hinden, R., Hoffman, E., Liaw, F., and Minshall, T.G. Transmission of flow labelled IPv4 on ATM data links Ipsilon version 1.0. *RFC 1954*. May 1996.

Partridge, C. *Gigabit Networking*. Addison-Wesley, Reading, MA, 1994.

Paxson, V. *Measurement and Analysis of End-to-End Internet Dynamics*. Ph.D. thesis. University of California at Berkeley. April 1997.

Postel, J. Domain name system structure and delegation. *RFC 1591*. March 1994.

Postel, J. Transmission control protocol. *RFC 793*. September 1981.

Ramanathan, R. Mobility support for Nimrod: Challenges and solution approaches. *RFC 2103*. February 1997.

Ramanathan, R. Multicast support for Nimrod: Requirements and solution approaches. *RFC 2102*. February 1997.

Rekhter, Y. Routing in a multi-provider Internet. *RFC 1787*. April 1995.

Rekhter, Y., Davie, B., Katz, D., Rosen, E., and Swallow, G. Cisco Systems' tag switching architecture overview. *RFC 2105*. February 1997.

Rekhter, Y., and Gross, P. Application of the border gateway protocol in the Internet. *RFC 1772*. March 1995.

Rekhter, Y., and Kandlur, D. "Local/Remote" forwarding decision in switched data link subnetworks. *RFC 1937*. May 1996.

Rekhter, Y., and Li, T. An architecture for IP address allocation with CIDR. *RFC 1518*. September 1993.

Renwick, J. IP over HIPPI. *RFC 2067*. January 1997.

Reynolds, J., and Postel, J. Assigned numbers. *RFC 1700*. October 1994.

Rigney, C. RADIUS accounting. *RFC 2139*. April 1997.

Rigney, C., Rubens, A., Simpson, W., and Willens, S. Remote authentication dial in user service (RADIUS). *RFC 2138*. April 1997.

Schneier, B. *Applied Cryptography: Protocols, Algorithms, and Source Code in C*. John Wiley and Sons, New York, 1994.

Schulzrinne, H. RTP profile for audio and video conferences with minimal control. *RFC 1890*. January 1996.

Schulzrinne, H., Casner, S., Frederick, R., and Jacobson, V. RTP: A transport protocol for real-time applications. *RFC 1889*. January 1996.

Simpson, W. PPP challenge handshake authentication protocol (CHAP). *RFC 1994*. August 1996.

Spohn, D.L. *Data Network Design*. McGraw-Hill, New York, 1993.

Spragins, J.D. *Telecommunications Protocols and Design*. Addison-Wesley, Reading, MA, 1992.

Stallings, W. *Data and Computer Communications,* 3rd ed. Macmillan, New York, 1991.

Stallings, W. *Handbook of Computer Communications Standards,* vols. 1 and 2. Howard W. Sams & Co., Indianapolis, 1987.

Stallings, W. *ISDN and Broadband ISDN,* 2nd ed. Macmillan, New York, 1992.

Stallings, W. *SNMP, SNMPv2 and CMIP: The Practical Guide to Network Management Standards*. Addison-Wesley, Reading, MA, 1993.

Steenstrup, M. Inter-domain policy routing protocol specification:Version 1. *RFC 1479*. July 1993.

Stevens, W. TCP slow start, congestion avoidance, fast retransmit, and fast recovery algorithms. *RFC 2001*. January 1997.

Stevens, W. *UNIX Network Programming*. Prentice Hall, Englewood Cliffs, NJ, 1990.

Tannenbaum, A.S. *Computer Networks,* 2nd ed. Prentice Hall, Englewood Cliffs, NJ, 1988.

Touch, J. TCP control block interdependence. *RFC 2140*. April 1997.

Traina, P. Autonomous system confederations for BGP. *RFC 1965*. June 1996.

Traina, P. Experience with the BGP-4 protocol. *RFC 1773*. March 1995.

Varadhan, K. BGP OSPF interaction. *RFC 1403*. January 1993.

Walrand, J., and Varaiya, P. *High-Performance Communication Networks*. Morgan Kaufmann, San Francisco, 1996.

Waters, G. User-based security model for SNMPv2. *RFC 1910*. February 1996.

Index

N

network access points
  as flow boundaries 127, 141
network analysis
  components of 3
  process 2–3
  trade-offs 2
network design
  capacity planning 1
  common design goals 179
  components of 3
  logical. *See* logical design.
  physical. *See* physical design.
  process 2–3
  traditional 1
network elements
  characteristics of 256
  definition of 256
network management
  as applied to the case study 280–281
  categories of 47, 256
  centralized and distributed monitoring 264–265
  configuration methods 268
  determining the requirement for monitoring nodes in the design 265–266
  generating configuration parameters 258
  guidelines for management data generation and storage 267
  in-band/out-of-band monitoring 262–263
  instrumentation for management 259
  locality of management data 267
  management protocols 259
  metrics and trend analysis 258
  monitoring and metering 256–257
  plans 278–279
  polling intervals for real-time analysis 258
  redundancy in monitoring methods 266
  sample SNMP interface parameters 260
  schemas 268
  stateful and stateless methods of generating management data 266
  storage types for management data 257
network management
  architectural issues 262–268
network management
  management traffic levels as a percentage of network capacity 265
network propagation delay
  as a delay threshold 71

network requirements 45–49
  enterprise 49
  existing network-layer and support services 46
  existing networks 45
  financial 49
  functional 47
  identifying constraints on the design 46
  interoperability 46
  network management 47
  performance 46
  scaling existing networks 45
  security 47
  security policies 48
network sizing
  as applied to the case study 219
  based on flow hierarchies 208
  based on functions and features of the design 209
  based on geography 206
  based on user concentrations 207
  and broadcast domains 209
NHRP 241
  See also interconnection mechanisms
non-real-time applications
  definition of 35

O

OC levels in the SONET hierarchy 192
optimizing security as a design goal 179
out-of-band monitoring
  definition of 263

P

packet filters
  as a security mechanism 272
pathchar
  example trace of 91
  as a utility to monitor service 58
peak data rate 58
peering
  definition of 320
performance
  modifiers 60
performance characteristics
  bus performance 42
  device driver performance 42
  memory performance 42
  OS performance 42
  processor (CPU) performance 42
  storage performance 42